CAMBRIDGE TEXTS IN THE
HISTORY OF POLITICAL THOUGHT

——

MICHAEL BAKUNIN
Statism and Anarchy

CAMBRIDGE TEXTS IN THE HISTORY OF POLITICAL THOUGHT

Series Editors:

RAYMOND GEUSS *Columbia University*
QUENTIN SKINNER *Christ's College, Cambridge*
RICHARD TUCK *Jesus College, Cambridge*

The series is intended to make available to students the most important texts required for an understanding of the history of political thought. The scholarship of the present generation has greatly expanded our sense of the range of authors indispensable for such an understanding, and the series will reflect those developments. It will also include a number of less well-known works, in particular those needed to establish the intellectual contexts that in turn help to make sense of the major texts. The principal aim, however, will be to produce new versions of the major texts themselves, based on the most up-to-date scholarship. The preference will always be for complete texts, and a special feature of the series will be to complement individual texts, within the compass of a single volume, with subsidiary contextual material. Each volume will contain an introduction on the historical identity and contemporary significance of the work or works concerned, as well as a chronology, notes on further reading and (where appropriate) brief biographical sketches of significant individuals mentioned in each text.

For a list of titles published in the series, please see end of book

MICHAEL BAKUNIN

Statism and Anarchy

TRANSLATED AND EDITED BY

MARSHALL S. SHATZ

*Professor in the Department of History,
University of Massachusetts at Boston*

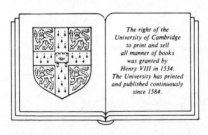

The right of the
University of Cambridge
to print and sell
all manner of books
was granted by
Henry VIII in 1534.
The University has printed
and published continuously
since 1584.

CAMBRIDGE UNIVERSITY PRESS

Cambridge

New York   Port Chester

Melbourne   Sydney

KH

Published by the Press Syndicate of the University of Cambridge
The Pitt Building, Trumpington Street, Cambridge CB2 1RP
40 West 20th Street, New York, NY 10011, USA
10 Stamford Road, Oakleigh, Melbourne 3166, Australia

First published 1990
Printed in Great Britain by Bath Press

British Library cataloguing in publication data

Michael Bakunin: *Statism and Anarchy*. – (Cambridge texts in the history of
political thought)
1. Russia. Anarchism. Bakunin, Mikhail. Biographies
I. Shatz, Marshall S. (Marshall Sharon) *1939*–
355'.83'0924

Library of Congress cataloguing in publication data.

Bakunin, Mikhail Aleksandrovich, 1814–1876.
[Gosudarstvennost' i anarkhiia. English]
Michael Bakunin, Statism and anarchy / translated, edited, and
with an introduction by Marshall S. Shatz.
p.   cm. – (Cambridge texts in the history of political thought)
Translation of: Gosudarstvennost' i anarkhiia.
Includes bibliographical references.
ISBN 0 521 36182 6. – ISBN 0 521 86973 8 (pbk.)
1. Anarchism. 2. State, The. I. Shatz, Marshall. II Title.
III. Title: Statism and anarchy. IV. Series.
HX833.B317513 1990
320.5'7 – dc20 – dc20 89–77393 CIP

ISBN 0 521 36182 6 hard covers
ISBN 0 521 36973 8 paperback

WV

12/23/05

Contents

Statism and Anarchy

I

3–8: the persecution of the International; 8–14: the supremacy of the German state over Europe; 14–26: the decline of the French state; the anti-state sentiments of the French workers.

II

26–33: the imminence of social revolution in Spain and Italy; 33–45: the weaknesses of the Austro-Hungarian Empire; the historical conflict between Slavs and Germans; the anti-state nature of the Slavs; pan-Germanism and pan-Slavism; 45–51: social revolution and the liberation of the Slavs; 51–56: the case of Serbia; 56–60: the Czechs.

III

60–77: German strength and Russian weakness; the dangers of pan-Slavism to the Russian state; 77–83: the character of the German military; 83–88: the Poles as a source of Russian vulnerability; 89–97: the rise of German power on the Baltic; 97–103: the folly of Russian expansion in the East.

Editor's Note

The preparation of this volume was made possible in part by a grant from the National Endowment for the Humanities, an independent federal agency. I am grateful to the Endowment and its staff for their support and encouragement.

I wish to express my thanks to Professor Paul Avrich of Queens College of the City University of New York, and Professor Paul Gagnon of the University of Massachusetts at Boston, who generously took the time to read parts of the manuscript and shared their wisdom with me.

Introduction

The reign of Nicholas I, it has often been noted, displays a curious paradox: one of the most repressive periods in the history of imperial Russia, it was also a time of remarkable intellectual and cultural creativity. In the 1830s and 1840s, under the very noses of the Third Section (Nicholas's political police), Westernizers, Slavophiles, liberals, and even socialists were discussing and developing their ideas. Some of the greatest classics of Russian literature were also being composed and published. Michael Bakunin's long intellectual journey, which would culminate in *Statism and Anarchy* of 1873, his last major work, had its beginnings in this bracing atmosphere.

Bakunin, as well as Peter Kropotkin, his successor as the foremost theorist of Russian anarchism, were both scions of the landed nobility, the most privileged class in the Russian Empire. They were not exceptional in this respect. Until about the 1860s nearly all of Russia's radicals and revolutionaries were nobles. In autocratic Russia, where no individual had political rights or even secure civil liberties or guarantees of free expression, even nobles could suffer oppression, if not of an economic kind. With the bulk of the Russian population enserfed until 1861 and the country as a whole socially and economically backward in comparison with Western Europe, only nobles had the education and exposure to Western ideas that enabled them to criticize existing conditions in ideological terms and articulate a vision of a freer and more just order of things. Thus, for much of the nineteenth century, the Russian intelligentsia, as such educated critics came to be called, consisted largely of sons (and some daughters) of the nobility. Bakunin stands as an extreme, but not untypical, example.

The contradictory social, political, and psychological conditions that generated the intelligentsia collided early in Bakunin's own life. Michael (Mikhail Aleksandrovich, to give him his full Russian name) Bakunin was born on May 18, 1814 – May 30 by the Western calendar, which was twelve days ahead of the Russian calendar then in use – at the family estate of Priamukhino (or Premukhino, as it is sometimes spelled), in Tver province, northwest of Moscow. His father, Alexander, had been sent to Italy at the age of nine and educated there, taking a doctor of philosophy degree at the University of Padua. He subsequently served as a Russian diplomat in Italy. Having retired to his estate, at the age of forty he married the eighteeen-year-old Varvara Muraveva, a member of the prominent and far-flung Muravev clan. They proceeded to have ten children, of whom Michael, the first son, was the third oldest. The Bakunins were a well-off and well-established gentry family, but they were neither illustrious nor rich. Though they owned some 500 "souls," or male serfs, their income was not lavish, especially when it came to providing education and dowries for so many children, and the family correspondence of Michael's early years is filled with references to financial worries.

The elder Bakunin educated his children at home, according to the principles of Rousseau and other Enlightenment figures in whose thought he himself had been steeped. The atmosphere of Priamukhino was idyllic, rich in intellectual stimulation, appreciation of art and nature, and spiritual elevation; it was also fraught with contradictions, for it had little to do with actual Russian life. In an autobiographical fragment composed shortly before his death, Bakunin wrote that he and his brothers and sisters were raised in a Western rather than a Russian spirit. "We lived, so to speak, outside Russian conditions, in a world full of feeling and fantasy but devoid of any reality."[1]

Like most educated Russians of his generation, the elder Bakunin was unperturbed by this contradiction. Having elevated the consciousness and self-consciousness of his sons and daughters, he nevertheless expected them to fulfill uncomplainingly their traditional

---

[1] "Contributions à la Biographie de Michel Bakounine," *La Société Nouvelle* (September 1896), p. 312.

duty to their family, class, and tsar. That meant careers as military officers or landowners for the boys, and as wives of military officers or landowners for the girls. Consciousness and reality soon came into sharp conflict for Michael, and to some extent for his sisters as well.

In 1828, at the age of fourteen, Bakunin was sent to St. Petersburg to prepare for entry into the Artillery School. It was not a happy encounter, either for Bakunin or for the Russian army. Although he received his officer's commission he was dismissed from the Artillery School in 1834 for disciplinary reasons and was sent to serve in a provincial garrison. He detested military life, and his letters of the time are filled with expressions of disgust for it. Although he referred on several occasions to the coarseness and crudeness of officer life, which contrasted so painfully with the cultured (and sheltered) upbringing he had had at Priamukhino, it appears to have been the constraints and petty discipline of military service that particularly grated on him. Finally, in 1835, much to his father's consternation, he left the military for good.

Having liberated himself from the shackles of military service, he also sought to liberate his sisters from the shackles of marriages, or prospective marriages, that he considered unworthy of them. As the oldest boy in the family, and the only male of the first five children, Michael became the leader of the older "cohort" of Bakunin off-spring. He was possessive of his sisters, and rather domineering in regard to them, but his intention was not to keep them from marrying – on the contrary, he would later try to match them up with some of his Moscow friends. His objection was to the kind of marriage to conventional gentry husbands that their parents had in mind, marria-ges in which neither love nor intellectual compatibility was considered relevant. His sisters, whose sensibilities had been cultivated as much as his, shared these qualms, although with more ambivalence. (In the end, he had only limited success in arranging their marital lives.) His quest for personal autonomy and self-development led him inexorably into rebellion against his father – who, it should be noted, was by no means a tyrant, and whom Bakunin genuinely loved and respected.

Bakunin's years at Priamukhino left a lasting mark on him. He was the center of a tight-knit family circle consisting of his four sisters, a few like-minded friends, and himself. It was a close, warm, and highly self-conscious little company, nurtured on the German romantic prose, poetry, and philosophy that was so popular with educated

Russians of the 1830s. Bakunin's letters, and those of the other members of the Priamukhino Circle, are filled with lofty philosophical concepts combined with more traditional religious sentiment. The rhetoric is abstract and romanticized, and not untypically adolescent in its self-centered introspection. What comes through clearly is the difficulty these young people faced in trying to reconcile their search for self-realization with the traditional patriarchal world in which they lived. Bakunin's solution was to create an alternative, ideal world of love and spiritual harmony, its intimacy and fraternal devotion sanctified by romantic literature and philosophy and intensified by its sense of embattlement against insensitive elders. He refers to the Priamukhino Circle in such terms as "our holy union," "this holy fraternity," "our little circle linked by holy love." The seeds of Bakunin's succession of intimate conspiratorial associations in later life, as well as his vision of the small, fraternal anarchist community, may well have been planted here.[2]

For all its warmth and emotional support, the world of Priamukhino was too small to contain Bakunin's restless spirit. He now completed the task of scandalizing his father by moving to Moscow and proclaiming his intention to study philosophy while earning his living as a mathematics tutor. Bakunin in fact gave very few lessons, subsisting instead on an allowance from his father and the assistance of friends. He did, however, immerse himself in the study of philosophy.

In Moscow, he became part of a circle of young intellectuals absorbed in the philosophical currents of the day. It was headed by Nicholas Stankevich, whose compelling personality and early death outshone any specific accomplishments, and it included the brilliant literary critic Vissarion Belinsky. In Moscow, Bakunin also made the acquaintance of such future luminaries as Alexander Herzen and Nicholas Ogarev, who were to achieve renown as radical journalists in emigration and remained his lifelong friends. The intellectuals in Moscow were just beginning to divide into the two camps of "Westernizers," who believed Russia should follow the general

---

[2] A. A. Kornilov, *Molodye gody Mikhaila Bakunina. Iz istorii russkogo romantizma* (Moscow: Izd. M. i S. Sabashnikovykh, 1915), pp. 195–97, 231–32; Arthur Lehning, "Bakunin's Conceptions of Revolutionary Organisations and their Role: A Study of his 'Secret Societies'," in C. Abramsky, ed., *Essays in Honor of E. H. Carr* (London: Macmillan, 1974), pp. 57–58.

course of political and social development already laid down by the West, and the "Slavophiles," who believed Russia should build on her own native culture and institutions, which had best been preserved by the unspoiled peasantry. Both groups would have their impact on Bakunin, for his later thought, like that of many nineteenth-century Russians, was to some degree an amalgam of the two: he would look to the "backward" but uncorrupted Russian peasants, and the Slavs in general, to be the first to put into practice the most advanced Western principles of socialism.[3]

Most of all, in his Moscow years, he studied Hegel, who now replaced Fichte as the philosopher in whom he sought the key to wisdom. As he says in *Statism and Anarchy*, in what is unmistakably an autobiographical remark, one had to have lived in those times to understand the passion with which Hegel's philosophy was embraced. Bakunin made a very serious study of at least parts of Hegel's doctrines, and his first original publication, in the journal *Moscow Observer*, was a Preface to his translation of two of Hegel's five *Gymnasium Lectures*. (He had previously published a translation of Fichte's lectures *On the Vocation of the Scholar*.)

Hegel's influence on his young Russian readers was twofold and contradictory. Some drew from Hegel's dictum "everything that is real is rational, and everything that is rational is real" a conservative, quietistic justification of the status quo. Others, however, drew from it precisely the opposite conclusion: if everything that is rational is real, then those elements of everyday life that are patently irrational, such as repression, or backwardness, are "unreal" and are destined to be swept away by the inexorable unfolding of the dialectic of history. In Herzen's famous phrase, the latter found in Hegel's philosophy "the algebra of revolution." From the perspective of the Anglo-American political tradition, Hegelian philosophy may seem an exceedingly abstract and circuitous way of arriving at a radical critique of the existing order. It must be recalled, however, that in the rigid autocracy of Nicholas I no autonomous political life was allowed, and any

---

[3] The best description of Moscow's intellectual life in this period appears in parts 1–4 of Alexander Herzen's memoirs, *My Past and Thoughts*, trans. by Constance Garnett, revised by Humphrey Higgens, with an introduction by Isaiah Berlin, 4 vols. (New York: Knopf, 1968). A good introduction to the subject is Isaiah Berlin, "A Marvellous Decade, 1838–48: The Birth of the Russian Intelligentsia," in Sidney Harcave, ed., *Readings in Russian History*, 2 vols. (New York: Crowell, 1962), 1, pp. 344–62; reprinted in Isaiah Berlin, *Russian Thinkers* (New York: Viking, 1978), pp. 114–35.

attempt to create one was treated as subversion. Lacking the opportunity for political activity or even political expression, those who wished to question the existing system had to find another, indirect approach. Since the young intellectuals of the day had no power other than the power of thought, Hegelianism, and idealist philosophy in general, with the primacy it gave to mind and consciousness, offered the most satisfying possibility, however abstract it may have been.[4] Thus, in a way that would undoubtedly have astonished its creator, Hegelian philosophy had the capacity to generate, or at least to validate, radicalism.

In general terms, the impact of Hegelianism in Russia was similar to its impact in Germany, where the Young, or Left, Hegelians – including Marx – were beginning to emerge. It has long been thought that it was only after he arrived in Berlin in 1840 and came in contact with Left Hegelian circles that Bakunin was "radicalized," and that he left Russia still a political conservative, or at most apolitical. In his 1838 Preface he had, after all, called for a "reconciliation with reality." A closer scrutiny of that article and of his other writings of the period, however, has brought this view into question and provided evidence that his Hegelianism had already begun to serve as a bridge between knowledge and the criticism of concrete reality, between philosophy and social action.[5] If so, then his later revolutionary stance was a logical result of a philosophical development that began well before he left Russia, rather than an abrupt, and inexplicable, transformation upon his arrival on German soil. Bakunin, who tended to deprecate his early interest in philosophy, a few years later characterized German philosophy as "the spiritual opium of all those who thirst for action and are condemned to inactivity."[6] The fact remains, however, that through such abstractions energetic young men like Bakunin found their way to revolution. This in turn helps to explain

[4] Martin Malia, *Alexander Herzen and the Birth of Russian Socialism, 1812–1855* (Cambridge, Mass.: Harvard University Press, 1961), is the best discussion of the role of idealist philosophy in Russia.

[5] Martine Del Giudice, "Bakunin's 'Preface to Hegel's "Gymnasium Lectures" ': The Problem of Alienation and the Reconciliation with Reality," *Canadian–American Slavic Studies*, 16, 2 (Summer 1982), 161–89.

[6] M. A. Bakunin, *Sobranie sochinenii i pisem, 1828–1876*, ed. Iu. M. Steklov, 4 vols. (Moscow: Izdatel'stvo vsesoiuznogo obshchestva politkatorzhan i ssyl'no-poselentsev, 1934–35), III, p. 415.

why devotion to abstract ideas could sometimes be a punishable offense in Nicholas's Russia.

In 1840, after a lengthy campaign, Bakunin persuaded his father to help finance a period of study in Berlin. His plan was to familiarize himself with German philosophy at its source, and then return to Russia to pursue a career as a university professor. His father was duly skeptical of his son's ability to settle down and embrace the pleasures of academic life, but he concluded that he had little choice but to agree. Since his family lacked sufficient funds to subsidize him fully, however, Bakunin arranged for a subvention from the wealthy and generous Herzen. Even in Moscow he had already acquired his lifelong habit of living off the benefactions of others – as did his later rival Marx, it should be noted. Perhaps it was fitting that a sworn enemy of the existing economic order should help to undermine it by observing so little bourgeois punctiliousness in regard to money matters. It was a practice that had unpleasant and sometimes unsavory consequences, however. For the rest of his life Bakunin would be trailed by an ever swelling chorus of unpaid creditors whose "loans" he never repaid. (Herzen, it should be emphasized, was not among them and always aided Bakunin unstintingly.) His behavior hardly stemmed from a lust for creature comforts – he never sought more than the bare minimum required to keep body and soul together and at times made do with less – nor can it be attributed simply to child-like fecklessness. Rather, it would seem that Bakunin, again like Marx, had such confidence in his destiny and in his mission that he was willing to endure the humiliation of depending on others to foot the bill.

That sense of mission was to drive him for the rest of his life, but as yet it had no specific content or objective. There is, for example, no indication in his early letters or writings that he gave Russia's peasants a thought, even though he had been raised on a serf estate. Like so many educated Russians of his time, he lived side by side with the peasants but in a world apart from them. What he took with him from Russia was a personal and intellectual framework within which concrete political and social ideals would begin to develop as a result of his sojourn in Western Europe. A few years later, in his famous "confession" to Nicholas I, to which we will return below, Bakunin provided an excellent formulation of his lifelong credo: "To look for

my happiness in the happiness of others, for my own worth in the
worth of all those around me, to be free in the freedom of others –
that is my whole faith, the aspiration of my whole life."[7] Throughout
his life Bakunin would seek to liberate both himself and others from
all external constraints on the development of their personalities, just
as he had sought to liberate himself, his sisters, and their friends from
the narrow conventions of family and caste. This effort, given shape
and direction by the myriad experiences and thoughts of subsequent
years, would culminate in his anarchist ideology.

Once settled in Berlin, where for a time he shared a flat with the
future novelist Ivan Turgenev, he attended only briefly to his
philosophical studies. Instead, he was drawn to the Left Hegelians,
and in October 1842 the first fruit of his leftward movement
appeared. It was an article in the Left Hegelian journal *Deutsche
Jahrbücher für Wissenschaft und Kunst* entitled "The Reaction in Germany: A Fragment from a Frenchman." He signed it with the
pseudonym Jules Elysard, so as not to attract the attention of watchful
Russian diplomats, and for good reason. Most of the article was cast
in the abstract terminology of Hegelian dialectics, but its subject was
the contemporary conflict between reaction and revolution. The last
few pages were overtly political, with references to Liberty, Equality,
and Fraternity and to the "spirit of revolution." Even in Russia, he
asserted, "dark clouds are gathering, heralding storm." The article
ended with the famous statement that became the virtual hallmark of
his subsequent career: "Let us therefore trust the eternal Spirit which
destroys and annihilates only because it is the unfathomable and
eternally creative source of all life. The passion for destruction is a
creative passion, too."[8]

In this article Bakunin referred briefly to the rights of the poor, and
he now began to examine the social question. Moving from Germany
to Switzerland, then to Paris, he became acquainted with the various
currents of socialism that were making increasing headway in Europe
at this time. He met almost everyone who was anyone in European

[7] *The Confession of Mikhail Bakunin. With the Marginal Comments of Tsar Nicholas I*,
translated by Robert C. Howes, with an introduction and notes by Lawrence D. Orton
(Ithaca: Cornell University Press, 1977), p. 92.

[8] James M. Edie *et al.*, eds., *Russian Philosophy*, 3 vols. (Chicago: Quadrangle Books,
1965), I, pp. 385, 403–06.

revolutionary and socialist circles of the 1840s, but it was in Paris that he encountered the two men whose views, in different ways, proved most crucial to him. One was Karl Marx, whom Bakunin first met in 1844. For all their bitter personal relations in later years, Bakunin had great respect for Marx's intellect, and adopted many of his criticisms of capitalism. In fact, he may have been the first Russian to familiarize himself closely with Marx's ideas.[9] The other was Pierre-Joseph Proudhon, with whom Bakunin became fast friends. Proudhon was the first to combine the critique of capitalism with anarchism's hostility to the state, and although Bakunin would later reject much of Proudhon's program he assimilated many of Proudhon's basic positions into his anarchist ideology. Meanwhile, the Russian government had learned that he was hobnobbing with European radicals and ordered him to return home. When he refused, he was stripped of his noble status and sentenced *in absentia* to hard labor in Siberia. By 1844 he had burned his bridges to his native land, though he still maintained contact with his family at Priamukhino.

The other issue on which he began to focus in the 1840s was the liberation of the Slavs, and particularly the Poles. In 1847, at a banquet in Paris commemorating the seventeenth anniversary of the Polish uprising of 1830–31, he gave an impassioned speech urging reconciliation between Poles and Russians in a joint revolutionary effort against their common enemy, the despotism of Nicholas I. By the time the revolutions of 1848 broke out, the social and national commitments to which he would henceforth adhere were firmly in place. Their precise definition, and the relationship between them, would be refined further in later years, but they continued to form the major axes of his revolutionary outlook.

Poland was a particularly sore spot for the Russian government, and at the instigation of the Russian ambassador Bakunin was expelled from France. The outbreak of the February Revolution in Paris found him in Brussels, but with the overthrow of Louis-Philippe and the installation of the provisional government he immediately returned to Paris. The upheavals of 1848 and 1849 at last gave him the opportunity for action, and he avidly pursued revolutions all over Europe. In Paris he immersed himself in radical circles. To quote his "confession" once again, he found the revolutionary atmosphere

---

[9] N. Pirumova, *Bakunin* (Moscow: Molodaia gvardiia, 1970), p. 72.

there "a feast without beginning and without end."[10] Equipped with funds and passports by the provisional government, he soon set off for the Duchy of Poznan, in the Prussian part of Poland, to agitate the Poles, but was prevented from reaching it. In June he participated in the Slav Congress in Prague, which had been called by the Czech leadership in response to the German National Assembly in Frankfurt to defend the interests of the Slavs against German as well as Hungarian expansion. He also participated in the insurrection which brought the congress to an end, although his role seems to have been a small one.

In December of 1848 he published an *Appeal to the Slavs*, the work that first drew the attention of a broad European public. Unlike the Czech leaders of the Slav Congress, who thought in terms of achieving national rights within a restructured Austrian Empire, Bakunin called for the overthrow of the despotic regimes in Prussia and Turkey, Austria and Russia, and their replacement by a free federation of Slavic peoples, or even a federation of European republics. "Our whole salvation lies in revolution, and nowhere else," he wrote.[11] Published in Leipzig as a pamphlet in German and Polish versions, it was also translated into Czech and French and was widely read and debated.[12]

Bakunin's overall objective in this period was to bring together the democratic forces of the Slavs, Hungarians, and Germans in a concerted revolutionary assault on the existing order throughout Central and Eastern Europe. After leaving Prague, Bakunin returned to Germany, while retaining contacts among the Czechs. At the beginning of May 1849, while living in Dresden, he was drawn into an insurrection that broke out against the king of Saxony.

The composer Richard Wagner became closely acquainted with Bakunin in Dresden, and although his account is not completely reliable he paints a vivid portrait of him in his autobiography. Wagner captures particularly well the magnetic attraction which this huge and self-assured man exerted on so many people who came in contact with him.

---

[10] Bakunin, *Confession*, p. 56.

[11] Bakunin, *Sobranie sochinenii*, III, p. 357.

[12] For an account of the publication and impact of the *Appeal*, see Lawrence D. Orton, "The Echo of Bakunin's *Appeal to the Slavs* (1848)," *Canadian–American Slavic Studies*, 10, 4 (Winter 1976), 489–501.

I was immediately struck by his singular and altogether imposing personality. He was in the full bloom of manhood, anywhere between thirty and forty years of age. Everything about him was colossal, and he was full of a primitive exuberance and strength . . . His general mode of discussion was the Socratic method, and he seemed quite at his ease when, stretched on his host's hard sofa, he could argue discursively with a crowd of all sorts of men on the problems of revolution. On these occasions he invariably got the best of the argument. It was impossible to triumph against his opinions, stated as they were with the utmost conviction, and overstepping in every direction even the extremest bounds of radicalism.[13]

According to Wagner, although Bakunin disapproved of the insurrection, which he found ill-conceived and inefficient, once it broke out he committed himself to it fully and behaved with "wonderful sangfroid." Wagner states that Bakunin proposed bringing all the insurgents' powder stores to the Town Hall to be blown up at the approach of the attacking troops. (Bakunin confirms this in his "confession," where he states also that he would not have boggled at setting fire to the city, for he could not understand why one should feel sorrier for houses than for people.[14]) Refusing as a matter of honor to flee even when the situation became hopeless, Bakunin was arrested with other leaders of the insurrection. The Saxon authorities tried him and sentenced him to death, then commuted the sentence and turned him over to the Austrians. They in turn tried him for his part in the Prague insurrection, sentenced him to death once again, commuted the sentence and extradited him to Russia. In May of 1851 he was conveyed in chains to St. Petersburg and placed in solitary confinement in the Peter-Paul Fortress, the main Russian prison for political offenders.

A few months later, Bakunin wrote one of his most controversial works, his "confession" to Nicholas I. He was informed that Nicholas wanted him to write an account of his transgressions "as a spiritual son writes to his spiritual father." Bakunin agreed and penned a "letter" ninety-six pages in length. After the Russian Revolution the

[13] Richard Wagner, *My Life*, authorized translation from the German, 2 vols. (New York: Dodd, Mead, 1911), I, p. 467.
[14] *Ibid.*, p. 492; for Wagner's account of Bakunin's participation in the insurrection, see *ibid.*, pp. 478–99. Bakunin, *Confession*, pp. 147–48.

document was found in the tsarist archives and published. Some have interpreted it as the abject apology of a man who had "cracked" under the strain of more than two years of incarceration. A closer examination of the "confession," however, reveals that that was far from the case. Nicholas seems to have wanted two things: repentance, and information on Bakunin's revolutionary accomplices, especially Poles. Bakunin disappointed him on both counts. While conceding that his actions had been criminal from Nicholas's point of view, and signing the document "a repentant sinner," Bakunin retracted none of his convictions. Furthermore, he explicitly refused to incriminate others and was careful to divulge only information he was sure Nicholas had from other sources.

Why, then, did Bakunin agree to write such a lengthy and detailed account of his thoughts and activities from the time of his arrival in Western Europe to the time of his arrest? Although we can hardly hope to enter into the state of mind of someone in Bakunin's position, part of his motivation appears to have been self-scrutiny, a desire to take stock of his life and his goals to date. The "confession" contains a number of introspective passages in which Bakunin seems to be addressing himself as much as Nicholas. In addition, he seems to have been taken with the idea of educating Nicholas. After all, how often did the Emperor of All the Russias have an opportunity to read an authentic revolutionary credo from a direct source? Bakunin probably had few illusions about persuading Nicholas of his views – although this cannot be entirely dismissed, for the idea of "revolution from above" died hard in many Russians, including Bakunin. Primarily, however, Bakunin appears to have wished to enlighten Nicholas, for whatever good it might do, as to the true nature of the progressive forces at large in contemporary Europe. Hence, in the guise of a letter of repentance, we find a detailed account of Bakunin's education in radicalism and his participation in efforts to topple governments across Europe.

In the course of the narrative, several themes appear that henceforth remain constant in Bakunin's thought in one form or another. Slav unity is one, coupled with an increasing strain of anti-Germanism, here directed mainly against the Austrian Empire. Anti-parliamentarism is also a prominent feature, for the events of 1848 and 1849 had deeply disillusioned Bakunin, like many other European radicals, as to the value of "bourgeois democracy" and constitutionalism. In turn, his disappointment at the failure of democratic revolution in Germany, which he analyzes at considerable length in *Statism and Anarchy*, may have reinforced his growing anti-German sentiment. In an odd passage that seems to reflect the very accusation he would later hurl against Marx, he told Nicholas that he favored a strong dictatorial government, especially for Russia, whose purpose would be to educate the people to the point that such dictatorship became unnecessary.[15] (He did not specify who was to head such a dictatorship, but this theme would recur several times in the course of his career.) He also admitted to harboring a "passion for destruction," reiterating the famous phrase from his article of 1842.[16]

The "confession," then, with due account taken of the circumstances in which it was written, stands as a detailed and self-revealing account of a vital period in Bakunin's life. That it elicited no mitigation of his sentence is not surprising. (In 1854, during the Crimean War, the government, apparently fearing an attack on St. Petersburg, moved him to the more remote Schlüsselburg Fortress.) Bakunin claimed that Alexander II, Nicholas's son, who came to the throne in 1855, upon reading his "letter" said that he saw no repentance in it at all,[17] and Nicholas seems to have been of the same mind. They were right, for Bakunin emerged from his long confinement with the same political views he held when he began it. This is clearly documented in a letter he smuggled past the prison censors to his family in 1854. Even after five years of solitude and physical deterioration, he declared that prison, far from altering his previous convictions, had made them "more fiery, more decisive, and more unconditional."[18] The rest of his life would bear out the truth of those words.

In 1857, fearing for his sanity as well as his physical condition, Bakunin was finally reduced to pleading for mercy, and his entreaties and those of his family succeeded. Alexander II released him from prison and allowed him to settle in Siberian exile for life. After a brief visit to his family's estate he arrived in Tomsk. For a man as gregarious and filled with restless energy as Bakunin, the loneliness and the inactivity of solitary confinement must have been unbearable. He now made up for lost time on both counts. In 1858 he met and

[15] Bakunin, *Confession*, p. 91.
[16] *Ibid.*, p. 103.
[17] M. P. Dragomanov, ed., *Pis'ma M. A. Bakunina k A. I. Gertsenu i N. P. Ogarevu* (Geneva: Georg et Co., 1896), p. 72.
[18] Bakunin, *Sobranie sochinenii*, IV, p. 245.

married Antonia Kwiatkowska, a comely eighteen-year-old of Polish parentage whose father worked for a private gold-mining company in Tomsk. It was a curious marriage in a number of respects. Bakunin was some twenty-six years older than his bride, and although she was educated she had little interest in his political activities. Even physically they seemed mismatched, for the enormous figure of Bakunin dwarfed his diminutive wife – like an elephant and a pony at the circus, as one of their acquaintances put it. Furthermore, in later years Antonia bore three children fathered by one of Bakunin's Italian political associates, Carlo Gambuzzi, whom she married after Bakunin's death. Nevertheless, Bakunin loved his wife, and her children, tenderly, and the marriage endured for the rest of his life.

The problem of political inactivity was resolved by Bakunin's bold escape from Siberia. (Not to be outdone, Peter Kropotkin in 1876 made an even more daring escape from a St. Petersburg military hospital.) Having persuaded the tsarist government to allow him to travel freely in Siberia to pursue a commercial career, he boarded a Russian ship on the Pacific coast and then transferred to an American vessel which took him to Yokohama. There he took another American ship to San Francisco, crossed the Isthmus of Panama, and after a stay in New York and a visit to Boston and Cambridge (where he dined with Longfellow), he sailed for England. At the end of 1861 he turned up on Alexander Herzen's doorstep in London.

Bakunin seems to have thought in terms of forming a triumvirate with Herzen and Ogarev, whose newspaper *The Bell*, published in London and smuggled into Russia, had become an influential voice of reform. It soon became clear that Bakunin's views were considerably more radical than those of his friends, and he craved a greater degree of political activism than their journalistic enterprise could offer him. When a new Polish insurrection broke out in January 1863, Bakunin felt impelled to make a personal contribution to the Polish cause, which he had championed so vigorously. He joined a quixotic expedition through the Baltic to land an armed Polish legion on the coast of Lithuania, but neither Bakunin nor the ship got any farther than Sweden. Probably the most gratifying moment of the whole episode was his reunion in May with his wife, Antonia, who, after an arduous journey from Siberia, at last caught up with him in Stockholm.

Bakunin now decided to move to Italy. He arrived there at the beginning of 1864 and remained until 1867, first in Florence and then in Naples. Italy proved to be one of the countries most receptive to Bakunin's views, and he exerted a strong influence on its budding socialist movement. It was in Naples in 1866 that Bakunin founded the International Brotherhood (an effort he had begun earlier in Florence), the first of the long and complex series of secret revolutionary organizations that marked his anarchist years.

Exactly when his views finally crystallized into full-fledged anarchism is difficult to determine. By July 1866, at the latest, he was voicing the categorical rejection of the state that formed the heart of his anarchist ideology.[19] In August 1867, in a series of articles written for an Italian newspaper, he explicitly used the word "anarchist" to characterize his views.[20]

Bakunin left Italy in the last months of 1867 and spent the rest of his life in Switzerland, where he could conduct his activities in greater safety. He joined the League of Peace and Freedom, a middle-class liberal organization founded in 1867 and based in Geneva. Serving on its central committee, he attempted to "radicalize" it, that is, to persuade it to adopt his anti-state and socialist views. As part of that campaign, he wrote an unfinished work entitled *Federalism, Socialism, and Anti-Theologism*, the first extended exposition of his anarchist principles. Having failed to bend the League to his purposes, he and his followers withdrew from it and created the International Alliance of Social Democracy.

The period from 1867 to 1874 was the most active and productive in Bakunin's life, and it was in these years that he wrote all of his major anarchist works. One element of his activities was an ill-advised attempt to influence revolutionary circles in his homeland through collaboration with Sergei Nechaev.

Nechaev appeared in Switzerland in 1869, claiming to be the head of a vast revolutionary conspiracy in Russia. He made a great impression on Bakunin, who helped produce a series of propaganda pamphlets for Nechaev to circulate in Russia, sought financing for his activities, and in general lent his name to Nechaev's enterprise. It gradually became clear that Nechaev in no way merited his confidence. A man of humble origins, he does seem to have hated the existing order, but it was a warped and unprincipled hatred which he

---

[19] Dragomanov, ed., *Pis'ma*, pp. 172–74.

[20] T. R. Ravindranathan, "Bakunin in Naples: An Assessment," *Journal of Modern History*, 53, 2 (June 1981), 201 n. 42.

was prepared to direct against his friends as well as his enemies.[21] Bakunin, for example, had received an advance from a publisher to translate Marx's *Capital* into Russian, and when he failed to deliver the translation Nechaev, without Bakunin's knowledge, wrote a threatening letter to the publisher demanding that he release Bakunin from his obligation. (Marx was to exploit this episode in his campaign against Bakunin in the International.) Nechaev also attempted to seduce Herzen's daughter in order to draw her into his schemes, and when he and Bakunin finally parted company he stole some of Bakunin's papers to use for blackmail. Worst of all, it transpired that in Moscow, where he did in fact form a small revolutionary circle, he had persuaded the other members to help him murder one of their number whom he claimed to be an informer. For this deed he was eventually extradited to Russia from Switzerland as a common criminal and spent the rest of his life in prison in particularly brutal conditions.

Bakunin's relationship with Nechaev, which lasted for more than a year, is one of the most closely examined episodes of his life. The greatest controversy has swirled around the authorship of the notorious "Catechism of a Revolutionary." This most famous literary product of the Nechaev affair is a horrifying credo of the revolutionary as nihilist, a cold-blooded individual who has severed all the personal ties and human feelings binding him to conventional society the better to destroy it. The "Catechism" was found by the Russian police and published in the course of prosecuting the Nechaevists. It had long been assumed that Bakunin was primarily, if not wholly, responsible for the composition of the document. Subsequently discovered evidence, however, indicates that Nechaev was the more likely author, though some contribution by Bakunin cannot be precluded.[22]

This does not absolve Bakunin of responsibility for entering into a partnership with such a sinister and unscrupulous figure. His initial attraction to Nechaev is not difficult to understand: Nechaev was young and energetic and claimed to be an authentic representative of

[21] For a biography of Nechaev, see Philip Pomper, *Sergei Nechaev* (New Brunswick, N. J.: Rutgers University Press, 1979).
[22] The documentation is provided in Arthur Lehning, ed., *Archives Bakounine*, IV: *Michel Bakounine et ses relations avec Sergej Nečaev, 1870–1872* (Leiden: Brill, 1971), and Michael Confino, *Violence dans la violence: le débat Bakounine-Nečaev* (Paris: Maspero, 1973).

the rising new generation in Russia and a direct link with the revolutionary movement. Wanting to believe him, Bakunin was too quick to accept Nechaev's claims – and much too slow to perceive their emptiness and Nechaev's ruthlessness.

Interestingly, Bakunin kept his collaboration with Nechaev separate from his other organizational activities both inside and outside the International. Those activities generated a welter of intertwining and overlapping associations, some with both public and secret manifestations, outer and inner circles, like the nesting wooden dolls of Russian folk art. Bakunin first joined the International in 1864, though he remained an inactive member. In the summer of 1868, he became a member of the International's Geneva Central Section. In September of the same year he formed the International Alliance of Social Democracy (essentially a successor to the International Brotherhood of 1866), which then asked to be admitted to the International. When the latter refused to admit it as a separate body, the International Alliance was dissolved – officially, at least – and in March 1869 was admitted as the Geneva Section of the International. (To make matters even more confusing, there was also a Russian Section in Geneva, whose members supported Marx against Bakunin.) In September of 1872, with a group of Italian and Spanish associates, Bakunin founded the Alliance of Social Revolutionaries, a sequel to (or possibly a continuation of) the Alliance of Social Democracy. A few months earlier, he had formed a Russian Brotherhood, consisting of himself and a handful of young Russian students in Zurich, and in July of 1872 he created with them and a few others the Slavic Section of Zurich, which affiliated with the Jura Federation of the International. Still other secret organizations may have existed, and the attempt to sort them out has bedeviled historians for a hundred years. In most cases, these were nothing more than small circles of like-minded intimates, for whom Bakunin delighted in drawing up elaborate statutes and statements of purpose.

At the same time Bakunin was producing an abundant mass of literature. He was an extraordinary letter-writer: at one point in 1870 he claimed that he had written "twenty-three big letters" in the past three days.[23] His letters are vigorous, direct, and often very revealing. His theoretical writings, on the other hand, consist mostly of

[23] Dragomanov, ed., *Pis'ma*, p. 300.

unfinished fragments, few of which were published in his lifetime. Nothing could better illustrate the difference in temperament between him and Marx than the sheer messiness of Bakunin's literary output. A good example is a major work entitled *The Knouto-Germanic Empire and the Social Revolution*, which he wrote in 1870–71. Like many of his works, it seemed to escape the control of its creator and take on a life of its own. He wrote to Ogarev, "understand that I started it as a pamphlet but am finishing it as a book. It's monstrous . . ."[24] And a monster it was, a great sprawling mass, never completed and bristling with fragments, variants, introductions, and addenda. Only part of it appeared in print at the time, but another section, published after Bakunin's death under the title *God and the State*, became the best known of Bakunin's works and has appeared in at least sixteen languages.

The outbreak of the Franco-Prussian War in 1870, and the events that followed it, evoked a strong response from Bakunin. His principal work on the subject was *Letters to a Frenchman on the Present Crisis*, published in September of 1870, an abridgment of a larger work. In a striking anticipation of Lenin's policy in the First World War of "turning the imperialist war into a civil war," Bakunin urged the French to turn their defensive war against the Germans into a popular revolution to transform the French state into a federation of autonomous communes – even at the risk of annihilating themselves and all their property.[25] A few days after the defeat of Louis Napoleon, having been informed of plans for a socialist uprising in Lyons, Bakunin resolved "to take my old bones there and probably to play my last role."[26] This was Bakunin's first opportunity to participate in a real insurrection since 1849. His influence made itself felt with the appearance in the city of a poster issued by the revolutionary committee calling for abolition of "the administrative and governmental machinery of the state,"[27] but the uprising itself was quickly suppressed. Bakunin conducted himself with resolution and was briefly arrested, but he managed to flee and made his way back to Switzerland in disguise.

[24] *Ibid.*, p. 321.
[25] Arthur Lehning, ed., *Archives Bakounine*, VI: *Michel Bakounine sur la guerre franco-allemande et la révolution sociale en France, 1870–1871* (Leiden: Brill, 1977), p. 20.
[26] *Ibid.*, p. xlix.
[27] *Ibid.*, p. 145.

He had already begun to connect the stunning victory of Germany over France with the "doctrinaire socialism" of the Marxists, and the next momentous event in his life, the schism in the International in 1872, confirmed that connection in his mind. Relations between Marx and Bakunin had never been warm, although it was only in the late 1860s that they erupted into open warfare. When the two met in Paris in 1844, Bakunin had admired Marx's erudition but not his personality. Then, in July of 1848, Marx, in his Cologne newspaper the *Neue Rheinische Zeitung*, published a report that the novelist George Sand had proof that Bakunin was a Russian government agent – a rumor that had been dogging Bakunin for some time. The paper subsequently printed Sand's denial of the story as well as Bakunin's protest, but the incident could not help but poison their future relations. (They met once again, in London in 1864, an encounter that was cordial but distant.) Furthermore, Marx was as scornful and distrustful of Russians as Bakunin was anti-German and anti-Semitic. Even Poland, whose independence both of them supported, drew them apart rather than together: to Marx, freedom for Poland signified a blow against Russia, the bastion of European reaction, whereas to Bakunin it represented the starting-point of Russia's liberation. Finally, it is hardly surprising that even an international organization was not capacious enough to contain two such domineering as well as divergent personalities. Nevertheless, the personal antagonism between them should not be unduly emphasized – for Bakunin as well as Marx their conflict involved fundamental differences of principle.

The storm which had been gathering for several years finally broke at the congress of the International held at The Hague in September 1872. Marx succeeded in having Bakunin (who was unable to attend the congress) expelled from the International on the grounds, for which no convincing proof was offered, that he had continued to maintain within the International a secret Alliance inimical to the International's objectives. For good measure, he was also accused of having engaged in fraud and intimidation in regard to his projected translation of Marx's *Capital*. In order to keep the General Council out of the hands of the Bakuninists (who by now probably constituted a majority of the International), Marx had The Hague Congress agree to transfer it from London to New York. In terms of the labor movement at the time, this was the equivalent of Siberian exile, and, as Marx well knew, it spelled the death of the old International.[28]

Statism and Anarchy, written in the following year, summarizes Bakunin's reactions to the tumultuous events of the early 1870s. It was his last major piece of writing. He now attempted to achieve a measure of stability in his life and security for his family. One of his Italian adherents, who had a private fortune, bought an estate called Baronata, near Locarno. The plan was to turn it into a kind of "safe house" for revolutionaries from neighboring Italy and elsewhere, while at the same time providing a home for the Bakunins. Among other benefits, vesting formal ownership in Bakunin's name would have provided him with the safety of Swiss citizenship. Like every other venture in Bakunin's life that involved money, this one ended disastrously. A succession of mishaps led to the near bankruptcy of Bakunin's friend and bitter recriminations between them. Bakunin and his long-suffering wife had to leave the property, and Bakunin's reputation suffered considerable damage. Perhaps in expiation of the fiasco, Bakunin in August of 1874 set off for Bologna to participate in another projected insurrection. It fizzled before it could even begin, and Bakunin returned to Switzerland without injury either to himself or to the established order. It was his last exploit. He spent his remaining days in growing distress from kidney and bladder ailments and on July 1, 1876, he died in Berne, where he had gone to seek medical treatment.

Bakunin's life and his thought are inseparably intertwined, for he drew his ideas from his experiences and personal encounters as well as from his reading – though the breadth of the latter should not be underestimated. Neither his life nor his thought can be understood in isolation from each other, but, on the other hand, neither entirely explains the other. For example, his commitment to popular spontaneity and self-rule was perfectly genuine, yet he was drawn throughout his life to the idea of a revolutionary "dictatorship." His celebration of destruction was not just an abstract vestige of Hegelian philosophy but manifested itself in graphic and concrete terms – yet in his personal behavior he was the kindest and least bloodthirsty of men. There is no ready explanation for such riddles, no neat dialectical

---

[28] A detailed history of the International from the anarchist point of view, which includes a good deal of information about Bakunin himself, is James Guillaume, *L'Internationale: documents et souvenirs (1864–1878)*, 4 vols. (Paris, 1905–10).

resolution of all the inconsistencies and contradictions in Bakunin's personality and ideas. While they continue to puzzle biographers and historians, however, they seem to have left Bakunin himself serenely untroubled.

Though technically incomplete, *Statism and Anarchy*, to a greater degree than most of Bakunin's writings, forms a cohesive whole. In fact, it is quite artfully constructed. Basically, it weaves together three main themes. One is the impact on Europe of the Franco-Prussian War and the rise of the German Empire. The second is Bakunin's criticism of the Marxists in the wake of the schism in the International. The third is a recapitulation of his fundamental anarchist views. The last is what gives the work its significance as a statement of anarchist principles, but in the context of the other two themes those principles take on a concrete, even programmatic character that is absent in more abstract works.

Much of *Statism and Anarchy* is a survey of the condition of Europe in the wake of the German victory over France and the advent of Bismarck. Like so many European radicals, Bakunin was shocked and dismayed at the abrupt eclipse of France, with its revolutionary and socialist traditions, and at the prospect of a Europe dominated by Germany. He feared that the forces of "statism," and hence of European-wide reaction, had been immeasurably strengthened by the rise of German power, and the forces of popular social and economic liberation weakened.

Unfortunately, Bakunin's elaboration of this theme is accompanied by a virulent Germanophobia. It may have stemmed in part from the Slavophile current of Russian thought, which regarded the Russian bureaucratic state as a German importation. It seems to have been implanted mainly by his experiences in the 1848 period, however: his adoption of the cause of the Austrian Slavs, his disillusionment with German liberalism, and, perhaps not least, his treatment at the hands of the Saxon and Austrian authorities after the Dresden insurrection. It emerged full-blown in the wake of the Franco-Prussian War, when his alarm at the political and military power of the German Empire coincided with his growing enmity toward Marx.

Bakunin's anti-German sentiments did sensitize him to some of the more ominous implications of Germany's rise. There is a certain prophetic quality to his warnings against unfulfilled German nationalist ambitions, acquiescence to authority, and militarism – just as there is a prophetic quality to his warnings of the possible consequences of Russian expansionism. He goes well beyond objective analysis, however, and his invective against the servility and docility of the Germans verges on a kind of racism.

Equally repellent, though less marked in this work than in some others, is Bakunin's anti-Semitism, which often appeared as a corollary to his anti-Germanism. Again, it is in part a weapon in his war against Marx. Not only was Marx himself Jewish as well as German, but some of those who helped him in his campaign against Bakunin were also Jewish. Bakunin's anti-Semitism, however, long antedated his conflict with Marx. It may be argued that such sentiments, however distasteful, do not negate Bakunin's anarchist principles.[29] It may also be argued that those principles are somehow deficient if even one so passionately committed to them was unable to surmount crude ethnic prejudices. The most that can be said for Bakunin is that he was hardly unique in this regard. In France, for example, at least until the Dreyfus affair, socialist and anarchist writers and artists frequently employed stereotypical anti-Semitic images of the Jew as capitalist or banker, or simply as a crude synonym for "bourgeois."[30] It should be noted also that Bakunin's consistent (though not uncritical) support and defense of the Poles – in regard to whom so many otherwise liberal Russians had a moral blind spot – was a remarkable example of adherence to principle.

The second major theme of *Statism and Anarchy* is its critique of Marxism. To the Marxists, the proletariat's participation in the political life of its respective nations seemed an effective way of pursuing the class struggle and ultimately achieving the supremacy of the proletariat and the elimination of the state. To the anarchists, however, any participation in "bourgeois politics" was inherently corrupting. One could fight the enemy or one could join the enemy, but one could not do both. To expect to use political methods to abolish political domination was a dangerous delusion.

A closely related issue concerned the structure and organization of

[29] Arthur Lehning, ed., *Archives Bakounine*, II: *Michel Bakounine et les conflits dans l'Internationale, 1872* (Leiden: Brill, 1965), p. xxvi n. 1.

[30] Michael R. Marrus, "Popular Anti-Semitism," and Philip Dennis Cate, "The Paris Cry: Graphic Artists and the Dreyfus Affair," in Norman Kleeblatt, ed., *The Dreyfus Affair: Art, Truth and Justice* (Berkeley: University of California Press, 1987), pp. 50–61, 62–95.

the International itself. If components of the International were to engage in contemporary political life, the organization required a certain amount of centralization in order to provide information, support, and coordination, and thus, at the very least, an enhanced role for the General Council. To the anarchists, the International must serve as a direct model for the new society, a microcosm of the free future order. Therefore they envisioned it as a true federation, with local sections enjoying the greatest possible degree of autonomy. Thus the debate over the powers of the General Council (and hence of Marx, who dominated it) was really a debate over basic issues of the International's strategy and objectives.

Bakunin contended that if the Marxists attempted to work through the state to achieve their ends, there could be only two results: either they would be drawn into the parliamentary system and would become indistinguishable from the bourgeois parties; or, if they ever came to power, they would form a new ruling elite over the masses. In twentieth-century terms, the result would be either West European Social Democracy or Leninism–Stalinism. Bakunin spelled out the second possibility in the most remarkable passage in *Statism and Anarchy*, his description of what a Marxist "dictatorship of the proletariat" would look like. Brief as it is, it is a chilling picture of Stalin's Russia some sixty years before the fact, and a prophecy of the rise of the "new class" long before Milovan Djilas made the term famous.

Interestingly enough, Marx, who had learned Russian in order to study Russian economic conditions, carefully read *Statism and Anarchy*. Sometime in 1874–75 he went through the work and made lengthy extracts and notes. His own comments on it are few but revealing. His chief criticism of Bakunin was that he did not pay enough attention to the economic preconditions of revolution. "Will," Marx complained, "not economic conditions, is the basis of his social revolution." There was much to be said for this judgment. What Marx did not perceive so clearly was that precisely the opposite criticism might be leveled against him. His only response to Bakunin's warning that socialism might produce a new ruling elite was to reiterate confidently that once economic conditions were changed and class rule came to an end, the state and all relations of political authority would necessarily disappear.[31] He would not entertain the possibility

---

[31] "Konspekt von Bakunins Buch 'Staatlichkeit und Anarchie'," in Karl Marx and Friedrich Engels, *Werke*, XVIII (Berlin: Dietz Verlag, 1981), p. 634.

that political domination was a product of will, and not solely of economic conditions, and that the former might persist even after the latter had been transformed.

It is in the attack on Marx that the literary artistry of *Statism and Anarchy* reveals itself. The discussion of Marx and his views appears only in the last third of the book. By the time Bakunin gets to Marx, however, he has so identified the Germans with "statism" that Marx's political outlook takes on a truly sinister cast. In the context which *Statism and Anarchy* has created, Marx becomes a kind of socialist Bismarck, promoting pan-German hegemony by other means. Whatever the fairness or accuracy of such a depiction – and it should be kept in mind that Marx, Lassalle, and the new German Social-Democratic Party, all of whom Bakunin lumps together, actually held different views on many issues – it is the product of a degree of literary skill for which Bakunin is rarely given credit.

In opposition to both statism and Marxism, Bakunin presents in broad outline the principles of "anarchy," as he calls what we would today term anarchism, and the anarchist society of the future. In the most general terms it can be said that each of the three competing political ideologies of the nineteenth century, liberalism, socialism, and anarchism, took its stand primarily on one element of the French Revolution's trinity, Liberty, Equality, and Fraternity. Anarchism joined socialism in rejecting nineteenth-century parliamentarism, or "bourgeois democracy," as a narrow conception of liberty which could be enjoyed only by the propertied classes as long as economic inequality prevailed. The anarchist critique of liberalism added little to that of the socialists, and the pages of *Statism and Anarchy* dealing with this subject are perhaps the least original – and, in retrospect, some of the most short-sighted – in the book. Much more original was anarchism's critique of Marxism as inherently unable to achieve the true economic equality it claimed to represent. Bakunin was the first to warn that Marxists in power might simply replace the capitalists they had chased out, leaving the position of the workers essentially unchanged, and after him it became a major component of anarchist thought.

Meanwhile, anarchism held that the key to true liberty and true equality was the third term of the revolutionary motto, fraternity. The word fraternity, or brotherhood, recurs throughout Bakunin's writings and appears in the name of several of his revolutionary organizations as well. Like other anarchists, Bakunin believed that social solidarity, a deep-rooted social and communal instinct, was an innate feature of human nature. If it failed to manifest itself consistently in contemporary society, that was only because it had been suppressed, or distorted, by the artificial structure of the state. To create a new and better society, therefore, did not require the reeducation of its inhabitants or the transformation of human nature, but only the release of the masses' pent-up natural instincts and social energies by destroying the institutions thwarting them. Hence the refrain that runs throughout *Statism and Anarchy*, the call for a new society organized "from below upward," composed of small, voluntary communities federating into larger associations for larger purposes. This was the structure that was to replace the state, with its hierarchical form of organization "from above downward." Such a social vision ultimately rested on an abiding faith in human brotherhood, for in the absence of the state, with its legal, administrative, and police structures, there would be little else to hold a community together.

And yet, in Appendix A of *Statism and Anarchy*, Bakunin sharply criticized the Russian peasant commune for the conformist pressures it exerted on the individual, a criticism he had expressed even more vehemently some years earlier.[32] He was unusual among Russian revolutionaries in this period, for most of them glorified the commune, believing it fraught with socialist potential. Bakunin seems to have sensed the possibility of conflict between the autonomy of the community and the freedom of the individual. This issue goes to the core of the anarchist outlook as a whole, for the small, face-to-face community lay at the very center of anarchism's ideals. Unfortunately, Bakunin failed to grapple with it further.

Bakunin's social objectives in turn helped to determine his concept of "social revolution," which occupied a particularly prominent place in *Statism and Anarchy*. The primary purpose of the revolution was to destroy the state and all its appurtenances; consequently, the popular forces most suitable for carrying it out were those segments of the population most alienated from the established order and with the least to lose from its demise. Bakunin often voiced suspicion of the sturdy, "class-conscious," urban proletarians upon whom Marx placed his hopes, for he regarded them as already partially

[32] Letter to Herzen and Ogarev, July 19, 1866, in Dragomanov, ed., *Pis'ma*, pp. 176–77.

"bourgeoisified," corrupted by middle-class values. Instead, he looked to the most destitute and desperate toilers: peasants, semi-urbanized laborers and artisans – what the Marxists would call the Lumpenproletariat. At times his vivid imagination led him to romanticize such elements as brigands and bandits, whom he chose to see as social rebels rather than social deviants. In *Statism and Anarchy*, as well as in other writings, he celebrates Razin and Pugachev, who led great popular uprisings in seventeenth- and eighteenth-century Russia, and at one point, in regard to the revolutions of 1848, he even refers to street urchins. Clearly, however, he regarded such individuals as instigators, or inspirers, of a popular revolution, not as a substitute for it.

The other force necessary for social revolution was what Bakunin referred to as the "intellectual proletariat," educated individuals who had turned their backs on their class of origin. They alone could provide organization, propaganda, and encouragement to the scattered and downtrodden masses. They must not attempt to direct the masses or to impose their own ideas or values on them, however, but must limit themselves to literary and organizational tasks. Exactly how such dedicated and strong-willed individuals were to be prevented from dominating or even dictating to the masses was unclear, and, as we have seen, Bakunin himself, like so many revolutionaries who came after him, was too impatient, and too domineering, to abide strictly by his own principles.

With his theory of social revolution, Bakunin at last brought together the social and national "tracks" he had been pursuing since the 1840s. For Bakunin believed that the popular forces most likely to demolish the "statist" order, and most capable of creating a new society "from below upward," were to be found in the Latin and Slavic countries. Spain, Italy, and Eastern Europe seemed to him to have retained to the greatest degree the large and destitute peasantry, the semi-peasant urban work force, and the disaffected intelligentsia characteristic of what we would today call an underdeveloped country. There, too, the peasants and even the working classes of the cities most fully retained their traditional character and forms of organization, hence the greatest sense of distance from the state. By contrast, in such countries as Germany and England, with their greater degree of civic development and public consciousness, the workers seemed increasingly drawn into the established structure.

Thus Bakunin looked to the southern and eastern fringes of Europe to initiate the anarchist revolution, and it was in these regions, notably Spain, Italy, and his homeland, Russia, that his ideas had the greatest impact and anarchism became a significant ideological force. More broadly, Bakunin's theory of revolution identified with remarkable accuracy the social forces and political environments that were to produce some of the most significant revolutions of the twentieth century.

Statism and Anarchy was aimed specifically at a Russian readership, and it is the only major work of Bakunin's anarchist period that he wrote in Russian rather than French. Composed in the summer of 1873, it was printed in Switzerland in an edition of 1,200 copies, almost all of which were destined for Russia. (It was published anonymously, but those interested in the contents had no difficulty learning who the author was.) Emigré revolutionaries had now established efficient networks for smuggling contraband literature across the porous Russian frontier, and most of the copies of the work were shipped safely to St. Petersburg, where they were distributed by revolutionary circles.[33]

Thus *Statism and Anarchy* succeeded in reaching its intended audience, and at a time when that audience was particularly receptive to the book's message – on the eve of the famous "to the people" movement of 1874. Bakunin, among others, had long been urging the educated youth to "go to the people," to immerse themselves in the life of the peasants, and in the "mad summer" of 1874, several thousand of them attempted to do just that. Leaving their homes, schools, and universities, they fanned out to the countryside to make direct contact with the Russian people. The movement was not a conspiracy, and the "Populists," as they came to be called, had no organizational center or direction. Some sought primarily to renounce their relative comforts and privileges and thereby give their lives greater meaning. Others, following the precepts of Peter Lavrov, viewed their mission as an educational one, a matter of preaching socialism to the peasants and, as we would term it today, "raising their consciousness." Still others, however, agreed with Bakunin's criti-

---

[33] Arthur Lehning, ed., *Archives Bakounine*, III: *Etatisme et anarchie, 1873* (Leiden: Brill, 1967), p. xxiv. The work was reprinted in 1906 in St. Petersburg. Editions were also published in Russia in 1919 and 1922, but without Appendices A and B.

cism of this program and sought to exhort and galvanize the peasants to insurrection on the model of the Razin and Pugachev uprisings. Unsurprisingly, the episode ended badly for its participants, and many hundreds of them were soon rounded up by the tsarist police.

The influence of *Statism and Anarchy* on the "to the people" movement was attested by a number of contemporary Russian activists. It was confirmed by the minister of justice himself, who, in a memorandum on the movement, attributed a particularly nefarious influence to Bakunin's writings and followers – perhaps the highest accolade a Russian revolutionary could receive.[34] Just how quickly and widely the book was disseminated can be judged by one curious example recently unearthed from the tsarist archives. In June of 1874, one A. I. Ivanchin-Pisarev, the owner of an estate in Iaroslavl province, northeast of Moscow, was investigated by the police. The investigation established that among other suspicious activities Ivanchin-Pisarev had been circulating a small library of subversive literature – including Bakunin's *Statism and Anarchy*.[35]

Although anti-state sentiment had been a marked feature of Russian revolutionary thought long before the appearance of *Statism and Anarchy*, the work helped to lay the foundations of a Russian anarchist movement as a separate current within the revolutionary stream. As in the West, the anarchists in Russia remained a minority voice among the radicals. Lacking any broad opportunity to put their own ideals into practice, one of their most important historical functions was to serve as critics of the more numerous and better organized Marxists. Reiterating and developing Bakunin's insight into the authoritarian proclivities of revolutionary intellectuals, they came to serve as a kind of conscience of the left. This role assumed particular relevance, as well as danger, when the Russian state in 1917 became the first to be ruled by avowed Marxists. Applying to the conditions of Soviet Russia their familiar warnings concerning the rise of a new socialist elite, anarchists were among the first critics of the Bolshevik dictatorship, and they were also among its first victims.[36]

[34] On the contemporary impact of *Statism and Anarchy*, see *ibid.*, pp. xxv–xxvi, and Franco Venturi, *Roots of Revolution: A History of the Populist and Socialist Movements in Nineteenth Century Russia*, translated by Francis Haskell (London: Weidenfeld and Nicolson, 1960), pp. 438, 506.
[35] Daniel Field, "Peasants and Propagandists in the Russian Movement to the People of 1874," *Journal of Modern History*, 59, 3 (September 1987), 419–20.
[36] Paul Avrich, ed., *The Anarchists in the Russian Revolution* (Ithaca: Cornell University

In a larger perspective, anarchism's foremost contribution to modern political thought has also, perhaps, been its critical voice. Whatever else anarchism might stand for, its defining feature is negation of the state and of political relationships. Consequently, anarchism has served the useful and provocative purpose of challenging the very validity of politics, the legitimacy of the political sphere of human life. It asks the simple but searching question, *is* man by nature made to live in a polis? One may or may not agree with the answer anarchism itself has given. By persistently and vigorously raising the question, however, anarchism, it might be said, has served as the conscience of political thought.

Press, 1973). The American anarchist Emma Goldman was in Russia in 1920 and 1921, and her autobiography, *Living My Life*, 2 vols. (New York: Knopf, 1931), contains a vivid account of those years. Even within the Communist Party itself, left-wing critics of official policies in the early years of Bolshevik rule frequently voiced sentiments the anarchists had been expressing for years. See Robert Vincent Daniels, *The Conscience of the Revolution: Communist Opposition in Soviet Russia*, (Cambridge, Mass.: Harvard University Press, 1960).

Principal events in Bakunin's life

Events occurring within Russia are dated according to the Old Style calendar then in effect, which in the nineteenth century was twelve days behind the Western calendar. The latter is used for events occurring outside Russia.

1814   *May 18*: born at Priamukhino, Tver province.

1828   Goes to St. Petersburg to study at Artillery School.

1835   Retires from military service.

1836   Moves to Moscow, joins Stankevich Circle.

1838   *March*: publishes Preface to Hegel's *Gymnasium Lectures*.

1840   *June*: leaves Russia to study philosophy in Berlin.

1842   *October*: publishes "Reaction in Germany."

1843   Moves to Zurich, meets Wilhelm Weitling.

1844   *February*: ordered home by Russian government.

        Settles in Paris, meets Marx and Proudhon.

        December: decree of Russian Senate strips him of noble status, sentences him *in absentia* to hard labor in Siberia.

1847   *November 29*: speaks at Polish banquet in Paris.

        December: expelled from France, moves to Brussels.

1848	*February*: returns to Paris after February Revolution.
	March: travels to Germany.
	June: participates in Slav Congress and insurrection in Prague.
	December: publishes *Appeal to the Slavs*.
1849	*May*: participates in Dresden insurrection.
1849–51	Tried and sentenced to death in Saxony, extradited to Austria; tried and sentenced to death in Austria, extradited to Russia.
1851	*May*: incarcerated in Peter-Paul Fortress, St. Petersburg.
	July–August: writes "Confession."
1854	*March*: transferred to Schlüsselburg Fortress.
1855	*February 18*: death of Nicholas I.
1857	*March*: released from prison, exiled to Siberia.
1858	*October 5*: marries Antonia Kwiatkowska in Tomsk.
1861	*July*: escapes from Siberia; sails via Japan to San Francisco.
	November–December: visits New York, Boston, Cambridge.
	December 27: arrives in London, joins Herzen and Ogarev.
1862	publishes *To Russian, Polish, and Other Slav Friends* and *The People's Cause: Romanov, Pugachev, or Pestel?*.
1863	*January*: Polish insurrection against Russia begins.
	February: leaves London to join Polish expedition for landing on Lithuanian coast.
	April–October: in Stockholm, gives speeches and writes articles on behalf of Polish revolution; reunited with his wife.

1864 *January*: arrives in Italy, visits Garibaldi, settles in Florence.

 September–November: travels to Stockholm and London, meets Marx again and joins International.

1865 Moves to Naples.

1866 Founds International Brotherhood.

1867 *September*: moves to Switzerland, joins League of Peace and Freedom.

 Writes *Federalism, Socialism, and Anti-Theologism.*

1868 Joins Geneva Section of International.

 Leaves League of Peace and Freedom, forms Alliance of Social Democracy.

1869 *March*: begins collaboration with Nechaev.

 September: attends Basle Congress of International.

 Settles in Locarno.

1870 *June*: breaks relations with Nechaev.

 September 2: defeat of France by Prussia at Sedan.

 Publishes *Letters to a Frenchman.*

 September 15: arrives in Lyons to participate in insurrection.

1870–71 Writes *The Knouto-Germanic Empire*, including section published posthumously as *God and the State.*

1871 *March–May*: Paris Commune.

 Writes *The Paris Commune and the Idea of the State.*

 Publishes *The Political Theology of Mazzini and the International.*

1872 *September*: expelled from International at The Hague Congress.

1873 Publishes *Statism and Anarchy.*

1874   *July–August*: travels to Bologna to participate in aborted insurrection.

        Moves to Lugano.

1876   *July 1*: dies in Berne.

Bibliographical note

Bakunin's writings

Most of Bakunin's works and letters are still available only in Russian or French; relatively little has been translated into English. The following are the two major editions of his works:

Bakounine, Michel. *Oeuvres* (*Works*). Edited by Max Nettlau and James Guillaume. 6 vols. Paris: Stock, 1895–1913. The series was left incomplete, but it remains the best starting point for an examination of Bakunin's anarchist writings.

Lehning, Arthur, ed. *Archives Bakounine* (*The Bakunin Archives*). 7 vols. in 8. Leiden: Brill, 1961– . An ongoing series, beautifully edited and produced. Each volume focuses on a particular topic and contains original texts, with French translations where required, supplementary material, and extensive annotations. The volumes to date deal with the years 1870 and after. A less expensive edition of the series is being issued in Paris: Editions Champ Libre, 1973– .

There are two other major collections:

Bakunin, M. A. *Sobranie sochinenii i pisem, 1828–1876* (*Collected Works and Letters*). Edited by Iu. M. Steklov. 4 vols. Moscow: Izdatel'-stvo vsesoiuznogo obshchestva politkatorzhan i ssyl'no-poselentsev, 1934–35. This collection brings together all of Bakunin's available letters and works from 1828 to 1861 and is very thoroughly annotated. Like the Nettlau–Guillaume *Oeuvres*, the series was left incomplete, but it is the only collection that covers Bakunin's early years. It has been reprinted in Vaduz, Liechtenstein: Europe Printing Establishment, 1970.

Dragomanov, M. P., ed. *Pis'ma M. A. Bakunina k A. I. Gertsenu i N. P. Ogarevu (Letters of M. A. Bakunin to A. I. Herzen and N. P. Ogarev)*. Geneva: Georg et Co., 1896. Contains Bakunin's letters to Herzen and Ogarev from 1860 to 1874, along with extensive appendices of Bakunin's writings and speeches. The 1968 reprint by Mouton, The Hague, is of the second edition, published in 1906 in St. Petersburg, which omitted the appendices. There are also German and French editions.

Aside from the present volume, the list of complete writings by Bakunin available in English is very short:

Bakunin, Michael. *God and the State*. With an introduction by Paul Avrich. New York: Dover, 1970. An unpublished segment of *The Knouto-Germanic Empire and the Social Revolution*, this became the most famous piece of writing by Bakunin. Other editions are also available.

Confino, Michael, ed. *Daughter of a Revolutionary: Natalie Herzen and the Bakunin–Nechayev Circle*. Translated by Hilary Sternberg and Lydia Bott. LaSalle, Ill.: Library Press, 1973. A collection of documents which includes a number of letters of 1870 by Bakunin.

The Confession of Mikhail Bakunin. With the Marginal Comments of Tsar Nicholas I. Translated by Robert C. Howes. Introduction and notes by Lawrence D. Orton. Ithaca: Cornell University Press, 1977. A well-translated and well-annotated edition of this important document.

Bakunin, Mikhail. *From out of the Dustbin: Bakunin's Basic Writings, 1869–1871*. Translated and edited by Robert M. Cutler. Ann Arbor: Ardis, 1985. A volume of Bakunin's journalistic writings, well translated and with a useful scholarly apparatus.

The following are anthologies of excerpts from Bakunin's writings:

Maximoff, G. P., ed. *The Political Philosophy of Bakunin: Scientific Anarchism*. Glencoe, Ill.: Free Press, 1953. A compilation of bits and snippets of Bakunin's works, arranged topically.

Dolgoff, Sam, trans. and ed. *Bakunin on Anarchy*. New York: Knopf,

1972. Extracts from a variety of writings drawn from Bakunin's entire career.

Lehning, Arthur, ed. *Michael Bakunin: Selected Writings*. Translated by Steven Cox and Olive Stevens. London: Jonathan Cape, 1973. Sizable selections constituting a representative sample of Bakunin's most important works.

The following contain significant selections from Bakunin's writings:

Edie, James M. *et al.*, eds. *Russian Philosophy*. 3 vols. Chicago: Quadrangle Books, 1965. Volume 1 contains "The Reaction in Germany" in entirety and excerpts from *The Paris Commune and the Idea of the State* and *God and the State*.

Shatz, Marshall S., ed. *The Essential Works of Anarchism*. New York: Bantam Books, 1971. Includes excerpts from *God and the State* and *Statism and Anarchy*.

Works on Bakunin

The following are some of the most useful and significant writings about Bakunin in English.

Avrich, Paul. *The Russian Anarchists*. Princeton, N.J.: Princeton University Press, 1967. A comprehensive history of the Russian anarchist movement.

Bakunin and Nechaev. London: Freedom Press, 1974. A convenient summary of the relationship, taking the latest research into account. Republished in Avrich, *Anarchist Portraits* (see below), pp. 32–52.

"Bakunin and the United States." *International Review of Social History*, 24 (1979), 320–40. Reprinted in Avrich, *Anarchist Portraits*, pp. 16–31. Bakunin's sojourn in America in 1861, and his impact on the American anarchist movement.

Anarchist Portraits. Princeton, N.J.: Princeton University Press, 1988. A collection of articles on anarchist figures, including several on Bakunin.

Berlin, Isaiah. "Herzen and Bakunin on Individual Liberty." In Ernest J. Simmons, ed., *Continuity and Change in Russian and Soviet Thought*. Cambridge, Mass.: Harvard University Press, 1955, pp. 473–99. Reprinted in Isaiah Berlin, *Russian Thinkers*.

New York: Viking, 1978, pp. 82–113. Argues that Herzen was more the true libertarian than Bakunin.

Brown, Edward J. *Stankevich and his Moscow Circle, 1830–1840.* Stanford: Stanford University Press, 1966. Depicts the young Bakunin in the context of the Russian intelligentsia.

Canadian–American Slavic Studies, 10, 4 (Winter 1976), *Special Issue: Michael Bakunin.* Articles on various aspects of his life and activities.

Carr, E. H. *Michael Bakunin.* London: Macmillan, 1937. Reprinted New York: Octagon Books, 1975. Still the most detailed and readable biography of Bakunin in English, but trivializes its subject and neglects even to mention *Statism and Anarchy.*

Cochrane, Stephen T. *The Collaboration of Nečaev, Ogarev and Bakunin in 1869: Nečaev's Early Years.* Osteuropastudien der Hochschulen des Landes Hessen: Ser. 2, Marburger Abhandlungen zur Geschichte und Kultur Osteuropas, vol. 18. Giessen: Wilhelm Schnitz Verlag, 1977. Carefully examines the contribution of each of the three to the literature produced during their collaboration.

Cole, G. D. H. *A History of Socialist Thought,* volume II: *Marxism and Anarchism, 1850–1890.* London: Macmillan, 1954. A good summary of Bakunin's ideas in a classic work.

Del Giudice, Martine. "Bakunin's 'Preface to Hegel's "Gymnasium Lectures" ': The Problem of Alienation and the Reconciliation with Reality." *Canadian–American Slavic Studies*, 16, 2 (Summer 1982), 161–89. A penetrating analysis of Bakunin's 1838 essay.

Esenwein, George R. *Anarchist Ideology and the Working-Class Movement in Spain, 1868–1898.* Berkeley: University of California Press, 1989. Details Bakunin's influence on the ideological development of Spanish anarchism.

Gerth, Hans, ed. and trans. *Minutes of The Hague Congress of 1872 with Related Documents.* Madison: University of Wisconsin Press, 1958. The proceedings of the congress at which Bakunin was expelled from the International.

Handlin, Oscar, ed. "A Russian Anarchist Visits Boston." *New England Quarterly*, 15, 1 (March 1942), 104–09. A first-hand account by Martin P. Kennard, a Boston businessman.

Herzen, Alexander. *My Past and Thoughts.* Translated by Constance Garnett, revised by Humphrey Higgens, with an introduction by

Isaiah Berlin. 4 vols. New York: Knopf, 1968. Volume III contains an oft-quoted character-sketch of Bakunin.

Hostetter, Richard. *The Italian Socialist Movement. I: Origins (1860–1882)*. Princeton, N.J.: Van Nostrand, 1958. Contains a good deal of information on Bakunin's activities in Italy and his impact on the early years of Italian socialism.

Kaplan, Temma. *Anarchists of Andalusia, 1868–1903*. Princeton, N. J.: Princeton University Press, 1977. Briefly traces Bakunin's influence in Spain.

Kelly, Aileen. *Mikhail Bakunin: A Study in the Psychology and Politics of Utopianism*. Oxford: Clarendon Press, 1982. An intellectual and psychological biography, informative but hostile to its subject.

Kenafick, K. J. *Michael Bakunin and Karl Marx*. Melbourne, 1948. A sympathetic treatment of Bakunin's views.

Lampert, E. *Studies in Rebellion*. London: Routledge and Kegan Paul, 1957. Contains a substantial chapter on Bakunin which emphasizes his darker sides.

Lehning, Arthur. "Bakunin's Conceptions of Revolutionary Organisations and their Role: A Study of his 'Secret Societies'." In C. Abramsky, ed., *Essays in Honor of E. H. Carr*. London: Macmillan, 1974, pp. 57–81. Sorts out the welter of conspiratorial groups Bakunin created in his anarchist period.

McClellan, Woodford. *Revolutionary Exiles: The Russians in the First International and the Paris Commune*. London: Frank Cass, 1979. The Russian revolutionaries in Switzerland, concentrating on those who supported Marx in the International.

Meijer, J. M. *Knowledge and Revolution: The Russian Colony in Zuerich (1870–1873)*. Assen: Van Gorcum, 1955. The Russian student colony on the eve of the "to the people" movement, with particular attention to the influence of Bakunin and Lavrov.

Mendel, Arthur. *Michael Bakunin: Roots of Apocalypse*. New York: Praeger, 1981. An unconvincing attempt at a psychobiography.

Pyziur, Eugene. *The Doctrine of Anarchism of Michael A. Bakunin*. Milwaukee: Marquette University Press, 1955. A superficial analysis, which finds that Bolshevism was the fulfillment of Bakunin's ideas.

Ravindranathan, T. R. *Bakunin and the Italians*. Montreal: McGill-Queen's University Press, 1989. A detailed and well-informed study of Bakunin's years in Italy and his influence on Italian socialism.

Saltman, Richard B. *The Social and Political Thought of Michael Bakunin*. Westport, Conn.: Greenwood Press, 1983. Attempts to define Bakunin's concept of freedom, relying heavily on English-language compilations of Bakunin's writings.

Shatz, Marshall S. "Michael Bakunin and his Biographers: The Question of Bakunin's Sexual Impotence." In Ezra Mendelsohn and Marshall S. Shatz, eds., *Imperial Russia, 1700–1917: State, Society, Opposition. Essays in Honor of Marc Raeff*. DeKalb, Ill.: Northern Illinois University Press, 1988, pp. 219–40. Deflates some of the myths about Bakunin that have taken root in the historical literature.

Thomas, Paul. *Karl Marx and the Anarchists*. London: Routledge and Kegan Paul, 1980. Contains a lengthy section on Bakunin and Marx, in the context of Marx's critique of anarchism.

Venturi, Franco, *Roots of Revolution: A History of the Populist and Socialist Movements in Nineteenth Century Russia*. Translated from the Italian by Francis Haskell, with an Introduction by Isaiah Berlin. London: Weidenfeld and Nicolson, 1960. An exhaustive history of the Russian revolutionary movement to 1881, with informative chapters on Bakunin's role in it.

For additional references, the reader may turn to two useful bibliographies:

Avrich, Paul. "Bakunin and his Writings." *Canadian–American Slavic Studies*, 10, 4 (Winter 1976), 591–96. A survey of the state of the literature by and about Bakunin as of the mid-1970s.

Cutler, Robert M., ed. *Mikhail Bakunin: From out of the Dustbin* (see above), "Bibliography," pp. 225–41. Contains a particularly extensive list of secondary works, including a number of obscure items.

Note on the translation

The Russian title Bakunin gave his work, *Gosudarstvennost' i anarkhiia*, can be rendered into English in several different ways. It is clear from the text that Bakunin uses the word *anarkhiia*, or anarchy, not to mean chaos or disorder but in the sense that we would use anarchism today. *Gosudarstvennost'*, however, can mean statism, in the sense of governmentalism, or it can mean statehood, and occasionally Bakunin also uses it to mean simply the state. As a result, the title is sometimes given as *Statehood and Anarchy*, or even as *Statism and Anarchism*. It seems to me that Bakunin most often uses the word in reference to belief in, or adherence to, the state – the state as an *ism*, to which he opposes his own belief in anarchism. Therefore, I have translated it statism, while retaining, at the sacrifice of symmetry, the word anarchy which Bakunin chose to use.

The original 1873 edition of *Statism and Anarchy* is a bibliographical rarity today. I have used the text established according to the original edition by Arthur Lehning in his *Archives Bakounine*, III: *Étatisme et anarchie, 1873* (Leiden: Brill, 1967), pp. 1–181. Only one attempt at a complete English translation has been made before: M. A. Bakunin, *Statism and Anarchy*, translated by C. H. Plummer, edited with an introduction by J. F. Harrison (New York: Revisionist Press, 1976). This translation is so faulty, however, as to be virtually unusable. Otherwise, the work has been available in English until now only in the form of excerpts.

Bakunin did not divide the book into chapters or parts. For ease of reading and reference I have created a few breaks in the text where the subject matter seemed to allow it. Footnotes marked with an asterisk (*) are Bakunin's. Footnotes designated by letter (*a*) have been supplied by the translator to explain certain terms Bakunin used and, where possible, to correct misstatements of historical fact or obvious misprints in the text. All of the endnotes are by the translator.

In transliterating Russian names, I have used the Library of Congress system in bibliographical citations but more conventional spelling in the text for the sake of readability.

Statism and Anarchy

The Struggle of the Two Parties in the International Working Men's Association

Foreword

I

The International Working Men's Association, which came into being scarcely nine years ago, has now attained such influence on the practical development of economic, social, and political issues throughout Europe that no political commentator or statesman can henceforth deny it his most serious, and frequently anxious, attention. The official, semi-official, and bourgeois world in general, the world of the fortunate exploiters of manual labor, views it with the kind of inner foreboding one experiences at the approach of a still mysterious and ill-defined but highly threatening danger. It regards the International as a monster that will surely devour the entire social, economic, and state order unless a series of energetic measures is taken simultaneously in all the countries of Europe to put an end to its rapid progress.

As we know, upon the conclusion of the recent war, which shattered the historic supremacy of the French state in Europe and replaced it with the even more odious and pernicious supremacy of state-supported pan-Germanism, measures against the International became a favorite topic of intergovernmental discussions. This is perfectly natural. By nature mutually antagonistic and utterly irreconcilable, states can find no other grounds for joint action than the concerted enslavement of the masses who constitute the overall basis and purpose of their existence. Prince Bismarck, of course, has been and will remain the chief instigator and moving spirit behind this new Holy Alliance. But he was not the first to come forward with his proposals. He ceded the dubious honor of taking this initiative to the humiliated government of the French state which he had just routed.

3

The foreign minister of the pseudo-national government, a true traitor to the republic but a faithful friend and protector of the Jesuit order, believing in God but scorning mankind, and scorned in turn by all honest defenders of the people's cause – the notorious rhetorician Jules Favre, who cedes only to Gambetta the honor of being the prototype of all lawyers, with pleasure took upon himself the role of malicious slanderer and denouncer. Among the members of the so-called Government of National Defense, he was without a doubt one of those who contributed most to the disarming of the national defense and the patently treasonous surrender of Paris to its arrogant, insolent, and merciless conqueror.[1] Prince Bismarck made a fool of him and abused him publicly. Yet, as though taking pride in his twofold shame, his own and that of France, which he had betrayed and maybe even sold out; impelled at one and the same time by a desire to please the great chancellor of the victorious German Empire who had put him to shame, and by his profound hatred of the proletariat in general and the world of the Paris workers in particular – Favre formally denounced the International, whose members, standing at the head of the working masses in France, had tried to provoke a national uprising against both the German conquerors and France's domestic exploiters, rulers, and traitors. A horrible crime, for which official, or bourgeois, France had to punish the people's France with exemplary severity!

Thus the first word uttered by the French state on the morrow of its terrible and ignominious defeat was a word of vilest reaction.

Who has not read Favre's memorable circular, in which crude lies and even cruder ignorance yield only to the impotent and frenzied malice of a republican renegade?[2] It is the desperate wail not of a single individual but of the whole of bourgeois civilization, which has depleted everything on earth and is condemned to death by its own ultimate exhaustion. Sensing the approach of its inevitable demise, with malicious desperation it latches onto anything that might prolong its pernicious existence. It appeals for help to all the idols of the past which bourgeois civilization itself once overthrew – God, the Church, the pope, patriarchal right, and, above all, as its most reliable means of salvation, police protection and military dictatorship, even though it be Prussian, as long as it safeguards "honest people" from the terrifying threat of social revolution.

Favre's circular found an echo, and where do you think – in Spain!

4

Sagasta, the ephemeral minister of the ephemeral Spanish King Amadeo, also wanted to please Prince Bismarck and immortalize his own name.[3] He too proclaimed a crusade against the International. Not contenting himself, though, with feeble and fruitless measures which elicited only the derisive laughter of the Spanish proletariat, he also wrote a bombastic diplomatic circular. What he got for it, however, doubtless with the approval of Prince Bismarck and his junior assistant Favre, was a well-deserved dressing-down from the more circumspect and less free government of Great Britain, and a few months later he was overthrown.

It appears, however, that Sagasta's note, though it spoke in the name of Spain, was conceived, if not composed, in Italy, under the direct supervision of the highly experienced King Victor Emmanuel, the lucky father of the luckless Amadeo.

In Italy, persecution of the International came from three different quarters. First, as one would have expected, it was damned by the pope himself. He did it in a most original fashion, in one general anathema lumping together all members of the International with Freemasons, Jacobins, rationalists, deists, and liberal Catholics.[4] According to the Holy Father's definition, anyone who does not blindly submit to his divinely inspired tirades belongs to this outcast association. Twenty-six years ago, a Prussian general defined communism in exactly the same way: "Do you know what being a communist means?" he said to his soldiers. "It means thinking and acting contrary to the royal thought and will of His Majesty the King."

It was not just the Roman Catholic pope, however, who damned the International Working Men's Association. The celebrated revolutionary Giuseppe Mazzini is much better known in Russia as an Italian patriot, conspirator, and agitator than as a metaphysician and deist and founder of a new church in Italy. But Mazzini himself, in 1871, right after the defeat of the Paris Commune, at the very moment when the brutal executors of the brutal Versailles decrees were shooting the disarmed communards by the thousands, deemed it useful and necessary to add to the Roman Catholic anathema and the state's police persecution his own malediction, supposedly patriotic and revolutionary but in essence utterly bourgeois and, moreover, theological.[5] He hoped his words would suffice to kill all sympathy in Italy for the Paris Commune and to nip in the bud the sections of the International that had just been formed there. Exactly the opposite

5

happened: nothing fostered the growth of such sympathy and the proliferation of the International's sections as much as his loud and solemn malediction.

The Italian government, hostile to the pope but even more hostile to Mazzini, was not asleep either. At first it did not understand the danger the International posed as it rapidly spread not just in the towns but even in the villages of Italy. It thought the new association would merely serve to counteract the progress of Mazzini's bourgeois republican propaganda, and in this regard it was not mistaken. But it quickly became convinced that propagandizing the principles of social revolution amidst an impassioned population which has been reduced to the utmost poverty and oppression by the government itself was more dangerous than all of Mazzini's political agitation and undertakings. The death of the great Italian patriot, which ensued soon after his angry outburst against the Paris Commune and the International, set the Italian government's mind at rest as far as the Mazzini party is concerned. Without its leader it henceforth will not pose the least danger to the government. It has visibly begun to disintegrate, and since its principles and its objectives, as well as its entire membership, are purely bourgeois, it is manifesting unmistakable symptoms of the decrepitude that afflicts all bourgeois initiatives in our time.

The International's propaganda and organization in Italy are something else again. The International addresses itself directly and exclusively to the milieu of the common laborer, which in Italy as in every other country of Europe concentrates within itself all the life, strength, and future of contemporary society. Its only allies from the bourgeois world are those few individuals who have come to hate the existing political, economic, and social order heart and soul, who have turned their backs on the class that begot them and have devoted themselves utterly to the people's cause. Such people are few, but they are precious – though, it goes without saying, only when they have learned to hate the general bourgeois desire to dominate and have suppressed within themselves the last vestiges of personal ambition. In such cases, I repeat, they are truly precious. The people give them life, elemental force, and a firm basis; in return, they bring the people practical knowledge, the habit of abstraction and analysis, and the ability to organize and form associations. These in turn create the conscious fighting force without which victory is inconceivable.

In Italy, as in Russia, quite a sizable number of young people of this kind have turned up, far more than in any other country. What is incomparably more important, however, is that Italy has a huge proletariat, endowed with an extraordinary degree of native intelligence but largely illiterate and wholly destitute. It consists of 2 or 3 million urban factory workers and small artisans, and some 20 million landless peasants. As I have already said, the oppressive and thieving government of the upper classes, under the liberal scepter of the king – the liberator and gatherer of the Italian lands[6] – has reduced this whole countless mass of people to such desperate straits that even those who defend the present government and have a personal interest in it are beginning to admit, and to say out loud both in parliament and in official journals, that it is impossible to proceed any further along this road, and that something must be done for the people before they go on a devastating rampage.

Indeed, perhaps nowhere else is social revolution as imminent as it is in Italy, not even in Spain, even though in Spain an official revolution is taking place while in Italy everything seems to be quiet. In Italy the people as a whole expect a social upheaval and consciously strive for it every day. You can imagine what a wide, sincere, and passionate welcome the Italian proletariat gave to the program of the International. Unlike many other countries of Europe, Italy does not have a separate stratum of workers who are to some degree privileged owing to their sizable wages, even boast of some literary education, and are so riddled with bourgeois principles, aspirations, and vanity as to be distinguishable from the bourgeoisie only by their circumstances, not by their sentiments. Particularly in Germany and Switzerland there are many such workers; in Italy, by contrast, there are very few, so few that they are lost in the crowd and have no influence at all. What predominates in Italy is that destitute proletariat to which Marx and Engels, and, following them, the whole school of German social democrats, refer with the utmost contempt. They do so completely in vain, because here, and here alone, not in the bourgeois stratum of workers, is to be found the mind as well as the might of the future social revolution.

We will talk about this at greater length later on. For now, let us confine ourselves to drawing the following conclusion: in Italy, precisely because of the decided predominance of the destitute proletariat, the propaganda and organization of the International Working Men's Association took on the most passionate and truly popular character. As a result, the International's influence was not confined to the towns but immediately embraced the village population as well.

Now the Italian government fully comprehends the danger of this movement and is trying with all its might to suppress it, but to no avail. It does not issue clamorous and bombastic diplomatic notes but acts as befits a police state, on the quiet; it smothers without explanations and without warning. In defiance of every law it shuts down all workers' associations, one after the other, with the exception only of those which count princes of the blood, government ministers, prefects, and other distinguished and respectable people as honorary members. It mercilessly persecutes the rest, seizing their records and funds and holding their members in its filthy jails for months at a time without trial and without even an inquest.

There is no doubt that in acting in this fashion the Italian government is guided not just by its own wisdom but by the advice and instructions of the great chancellor of Germany, just as in the past it obediently followed the orders of Napoleon III. The Italian state finds itself in a peculiar position: by virtue of the size of its population and the extent of its territory, it should count as one of the great powers; as it is, though, financially ruined, corruptly organized, for all its efforts very badly disciplined, and, moreover, detested by the masses and even by the petty bourgeoisie, its real strength barely enables it to be deemed a power of the second magnitude. Therefore it needs a patron, a master outside of Italy, and it seems perfectly natural that with the fall of Napoleon III Prince Bismarck should take his place as the *indispensable ally* of this monarchy, which was created by Piedmontese intrigue on soil prepared by the patriotic efforts and exploits of Mazzini and Garibaldi.[7]

The hand of the great chancellor of the pan-German empire now makes itself felt not just in Italy but throughout Europe, with the possible exceptions of England (which, however, does not look upon this emerging power with equanimity), and Spain, which was shielded from Germany's reactionary influence, at least at first, by its revolution as well as its geographical location. The new empire's influence is explained by its astounding victory over France. Everyone recognizes that by virtue of its circumstances, the enormous resources it has conquered, and its own internal organization, it now ranks incontestably first among the great European powers and is in a position to

8

make each of the others feel its supremacy. That its influence must necessarily be reactionary cannot be doubted.

Germany in its present form, unified by the brilliant and patriotic duplicity* of Prince Bismarck, relies on the one hand on the exemplary organization and discipline of its army, which is prepared to suppress or cut down anything on earth and to commit every conceivable atrocity, at home or abroad, at the mere nod of its king-emperor. It relies on the other hand on the patriotism of its loyal subjects; a boundless national ambition that goes back into ancient history; and the equally boundless worship of authority, and obedience to it, for which the German nobility, the German bourgeoisie, the German bureaucracy, the German Church, the entire guild of German scholars, and often, alas, under their combined influence, the German people, too, are all distinguished to this day. Germany, I say, proud of the despotic-constitutional power of its autocrat and sovereign, represents and embodies one of the two poles of contemporary social and political development: the pole of statism, the state, reaction.

Germany is a state par excellence, as France was under Louis XIV and Napoleon I, as Prussia has never ceased to be. From the time Frederick II completed the creation of the Prussian state the question was, who would swallow up whom, Germany – Prussia, or Prussia – Germany? As it turned out, Prussia swallowed up Germany. Therefore, as long as Germany remains a state, regardless of any pseudo-liberal, constitutional, democratic, or even social-democratic forms, it will of necessity be the paramount representative and constant source of every kind of despotism that may arise in Europe.

Indeed, ever since the historical formation of the modern concept of the state in the mid-sixteenth century, Germany (including the Austrian Empire to the extent that it is German) has never ceased to be the main center of all reactionary movements in Europe, even when the great crowned free-thinker Frederick II was corresponding with Voltaire. As a clever statesman, student of Machiavelli and teacher of Bismarck, he cursed everyone, God and man, including, of course, his correspondents the philosophes. He believed only in his "reason of state," relying, as always, on "the divine force of many battalions" ("God is always on the side of the strong battalions," he used to say), as well as on his economy and the utmost perfection of

* In politics, as in high finance, swindling is considered valorous.

his internal administrative apparatus (a mechanical and despotic one, it goes without saying). In his opinion, and in ours as well, this is what really constitutes the entire essence of the state. Everything else is just a harmless grace-note, its purpose being to beguile the tender feelings of people who cannot bear to face the harsh truth.

Frederick II perfected and completed the state machine which his father and grandfather put together and for which his ancestors paved the way. In the hands of his worthy successor Prince Bismarck, this machine became an instrument for the conquest and potential Prusso-Germanization of Europe.

As we have said, from the Reformation onward Germany never ceased to be the principal source of all reactionary movements in Europe. From the middle of the sixteenth century to 1815 the initiative for these movements belonged to Austria. From 1815 to 1866 it was shared between Austria and Prussia, although the former predominated while it was governed by old Prince Metternich, that is, until 1848. In 1815 our own Tatar-Germanic Imperial Knout of All the Russias joined this Holy Alliance of purely German reaction, more as a devoted admirer than an active participant.

Impelled by a natural desire to evade their grave responsibility for all the abominations committed by the Holy Alliance, the Germans try to convince themselves and others that their chief instigator was Russia. We are not the ones to defend imperial Russia. Because of our deep love for the Russian people, because we passionately desire their utmost progress and liberty, we abhor that vile Empire of All the Russias as no German can. In contrast to the German social democrats, whose program has as its prime objective the creation of a pan-German state, Russian social revolutionaries strive first of all for the complete destruction of our state, convinced as we are that as long as the principle of the state, in whatever form, hangs over our people, they will be poverty-stricken slaves. Therefore, not out of a desire to defend the policies of the Petersburg cabinet, but in the name of truth, which is always and everywhere useful, we reply to the Germans as follows.

Imperial Russia, in the person of two of its crowned heads, Alexander I and Nicholas I[8], did in fact give the appearance of intervening very actively in the internal affairs of Europe. Alexander roamed Europe from one end to the other and made a lot of fuss and noise; Nicholas scowled and made threats. But that was as far as it all went.

They did nothing – not because they did not want to, but because they could not, not being allowed to by their friends, the Austrian and Prussian Germans. They were granted only the honorific role of bogeyman, while Austria, Prussia, and eventually, under their supervision and with their permission, the French Bourbons (against Spain) acted.

Only once did the Russian Empire go beyond its own frontiers, in 1849, and then in order to save the Austrian Empire, which was in the throes of the Hungarian uprising. In this century Russia has twice suppressed a Polish revolution, and both times with the aid of Prussia, which was just as interested in preserving Polish bondage as Russia was. It goes without saying that I am speaking of imperial Russia. A Russia of the people is inconceivable without Polish freedom and independence.[9]

Who can doubt that by its very nature the Russian Empire can wish to exert on Europe only the kind of influence that is most pernicious and opposed to freedom, that it greets every new act of state brutality and triumphant repression, every fresh instance of a popular uprising drowned in the people's blood, in any country whatsoever, with the most heartfelt sympathy? But that is not the question. The question is the extent of its real influence: by virtue of its intelligence, power, and wealth, does it occupy such a dominant position in Europe as to have a determining voice in European affairs?

We need only take a careful look at the history of the last sixty years, and at the very nature of our Tatar-Germanic empire, to answer no. Russia is far from being as strong a power as it is fondly depicted in the boastful imaginations of our *kvass* patriots,[a] the infantile imaginations of the western and southeastern pan-Slavists, or the senile or panic-stricken imaginations of Europe's servile liberals, who are ready to bow down before any military dictatorship, domestic or foreign, as long as it delivers them from the terrible danger their own proletariat poses. Anyone who looks soberly, guided neither by hope nor by fear, at the actual circumstances of the Petersburg empire today, knows that on its own initiative, unless summoned by one of the great Western powers and in close alliance with it, it has never undertaken anything in the West or against the West, nor can it. Its entire policy from time immemorial has consisted of attaching itself to a

[a] *Kvass* is a mildly alcoholic, generally home-brewed Russian beverage made from bread. The term "*kvass* patriots" denotes unreflecting Russian chauvinists.

foreign enterprise one way or another. And ever since the rapacious partition of Poland, which, as everyone knows, was conceived by Frederick II – who intended to propose to Catherine II that they divide up Sweden in the same way – Prussia is the Western power that has continually rendered this service to the Russian Empire.

In regard to the revolutionary movement in Europe, Russia in the hands of Prussian statesmen served as a bogeyman, and often, too, as a screen behind which the Prussians very skillfully concealed their own aggressive and reactionary enterprises. Once the Prusso-German army won its stunning series of victories in France, however, once French hegemony in Europe was definitively overthrown and replaced by pan-German hegemony, such a screen was no longer needed, and the new empire, which has fulfilled the most cherished dreams of German patriotism, emerged openly in all the glory of its aggressive might and systematic reaction.

Yes, Berlin has now become the manifest head and capital of all vigorous and effective reaction in Europe, and Prince Bismarck its chief guide and prime minister. I say vigorous and effective, not outmoded, reaction. Outmoded, senile reaction, predominantly Roman Catholic, still wanders like a sinister but impotent ghost through Rome, Versailles, to some degree Vienna and Brussels. Another kind, knouto-Petersburg reaction, not a ghost, perhaps, but nonetheless senseless and without a future, continues to commit outrages within the confines of the Russian Empire. But vigorous, intelligent, truly powerful reaction from now on will be concentrated in Berlin and disseminated to all the countries of Europe from the new German Empire run by the statist – and thereby utterly anti-popular – genius of Prince Bismarck.

This reaction is nothing other than the ultimate realization of the anti-popular idea of the modern state, the sole objective of which is to organize the most intensive exploitation of the people's labor for the benefit of capital concentrated in a very small number of hands. It signifies the triumphant reign of the Yids,[a] of a bankocracy under the powerful protection of a fiscal, bureaucratic, and police regime which relies mainly on military force and is therefore in essence despotic, but cloaks itself in the parliamentary game of pseudo-constitutionalism.

[a] Here, as in other places in the text, Bakunin uses the derogatory Russian term for Jew, *zhid*.

To achieve their fullest development, modern capitalist production and bank speculation require enormous centralized states, which alone are capable of subjecting the many millions of laborers to their exploitation. A federal organization, from below upward, of workers' associations, groups, communes, districts, and, ultimately, regions and nations – the sole condition for real as opposed to fictitious freedom – is as contrary to their essence as any kind of economic autonomy is incompatible with them. They get along very nicely, though, with so-called *representative democracy*. This latest form of the state, based on the pseudo-sovereignty of a sham popular will, supposedly expressed by pseudo-representatives of the people in sham popular assemblies, combines the two main conditions necessary for their success: state centralization, and the actual subordination of the sovereign people to the intellectual minority that governs them, supposedly representing them but invariably exploiting them.

When we come to speak of the social and political program of the Marxists, the Lassalleans,[10] and the German social democrats in general, we will have occasion to examine this factual truth more closely and to elucidate it. Let us turn our attention now to another side of the question.

Any exploitation of the people's labor is a bitter pill for them, whatever the political forms of sham popular sovereignty and sham popular freedom that may gild it. Therefore no people will readily submit to it, however docile they may be by nature and however accustomed they may have grown to obeying authority. It requires constant coercion and compulsion, meaning police surveillance and military force.

The modern state, in its essence and objectives, is necessarily a military state, and a military state necessarily becomes an aggressive state. If it does not conquer others it will itself be conquered, for the simple reason that wherever force exists, it absolutely must be displayed or put into action. From this again it follows that the modern state must without fail be huge and powerful; that is the indispensable condition for its preservation.

The modern state is analogous to capitalist production and bank speculation (which ultimately swallows up even capitalist production). For fear of bankruptcy, the latter must constantly broaden their scope at the expense of the small-scale production and speculation which they swallow up; they must strive to become unique, universal, world-wide. In just the same way the modern state, of necessity a military state, bears within itself the inevitable ambition to become a world-wide state. But a world-wide state, which obviously is unrealizable, could in any event exist only in the singular; two such states, side by side, are a logical impossibility.

Hegemony is only a modest, possible display of this unrealizable ambition inherent in every state. But the primary condition for hegemony is the relative impotence and subordination of at least all surrounding states. Thus the hegemony of France, as long as it existed, was conditional upon the impotence of Spain, Italy, and Germany. To this day French statesmen – and foremost among them, of course, Thiers – cannot forgive Napoleon III for having allowed Italy and Germany to unify and consolidate themselves.

Now France has vacated its position and has been replaced by the German state, which in our opinion is the only real state in Europe today.

The French people without a doubt still have a great role to play in history, but France's career as a state is over. Anyone who knows anything about the character of the French will concur that if France was long able to be the preeminent power, it is absolutely impossible for it to be a second-rank state, or even one that is merely the equal of others. As a state, and as long as it is governed by statesmen, whether Thiers, Gambetta, or even dukes of Orleans, it will never become reconciled to its humiliation. It will make preparations for a new war and will seek revenge and the restoration of its lost preeminence.

Will it succeed? Decidedly not. There are a number of reasons for this; let us mention the two main ones. Recent events have shown that patriotism, the highest *state* virtue, the heart of the state's strength, no longer exists at all in France. In the upper classes it now manifests itself only in the form of national vanity. But even that vanity has grown so weak, it has been extirpated to such a degree by bourgeois expediency and the bourgeois habit of sacrificing all *ideals* to *practical interests*, that during the last war it could no longer even temporarily, as it used to be able to do, make selfless heroes and patriots out of shopkeepers, dealers, stock-market speculators, officers, generals, bureaucrats, capitalists, landowners, and Jesuit-educated nobles. They all behaved like cowards and traitors, scurrying to save their property and taking advantage of France's misfortune to intrigue against France. In the most brazen fashion they tried to outdo each other in seeking the favor of the merciless and arrogant conqueror who had become the arbiter of France's fate. One and all, they preached submission and humility and prayed for peace at any price . . . Now all these depraved windbags have become nationalists again and boast of it, but this absurd and repulsive clamor of cheap heroes cannot drown out the resounding testimony of their baseness of yesterday.

Incomparably more important is the fact that not even the rural population of France displayed a single drop of patriotism. Indeed, contrary to general expectations, the French peasant, from the moment he became a property-owner, ceased to be a patriot. In Joan of Arc's time he bore France on his shoulders all by himself. In 1792 and subsequently he defended her against a military coalition of the whole of Europe. But the situation was different then: thanks to the cheap sale of church and noble estates he had become the owner of the land he formerly worked as a slave, and he rightly feared that in the event of defeat the émigré nobles would return on the heels of the German troops and take back the property he had just acquired. Now, however, he did not have that fear and regarded with utter indifference the shameful defeat of his dear fatherland. Except in Alsace and Lorraine, where, strangely enough, as a kind of joke on the Germans, who stubbornly regard them as purely German provinces, unmistakable signs of patriotism manifested themselves, throughout central France the peasants drove away the French and foreign volunteers who had taken up arms to save France. They refused them everything and often even handed them over to the Prussians, while greeting the Germans most hospitably.

One can say quite truthfully that patriotism has been preserved only in the urban proletariat.

In Paris, as in all the other provinces and towns of France, the proletariat alone wanted and demanded the arming of the nation and war to the death. And a strange thing happened: this brought down upon it all the hatred of the propertied classes, as though they were offended that their "younger brothers" (Gambetta's expression) were displaying more virtue, more patriotic devotion than their elders.

To a certain degree, however, the propertied classes were right. What motivated the urban proletariat was not pure patriotism in the old and strict sense of the word. Real patriotism is, of course, a highly honorable sentiment, but it is at the same time a narrow, exclusive, anti-humanistic, often simply bestial one. The only consistent patriot is the person who passionately loves his fatherland and everything that is his own, while passionately hating everything foreign, exactly like our Slavophiles.[11] Not even a trace of such hatred has remained within the French urban proletariat. On the contrary, in recent decades – since 1848, say, or even much earlier – under the influence of socialist propaganda it has developed a positively fraternal attitude toward the proletariat of all countries, along with an equally decided indifference to the so-called grandeur and glory of France. The French workers opposed the war undertaken by the last Napoleon, and on its eve, in a manifesto signed by the Paris members of the International, loudly declared their sincere fraternal attitude toward the workers of Germany. Even when German troops entered France, the workers took up arms not against the German people but against German military despotism.

The war began exactly six years after the founding of the International Working Men's Association and just four years after its first Congress in Geneva. In such a short time, not only in the French proletariat but among the workers of many other countries, especially the Latin ones, the International's propaganda had succeeded in giving rise to a world of ideas, opinions, and sentiments that were entirely new and extraordinarily broad-minded. It gave birth to a common international passion which absorbed nearly all the prejudices and narrow-mindedness of patriotic or parochial passions.

This new outlook found triumphant expression in 1868 at a popular meeting – and where do you think, in what country? In Austria, in Vienna, in response to a series of political and patriotic proposals which the bourgeois democrats of south Germany and Austria made jointly to the Viennese workers and which would have led to the solemn recognition and proclamation of a pan-German, one and indivisible fatherland. To their horror, the bourgeois democrats heard the following reply: "What is this talk about a German fatherland? We are workers, and you are the ones who exploit us, who endlessly deceive and oppress us. All workers, whatever country they belong to, the exploited and oppressed proletarians of the whole world, are our brothers, and all bourgeois, the oppressors, rulers, overseers, and exploiters, are our enemies. The international camp of workers is our one and only fatherland; the international world of exploiters is a country alien and hostile to us."

And to demonstrate the sincerity of their words the Viennese workers immediately sent a congratulatory telegram "to our Parisian brothers, the pioneers of world-wide worker emancipation."

This reply of the Viennese workers, which, all political considerations aside, came straight from the depths of popular instinct, caused a great stir in Germany at the time. It frightened all the bourgeois democrats, including the party's veteran leader, the venerable Dr. Johann Jacoby,[12] and offended not only their patriotic sentiments but the statist creed of the school of Lassalle and Marx. Probably on Marx's advice, Liebknecht, who is now considered one of the leaders of the social democrats in Germany but at that time was still a member of a bourgeois-democratic party (the defunct People's Party), immediately set out from Leipzig to Vienna to negotiate with the Viennese workers, whose "political tactlessness" had provoked such a scandal.[13] One has to do him justice: he was so successful that a few months later, in August 1868, at the Nuremberg Congress of German Workers, all the representatives of the Austrian proletariat without any protest subscribed to the narrow patriotic program of the Social-Democratic Party.[14]

But this only exposed the profound distinction that exists between the political orientation of the party's leaders, who are more or less educated and bourgeois, and the revolutionary instinct of the German, or at least the Austrian, proletariat itself. True, in Germany and in Austria this popular instinct has been suppressed and constantly diverted from its real objective by the propaganda of a party more political than social-revolutionary, and since 1868 it has made little progress and has been unable to pass into the people's consciousness. By contrast, in the Latin countries, Belgium, Spain, Italy, and especially France, which are free of this yoke and this systematic corruption, it has undergone broad development, in full freedom, and has in fact turned into the revolutionary consciousness of the urban factory proletariat.*

As we have already noted, this consciousness of the universal character of social revolution and the solidarity of the proletariat of all

---

* There is no doubt that the efforts of the English workers, who strive only for their own emancipation or the betterment of their own lot, redound to the benefit of all mankind. But the English do not know this and do not seek it. The French, on the contrary, know it and seek it, which in our opinion constitutes an enormous difference in favor of the French and gives all of their revolutionary movements a truly universal significance and character.

countries, which is still so undeveloped among the workers of England, arose long ago within the French proletariat. It knew back in the 1790s that in struggling for its own equality and freedom it was liberating all mankind.

Those great words – liberty, equality, and fraternity of the whole human race – today are often used as empty phrases but at that time were sincerely and deeply felt, and they are found in all the revolutionary songs of the day. They underlay the new social faith and social-revolutionary passion of the French workers, becoming part of their nature, so to speak, and determining, even unconsciously and involuntarily, the direction of their thoughts, aspirations, and actions. When he makes a revolution, every French worker is fully convinced that he is making it not just for himself but for the whole world, and far more for the world than for himself. Practical politicians and radical republicans of Gambetta's ilk have tried in vain to divert the French proletariat from this cosmopolitan orientation and convince it that it ought to concentrate on its own exclusively national concerns, which are bound up with the patriotic idea of the grandeur, glory, and political supremacy of the French state, that it ought to secure its own freedom and well-being within the state before dreaming about the liberation of all mankind or of the whole world. Their efforts seem very sensible but are of no avail – you cannot remake nature, and this dream has become part of the nature of the French proletariat and has driven the last vestiges of state patriotism from its imagination and its heart.

The events of 1870–71 demonstrated this fully. In every city of France the proletariat demanded a universal call to arms and the formation of a militia against the Germans. There is no doubt that it would have realized its intentions had it not been paralyzed on the one hand by the ignominious fear and wholesale treachery of the majority of the bourgeois class, which preferred a thousand times over to submit to the Prussians rather than put weapons in the hands of the proletariat; and, on the other, by the systematically reactionary counteractivity of the Government of National Defense in Paris and the equally anti-popular opposition of the dictator and patriot Gambetta in the provinces.

In arming themselves against the German conquerors, however, to the extent that it was possible under the circumstances, the French workers were firmly convinced that they would be struggling as much for the freedom and rights of the German proletariat as for their own. Their concern was not with the grandeur and honor of the French state but with the proletariat's victory over the hated military force that was serving in the hands of the bourgeoisie as an instrument for enslaving them. They hated the German soldiers not because they were Germans but because they were soldiers. The troops Thiers used against the Paris Commune were pure French, but they committed in a few days more crimes and atrocities than the German army did in the entire war. From now on, in relation to the proletariat, all troops, domestic or foreign, will be enemies, and the French workers know it. Therefore their militia was not in any way a patriotic one.

The uprising of the Paris Commune against the Versailles *popular* assembly and against the savior of the fatherland, Thiers, carried out by the Paris workers in full view of the German forces which still surrounded the city, reveals and fully clarifies the one passion motivating the French proletariat today. Henceforth it will have and can have no other cause, no other objective, and no other war than a social-revolutionary one.

On the other hand, the uprising fully explains the unbridled frenzy that seized the hearts of the Versailles rulers and representatives, as well as the unprecedented atrocities committed under their direct supervision and with their blessing against the defeated communards. From the standpoint of state patriotism, the Parisian workers had in fact committed a terrible crime: in full view of the German army which had just routed the fatherland, shattered its national might and grandeur, and struck at the very heart of national honor, the workers, in the throes of a wild, cosmopolitan, social-revolutionary passion, proclaimed the complete abolition of the French state, the dissolution of France's state unity as incompatible with the autonomy of France's communes. The Germans had merely diminished the frontiers and power of the political fatherland, while the workers wanted to annihilate it completely, and as though to flaunt their treasonous objective they threw down into the dust the Vendôme column, the majestic witness to France's past glory.[15]

From a political and patriotic point of view, what crime could compare with such unheard-of sacrilege! And remember that the Paris proletariat did not commit it accidentally, under the influence of demagogues, nor in one of those moments of frenzied enthusiasm which one frequently encounters in the history of any nation, and especially the French. No, this time the Paris workers acted calmly and consciously. Their factual rejection of state patriotism was obviously an expression of strong popular passion, and not a fleeting passion but a deep, one might say carefully considered, one which transformed itself into the people's consciousness. This passion suddenly revealed itself before the frightened world as a bottomless pit ready to swallow up the whole of the existing social order, with all its institutions, comforts, privileges, and its entire civilization . . .

With a clarity as terrible as it is unmistakable, these events demonstrated that henceforth there can be no reconciliation between the wild, hungry proletariat, gripped by social-revolutionary passions and striving persistently for the creation of another world based on the principles of human truth, justice, liberty, equality, and fraternity (principles tolerated in respectable society only as the innocuous subject of rhetorical exercises), and the well-fed, educated world of the privileged classes, defending with desperate energy the state, legal, metaphysical, theological, and military and police order as the last stronghold now safeguarding their precious privilege of economic exploitation. Between these two worlds, I say, between the common laborers and educated society – which, as we all know, embodies every conceivable merit, beauty, and virtue – no reconciliation is possible.

It is war to the death, not just in France but in the whole of Europe, and it can end only in the decisive victory of one side and the decisive defeat of the other!

Either the bourgeois educated world must subdue and enslave the elemental force of the rebellious people so as to compel the laboring masses to work as before by force of bayonet, knout, or rod (blessed, of course, by some God or other and rationally explained by science) – which would lead directly to the full restoration of the state in its sincerest form, a military dictatorship or empire, the only form possible at the present time; or the workers will at last throw off their hated, centuries-old yoke and eradicate bourgeois exploitation and the bourgeois civilization that is based upon it – which means the triumph of social revolution, the obliteration of everything that bears the name of the state.

The state on one side, social revolution on the other – those are the two poles whose antagonism constitutes the very essence of contemporary public life throughout Europe, though it is more palpable in France than in any other country. The world of the state, which embraces the whole of the bourgeoisie, including, of course, the bourgeoisified nobility, has found its focal point, its ultimate refuge and last defense, at Versailles. The social revolution, which suffered a terrible defeat in Paris but was by no means extinguished and not even vanquished, now embraces, as it always has, the entire urban factory proletariat and is already beginning to engage the rural population too with its tireless propaganda, at least in the south of France, where it is being conducted and disseminated on a very large scale. This hostile confrontation of two henceforth irreconcilable worlds is the second reason why it is absolutely impossible for France to become once again the paramount, predominant state.

All the privileged strata of French society would doubtless love to restore their fatherland to that brilliant and imposing position. At the same time they are so filled with the passion for acquisition, for enrichment at whatever cost, and with anti-patriotic selfishness, that in order to achieve their patriotic objective they are prepared to sacrifice the possessions, life, and freedom of the proletariat, to be sure, but will not renounce a single one of their own privileges and would rather submit to a foreign yoke than give up their property or agree to the equalization of economic conditions or rights.

What is now taking place before our eyes fully confirms what we have said. When Thiers's government officially announced to the Versailles assembly that a final treaty had been concluded with the Berlin cabinet under which the German troops in September would evacuate the French provinces they still occupied, the majority of the assembly, representing a coalition of the privileged classes, hung their heads. French stocks, representing their interests in a more real and vital sense, plummeted, as though after a state catastrophe . . . It turned out that the presence of the victorious German army, which was hateful, coercive, and shameful for France, was comfort, support, and salvation for the privileged French patriots, the representatives of bourgeois valor and bourgeois civilization, and its prospective departure was synonymous to them with a death sentence.

So the strange patriotism of the French bourgeoisie seeks its salvation in the ignominious subjugation of the fatherland. Should anyone still have doubts on this score, we can point to any conservative French journal. It is well known how frightened, agitated, and infuriated all the branches of the reactionary party – Bonapartists, legitimists, and Orleanists – were at the election of Barodet[16] as deputy from Paris. But who is this Barodet? One of the numerous mediocrities of Gambetta's party, a conservative by position, instinct, and inclination but with democratic and republican phrases, which, however, by no means impede but, on the contrary, very much assist the implementation of the most reactionary measures – in a word, a man between whom and revolution there is not and never has been anything in common and who in 1870 and 1871 was one of the most ardent defenders of the bourgeois order in Lyons. But now, like many other bourgeois patriots, he finds it advantageous to operate under the standard of the by no means revolutionary Gambetta. Paris elected him in order to spite the president of the republic, Thiers, and the monarchist, pseudo-popular assembly reigning in Versailles. And the election of this insignificant individual was enough to get the whole conservative party worked up! And do you know what their main argument was? The Germans!

Open any journal and you will see how they threaten the French proletariat with the justifiable wrath of Prince Bismarck and his emperor – what patriotism! Indeed, they simply call upon the Germans for help against the French social revolution that threatens them. In their idiotic fright they even took the innocuous Barodet for a revolutionary socialist.

These sentiments of the French bourgeoisie hold out little hope of restoring the state power and supremacy of France by means of the patriotism of the privileged classes.

The patriotism of the French proletariat does not offer much hope either. The frontiers of its fatherland have now expanded to embrace the proletariat of the entire world in opposition to the whole bourgeoisie, including, of course, that of France. The declarations of the Paris Commune are categorical in this regard, while the sympathies which the French workers are now so clearly expressing for the Spanish revolution prove that the era of state patriotism has passed for the French proletariat just as it has for the privileged classes. This is particularly true in the south of France, where the proletariat is manifesting an explicit desire for fraternal union with the Spanish proletariat and even for a popular federation with it based on emancipated labor and collective property, in defiance of all national distinctions and state boundaries.

Given the absence of patriotism in all strata of French society and the open and implacable war now going on between them, how is a strong state to be restored? All the statesman's skills of the aged president of the republic will go for naught, and all the terrible sacrifices he has made on the altar of the political fatherland, such as the inhuman slaughter of the many tens of thousands of Paris communards, including women and children, and the equally inhuman deportation of tens of thousands of others to New Caledonia, will unquestionably prove useless.

In vain Thiers struggles to reestablish credit and restore domestic calm, the old order, and the military power of France. The edifice of the state, rocked to its very foundations again and again by the antagonism between proletariat and bourgeoisie, is cracking and splitting and threatens to collapse at any moment. How is such an old, incurably ill state to contend with the young and still robust German state?

Henceforth, I repeat, France's role as the paramount power is over. The era of French political power has passed as irrevocably as the era of French literary classicism, monarchical and republican. All the old foundations of the state have rotted, and Thiers strives in vain to build his conservative republic – the old monarchist state with a renovated pseudo-republican façade – upon them. Likewise Gambetta, the leader of the present radical party and Thiers's heir apparent, promises in vain to build a new state, supposedly a sincerely republican and democratic one, on supposedly new foundations, because those foundations do not and cannot exist.

At the present time a serious, strong state can have but one sound foundation – military and bureaucratic centralization. Between a monarchy and the most democratic republic there is only one essential difference: in the former, the world of officialdom oppresses and robs the people for the greater profit of the privileged and propertied classes, as well as to line its own pockets, in the name of the monarch; in the latter, it oppresses and robs the people in exactly the same way, for the benefit of the same classes and the same pockets, but in the name of the people's will. In a republic a fictitious people, the "legal nation" supposedly represented by the state, smothers the real, live people. But it will scarcely be any easier on the people if the cudgel with which they are beaten is called the people's cudgel.

The social question, the passion for social revolution, has now seized the French proletariat. That passion must either be satisfied or bridled and subdued. It can be satisfied, however, only when the state's power of coercion, the last bulwark of bourgeois interests, collapses. This means that no state, howsoever democratic its forms, not even the reddest *political* republic – a people's republic only in the sense of the lie known as popular representation – is capable of giving the people what they need: the free organization of their own interests from below upward, without any interference, tutelage, or coercion from above. That is because no state, not even the most republican and democratic, not even the pseudo-popular state contemplated by Marx, in essence represents anything but government of the masses from above downward, by an educated and thereby privileged minority which supposedly understands the real interests of the people better than the people themselves.

Thus it is absolutely impossible for the propertied and governing classes to satisfy the people's passion and the people's demands. One instrument remains – *state coercion*, in a word the *state*, for the state *means* coercion, domination by means of coercion, camouflaged if possible but unceremonious and overt if need be. Gambetta is just as much a representative of bourgeois interests as Thiers himself; he too wants a strong state and the unconditional domination of the middle class, with the addition, perhaps, of the bourgeoisified stratum of workers, which in France makes up a very insignificant part of the proletariat as a whole. The difference between him and Thiers consists entirely of the fact that the latter, swayed by the biases and prejudices of his time, seeks support and salvation only from the extremely rich bourgeoisie and views with suspicion the tens or even hundreds of thousands of new claimants to government office from the petty bourgeoisie and the aforementioned class of workers who aspire to the bourgeoisie; while Gambetta, spurned by the upper classes who hitherto have been the exclusive rulers of France, seeks to base his political power, his republican-democratic dictatorship, on the vast and purely bourgeois majority who until now have been left out of the rewards and honors of state administration.

He is convinced, however, and quite rightly, we believe, that once he succeeds in seizing power with the help of this majority, the richest classes, the bankers, big landowners, merchants, and industrialists, in short, all the important speculators who have enriched themselves more than anyone else on the people's labor, will turn to him, accept him, and seek his alliance and friendship. Nor, of course, will he spurn them, for as a true statesman he knows all too well that no state, particularly a strong one, can exist without their alliance and friendship.

This means that Gambetta's state will be just as oppressive and ruinous for the people as any of its more candid but no more coercive predecessors. And precisely because it will be decked out in broad democratic forms it will provide the rich and rapacious minority with a stronger and more reliable guarantee of their peaceful and intensive exploitation of the people's labor.

As a statesman of the modern school, Gambetta has no fear at all of the most broadly democratic forms or of universal suffrage. He knows better than anyone how little assurance they offer to the people and how much to the individuals and classes who exploit them. He knows that governmental despotism is never so fierce and so powerful as when it rests on the fictitious representation of a fictitious popular will.

Therefore, should the French proletariat get carried away by the promises of this ambitious lawyer, should Gambetta manage to fit this unruly proletariat onto the Procrustean bed of his democratic republic, there is no doubt that he would succeed in restoring the French state to its former grandeur and supremacy.

But that is the problem, he cannot succeed. There is no force on earth, no political or religious instrument now capable of stifling the desire for economic liberation and social equality in the proletariat of any country, and especially in the French proletariat. Whatever Gambetta may do, whether he threatens with bayonets or caresses with words, he will not be able to cope with the herculean force now latent in that desire, and he will never succeed in harnessing the laboring masses as before to the glittering chariot of the state. His flights of oratory will not fill in and smooth over the abyss that irrevocably separates the bourgeoisie from the proletariat, will not put an end to the desperate struggle between them. That struggle will require the application of all of the French state's resources and strength, so that it will have none left to maintain its external supremacy among the European states. How, then, is it to vie with Bismarck's empire?

Whatever the French state patriots may say, and however they may boast, France as a state is condemned henceforth to occupy a modest, distinctly secondary position. Moreover, it will have to subordinate itself to the supreme leadership, the friendly tutelage, of the German Empire, just as the Italian state before 1870 subordinated itself to the policies of the French Empire.

It is a position that may be quite profitable for the French speculators who are finding considerable consolation on the world market, but it is a highly unenviable one from the point of view of national vanity, with which the French state patriots are so replete. Until 1870 one might have thought this vanity strong enough to thrust even the staunchest and most stubborn defenders of bourgeois privilege into social revolution, if only to save France from the shame of being vanquished and subjugated by the Germans. But after 1870 no one will expect this of them; everyone knows that they will agree to any kind of shame, even submission to German protection, rather than renounce their profitable dominion over their own proletariat.

Is it not clear that the French state will never regain its former power? But does that mean that France's universal and progressive role has come to an end? Not at all. It means only that France, having irretrievably lost its grandeur as a state, will have to seek new grandeur in social revolution.

II

But if not France, then what other state in Europe can compete with the new German Empire?

Certainly not Great Britain. In the first place, England has never been a state in the strict, modern sense of the word, that is, in the sense of military, police, and bureaucratic centralization. Rather, England represents a federation of privileged interests, an autonomous society in which a landed aristocracy predominated at first and a monied aristocracy now predominates along with it, but in which, just like France though in somewhat different forms, the proletariat clearly and threateningly strives for the equalization of economic conditions and political rights.

England's influence on the political affairs of continental Europe has always been great, to be sure, but it was based much more on wealth than on the organization of military force. Today, as everyone knows, it has diminished considerably. A mere thirty years ago, England would not have tolerated with such equanimity the Germans' conquest of the Rhine provinces, or the restoration of Russian predominance on the Black Sea, or the Russians' campaign against Khiva.[17] Such systematic acquiescence on its part demonstrates its unmistakable political bankruptcy, which grows with each passing year. The main reason for that bankruptcy is the antagonism between the world of the common laborers and the world of the exploiting, politically dominant bourgeoisie.

In England, social revolution is much more imminent than people think, and nowhere else will it be as fierce, for nowhere else will it encounter such desperate and well-organized resistance.

Spain and Italy need not even be mentioned. They will never become threatening or even strong states, not because they lack the material resources but because in both countries the spirit of the people draws them ineluctably toward an entirely different objective.

Spain, led astray from its normal course by Catholic fanaticism and the despotism of Charles V and Philip II, and suddenly enriched not by its people's labor but by American silver and gold, in the sixteenth and seventeenth centuries tried to assume the unenviable honor of establishing a universal monarchy by force. It paid dearly for that. The period of its power was precisely the beginning of its intellectual, moral, and material impoverishment. After the brief and unnatural exertion of all its forces, which made it feared and hated by the whole of Europe and even succeeded in halting for a moment – but only for a moment – the progressive movement of European society, it seemed suddenly to have exhausted itself and fell into an extreme state of torpor, enfeeblement, and apathy. So it remained, utterly disgraced by the monstrous and idiotic rule of the Bourbons, until Napoleon I's predatory invasion aroused it from its two-centuries-long slumber.

It turned out that Spain had not died. It delivered itself from a foreign yoke by means of a purely popular uprising and demonstrated that the masses, ignorant and unarmed, are capable of resisting the best armies in the world as long as they are animated by a strong and unanimous passion. Even more, Spain demonstrated that for the preservation of a people's liberty, strength, and passion, ignorance is preferable to bourgeois civilization.

In vain the Germans plume themselves on their own national – but far from popular – uprising of 1812 and 1813, and compare it with that of Spain. The Spaniards rose up defenseless against the enormous might of a hitherto invincible conqueror; the Germans, however, rose up against Napoleon only after the total defeat inflicted on him in Russia. Until then there was no instance of any German village or any German town daring to offer even the least resistance to the victorious French armies. The Germans were so used to obedience, that cardinal state virtue, that the conquerors' will became sacred to them as soon as it effectively replaced the will of the domestic authorities. The Prussian generals themselves, surrendering their fortresses, strongholds, and capitals one after the other, repeated the memorable words of the Berlin commandant at the time, which became proverbial: "Order is the first duty of the citizen."

The Tyrol was the lone exception. There, Napoleon met truly popular resistance. But the Tyrol, as everyone knows, constitutes the most backward and uneducated part of Germany, and its example found no imitators in any of the other provinces of enlightened Germany.

A popular uprising, elemental, chaotic, and merciless in nature,[18] always presupposes a great loss and sacrifice of property, the people's own and that of others. The masses are always ready for such sacrifices; they constitute a rude, untamed force, capable of accomplishing heroic feats and achieving seemingly impossible objectives, precisely because they have very little property or none at all and are therefore not corrupted by it. When it is required for defense or for victory, they will not stop short of razing their own villages and towns, and since property for the most part belongs to others, they frequently evince a real passion for destruction.[19] This negative passion is far from sufficient for achieving the ultimate aims of the revolutionary cause. Without it, however, that cause would be inconceivable, impossible, for there can be no revolution without widespread and passionate destruction, a destruction salutary and fruitful precisely because out of it, and by means of it alone, new worlds are born and arise.

Such destruction is incompatible with bourgeois consciousness, with bourgeois civilization, for the latter is built entirely on the fanatical worship of property. A burgher or a bourgeois would sooner give up his life, liberty, and honor than renounce his property. The very idea that it might be encroached upon, that it might be destroyed for any purpose whatsoever, strikes them as sacrilege. That is why they will never agree to the obliteration of their own cities and homes, even when the country's defense requires it, and that is why the French bourgeoisie in 1870 and the German burghers right up to 1813 submitted so readily to their fortunate conquerors. We have seen that the possession of property was enough to corrupt the French peasantry and extinguish its last spark of patriotism.

To say a final word about Germany's so-called national uprising against Napoleon, let us reiterate that in the first place it ensued only when his shattered forces were fleeing Russia, and when the Prussian and other German corps, which not long before had been part of Napoleon's army, had gone over to the Russian side. In the second place, even then there was, strictly speaking, no universal popular uprising in Germany. The towns and villages remained calm, and only volunteer detachments of young people, students for the most part, were formed, and they were immediately incorporated into the regular army, something completely contrary to the method and spirit of popular uprisings.

In short, in Germany youthful citizens, or, more precisely, loyal subjects, incited by the heated sermons of their philosophers and inflamed by the songs of their poets, took up arms to defend and restore the German state, for at this time the idea of a pan-German state had also awakened in Germany. Meanwhile, the Spanish people to a man rose up to defend the freedom of their homeland and the independence of national life against an arrogant and powerful marauder.

Since then, Spain has not gone back to sleep but for sixty years has tormented itself in search of new forms for a new life. Poor Spain, what has it not tried – from absolute monarchy, twice restored, to the constitution of Queen Isabella, from Espartero to Narváez, from Narváez to Prim, and from the latter to King Amadeo, Sagasta, and Zorilla.[20] Spain seemed to be trying out all the conceivable forms of constitutional monarchy, and they all proved too constricting, ruinous, impossible. Now a conservative republic, the dominion of speculators, rich property-owners, and bankers under republican forms, is turning out to be equally impossible. A petty-bourgeois political federation of the Swiss type will rapidly prove impossible too.

The demon of revolutionary socialism has taken possession of Spain in earnest. The peasants of Andalusia and Estremadura, without asking anyone's permission or waiting for anyone's instructions, have been seizing the estates of the former landowners. Catalonia, led by Barcelona, is loudly declaring its independence, its autonomy. The people of Madrid are proclaiming a federal republic and refusing to subordinate their revolution to the future edicts of the constituent assembly. In the northern provinces, which were supposed to be in the grip of Carlist reaction, a social revolution is manifestly occurring: *fueros*[a] and the independence of provinces and communes are being proclaimed, and all judicial and civil documents are being burned. Throughout Spain soldiers are fraternizing with the people and ousting their officers. General bankruptcy, public and private, has begun – the primary condition for social and economic revolution.

In a word, there is havoc and utter disintegration, and everything is collapsing of its own accord, smashed or broken as a result of its own decay. There are no revenues, no army, no courts, no police; there is no state power, there is no state. Only the people remain, strong and fresh, possessed now by a single social-revolutionary passion. Under the collective leadership of the International and the Alliance of Social Revolutionaries,[21] they are rallying and organizing their forces, preparing to establish their own world of the liberated workingman on the ruins of the disintegrating state and bourgeois world.

Italy is just as close to social revolution as Spain. There, too, despite all the endeavors of the constitutional monarchists, and even the heroic but futile efforts of the two great leaders, Mazzini and Garibaldi, the idea of the state has never been accepted, nor will it ever be, for it is contrary to the true spirit and the contemporary instinctive desires and material demands of the innumerable rural and urban proletariat.

Like Spain, Italy long ago and irrevocably lost the centralizing and autocratic traditions of ancient Rome, traditions preserved in the books of Dante and Machiavelli, and in modern political literature, but not at all in the living memory of the people. Italy, I say, has preserved only the living tradition of absolute autonomy, autonomy not even of the province but of the commune. This is the sole political concept existing among the people. Add to it the historical and ethnographic diversity of provinces which speak such different dialects that the inhabitants of one have difficulty understanding the inhabitants of another, and sometimes cannot understand them at all. Then it becomes clear how far Italy is from realizing the modern political ideal of state unity. But this in no way signifies that Italy is socially disunited. On the contrary, for all the differences in dialects, customs, and mores, there is a common Italian character-type by which an Italian can immediately be distinguished from a member of any other nation, even a southern one.

---

[a] *Fueros* were charters of local liberties granted by medieval Spanish kings.

Furthermore, a real community of material interests and an astonishing identity of moral and intellectual aspirations unite all the Italian provinces and bind them very closely together. It is remarkable, however, that all these interests and aspirations are directed against forcible political unity and are leading instead to the establishment of social unity. It can be said, and proved with countless facts drawn from current Italian life, that Italy's forcible political or state unity resulted in social disunity, and that consequently the abolition of the contemporary Italian state will assuredly result in its voluntary social unification.

All of this applies, of course, only to the masses, for in the upper strata of the Italian bourgeoisie, as in other countries, state unity was accompanied by the social unity of the class of privileged exploiters of the people's labor, a unity which is now being developed and expanded.

That class is now designated in Italy by the general term *Consorteria*.[22] The *Consorteria* embraces the entire official world, the bureaucracy and the army, the police and the courts; the entire world of big property-owners, industrialists, merchants, and bankers; official and semi-official lawyers and writers, as well as the whole of parliament, the right wing of which now enjoys all the benefits of government while the left strives to take the government into its own hands.

Thus in Italy, as everywhere else, there exists a united and indivisible political world of predators, sucking the country dry in the name of the state and, for the greater benefit of the latter, reducing the former to an extreme degree of poverty and desperation.

The most terrible poverty, however, even when it strikes a proletariat numbering in the many millions, is not a sufficient guarantee of revolution. Nature has given man an astonishing and, indeed, sometimes despairing, patience, and the devil knows what he will not endure when, along with poverty that condemns him to unheard-of privations and slow starvation, he is also endowed with obtuseness, emotional numbness, lack of any consciousness of his rights, and the kind of imperturbability and obedience that particularly characterize the east Indians and the Germans, among all nations. Such a fellow will never take heart; he will die, but he will not rebel.

But when he is driven to desperation, revolt becomes more of a possibility. Desperation is a sharp, passionate feeling. It draws him out of his dull, somnolent suffering and at least presupposes a more or less clear awareness that better conditions are possible, though he has no hope of achieving them.

In the end, no one can remain in a state of desperation for long; it rapidly leads a man either to death or to action. To what kind of action? Obviously, action to liberate himself and to achieve the conditions for a better existence. In desperation even a German will stop philosophizing; but it takes a great many insults and a great deal of oppression, suffering, and misfortune to drive him to it.

Not even poverty and desperation, however, are enough to provoke a social revolution. They are capable of producing personal or, at most, local rebellions, but they are insufficient for arousing the people en masse. That requires a popular ideal, which always develops historically, from the depths of popular instinct, an instinct nurtured, broadened, and illuminated by a series of significant events, painful and bitter experiences – it requires a general conception of one's rights and a profound, passionate, one might say religious, belief in those rights. When such an ideal and such a belief are found in a people together with a poverty that drives them to desperation, then a social revolution is inevitable, it is imminent, and there is no force that can prevent it.

The Italian people are in precisely such a situation. Their poverty, and the sufferings of every kind that they have endured, are terrible and do not fall far short of the poverty and sufferings that weigh upon the Russian people. But at the same time the Italian proletariat to a much greater degree than ours has developed a passionate revolutionary consciousness which day by day grows clearer and stronger. Intelligent and passionate by nature, the Italian proletariat is at last beginning to understand what it needs and what it must desire for its complete and comprehensive liberation. In this respect the International's propaganda, which has been conducted energetically and on a broad scale only in the last two years, has rendered the proletariat an enormous service. It has given it, or, more accurately, has awakened within it, the ideal traced in broad outline by its deepest instinct, without which, as we have said, a popular uprising is absolutely impossible whatever the people's sufferings.* It has shown the proletariat the objective it must achieve and at the same time has indicated to it the ways and means of organizing a popular force.

What this ideal represents for the people is, of course, first of all an

* See Appendix A at the end of this Introduction.

end to want, an end to poverty, the full satisfaction of all material needs through collective labor equal and obligatory for all; then, an end to all masters and to domination of every kind, and the free construction of popular life in accordance with popular needs, not from above downward, as in the state, but from below upward, by the people themselves, dispensing with all governments and parliaments – a voluntary alliance of agricultural and factory worker associations, communes, provinces, and nations; and finally, in the more distant future, universal human brotherhood triumphing on the ruins of all the states.

It is remarkable that in Italy, as in Spain, Marx's state-communist program has had no success whatsoever. Instead, what has been widely and passionately adopted is the program of the notorious Alliance or League of Social Revolutionaries, which declared relentless war on every kind of domination, governmental tutelage, hierarchy, and authority.

Under these conditions a nation can liberate itself and can build its own life on the basis of the broadest freedom of each and all, but it can no longer threaten the freedom of other nations in any way. Therefore, neither on the part of Spain nor on the part of Italy should one anticipate a policy of aggression, but rather an imminent social revolution.

Small states such as Switzerland, Belgium, Holland, Denmark, and Sweden, for the same reasons but chiefly because of their political insignificance, threaten no one. On the contrary, they have good reason to fear annexations on the part of the new German Empire.

Austria, Russia, and Prussian Germany are left. As far as Austria is concerned, are we not speaking of an incurable invalid taking rapid strides toward the grave? This empire, a creation of dynastic ties and military force, is composed of four mutually antagonistic races with little love lost among them; it is dominated by the German race, which is unanimously detested by the three others and numerically amounts to scarcely a quarter of the total population; and it is half made up of Slavs who are demanding autonomy and were recently divided between two states, one Magyar-Slavic and the other German-Slavic.[23] Such an empire could be held together only as long as military and police despotism prevailed within it. In the course of the last twenty-five years it suffered three mortal blows. A first defeat was inflicted on it by the revolution of 1848, which put an end to the old regime and the government of Prince Metternich. Since then it has maintained its decrepit existence by taking heroic measures and a wide variety of restorative tonics. In 1849, having been saved by Emperor Nicholas, under the administration of an arrogant oligarch, Prince Schwarzenberg, and a Slavophile Jesuit, Count Thun, who drafted the concordat with Rome, it began to seek salvation in the most desperate clerical and political reaction and in the introduction of the most complete and ruthless centralization in all its provinces, in defiance of national differences.[24] But a second defeat, inflicted on it by Napoleon III in 1859, proved that military and bureaucratic centralization could not save it.

Since then it has gone in for liberalism. It summoned from Saxony the inept and hapless rival of Prince (then still Count) Bismarck, Baron Beust, and began desperately to liberate its peoples.[25] While liberating them, however, it also wanted to preserve its state unity – that is, to solve a problem that is simply insoluble.

It had to satisfy simultaneously the four principal nationalities inhabiting the empire, the Slavs, Germans, Magyars, and Romanians,* who are not only extremely divergent by nature, language, character, and cultural level, but for the most part regard each other with hostility and therefore can be kept together within the state only by means of governmental constraint.

It had to satisfy the Germans, the majority of whom seek to attain the most liberal-democratic constitution while demanding loudly and insistently that they retain their *ancient right* to political supremacy within the Austrian monarchy, regardless of the fact that together with the Jews they make up only a quarter of its total population.

Is this not new evidence of that truth which we never tire of asserting, in the conviction that the quickest resolution of all social problems depends on its universal comprehension: that the state, any state, be it vested in the most liberal and democratic forms, is necessarily based on domination, on force, that is, on despotism – covert, perhaps, but all the more dangerous?

The Germans, statists and bureaucrats by nature, it may be said, base their pretensions on their historic rights (meaning rights of

* Of the 36 million inhabitants, these nationalities are distributed as follows: approximately 16,500,000 Slavs (5 million Poles and Ruthenians; 7,250,000 other north Slavs: Czechs, Moravians, Slovaks; and 4,250,000 south Slavs), approximately 5,500,000 Magyars, 2,900,000 Romanians, 600,000 Italians, 9,000,000 Germans and Jews, and some 1,500,000 others.

conquest and antiquity), on the one hand, and on the fancied superiority of their culture, on the other. At the end of this foreword we will
have occasion to indicate how far their pretensions go. For now let us
confine ourselves to the Austrian Germans, though it is very difficult
to separate their pretensions from those of the Germans in general.

The Austrian Germans in recent years came to the grudging
realization that they had to renounce domination over the Magyars, at
least for the time being, and finally recognized their right to an
independent existence. Of all the nationalities inhabiting the Austrian
Empire, the Magyars, after the Germans, are the most state-minded.
Despite the most brutal persecutions and the most drastic measures
by which the Austrian government in the nine years from 1850 to
1859 tried to overcome their stubbornness, they not only refused to
renounce their national independence but asserted their right (also an
historic one, in their opinion) to political supremacy over all the other
nationalities inhabiting the Kingdom of Hungary, regardless of the
fact that they themselves make up not much more than a third of the
kingdom's population.*

Thus the hapless Austrian Empire split up into two states, almost
equal in strength and united only under a single crown – the
Cisleithan, or Slavic-German state, with 20,500,000 inhabitants (of
whom 7,200,000 are Germans and Jews, 11,500,000 Slavs, and
approximately 1,800,000 Italians and other nationalities), and the
Transleithan, Hungarian, or Magyar-Slavic-Romanian-German
state.

It is remarkable that neither of these two states, even in its internal
structure, offers any assurance of vigor, current or future.

Within the Kingdom of Hungary, despite its liberal constitution
and the unquestionable adroitness of its Magyar rulers, racial conflict,
that chronic disease of the Austrian monarchy, has not abated in the
least. The majority of the population, subordinated to the Magyars,
dislikes them and will never voluntarily agree to bear their yoke. The
result is an unrelenting struggle between them, in which the Slavs rely
on the Turkish Slavs and the Romanians on the fraternal population
of Wallachia, Moldavia, Bessarabia, and Bukovina. The Magyars,
constituting but a third of the population, like it or not must seek

* The Kingdom of Hungary numbers 5,500,000 Magyars, 5,000,000 Slavs,
2,700,000 Romanians, 1,800,000 Jews and Germans, and some 500,000 others – a total
of 15,500,000 inhabitants.

support and protection in Vienna. Imperial Vienna, meanwhile, which cannot stomach the secession of the Magyars, like all decaying and declining dynastic governments nourishes the secret hope of a miraculous restoration of its lost power. It is delighted at these internal discords which prevent the Kingdom of Hungary from achieving stability, and it covertly stirs up Slavic and Romanian passions against the Magyars. The Magyar rulers and politicians know this and return the favor by maintaining secret relations with Bismarck, who, foreseeing an inevitable war against an Austrian Empire doomed to extinction, makes advances to the Magyars.

The Cisleithan or German-Slavic state finds itself in no better a situation. Here, little more than 7 million Germans, including Jews, assert the claim to govern 11.5 million Slavs.

This pretension, it goes without saying, is a strange one. One might say that it has been the historic mission of the Germans since ancient times to conquer the Slavic lands, to exterminate, subjugate, and civilize – that is, to Germanize or petty-bourgeoisify – the Slavs. Hence a deep historical and mutual hatred arose between them, conditioned on both sides by the special situation of each one.

The Slavs hate the Germans as peoples who have been vanquished but not reconciled, and in their hearts not subdued, hate all conquerors. The Germans hate the Slavs as masters customarily hate their slaves: they hate them for their hatred, which they, the Germans, have earned from the Slavs. They hate them for the involuntary and incessant fear aroused within them by the Slavs' inextinguishable thought and hope of liberation.

Like all conquerors of a foreign land and subjugators of an alien people, the Germans with consummate injustice hate and scorn the Slavs simultaneously. We have already said why they hate them; they scorn them because the Slavs have been unable and unwilling to be Germanized. It is remarkable that the Prussian Germans bitterly and in all seriousness reproach the Austrian Germans, and practically accuse the Austrian government of treason, for being unable to Germanize the Slavs. In their view, and in actual fact, this constitutes the greatest crime against the patriotic interests of all Germans, against *pan-Germanism*.

Threatened, or, more accurately, persecuted from all sides but not completely crushed by this detested pan-Germanism, the Austrian Slavs, with the exception of the Poles, have countered it with another highly repugnant absurdity, another ideal that is no less opposed to freedom and lethal for the people – pan-Slavism.*

We do not claim that all the Austrian Slavs, even aside from the Poles, worship this ideal, which is as grotesque as it is dangerous – let us note in passing that the Turkish Slavs, for all the intrigues of the Russian agents who are always hanging around them, have shown very little sympathy for it. It is nonetheless true that the hope of deliverance and a deliverer from Petersburg is quite widespread among the Austrian Slavs. Their fierce, and, let us add, perfectly justifiable, hatred has driven them to such a degree of folly that they have forgotten or are ignorant of all the catastrophes Lithuania, Poland, Ukraine,*a* and even the Great Russian people themselves have suffered under Muscovite and Petersburg despotism, and have come to expect salvation from our Tsar-Knout of All the Russias!

That such ridiculous expectations could have arisen among the Slavic masses is not surprising. They know no history, nor do they know Russia's internal situation. All they have heard is that as a joke on the Germans, and in defiance of them, a huge, supposedly purely Slavic Empire has arisen, so powerful that the hated Germans tremble before it. The Germans tremble, hence the Slavs must rejoice; the Germans hate, therefore the Slavs must love.

That is all very natural. But it is strange, sad, and unforgivable that within the educated class in the Austro-Slavic lands a whole party has been created, headed by experienced, intelligent, knowledgeable people who openly advocate pan-Slavism – or, at least, as some of them would have it, the liberation of the Slavic people by means of the

---

* We are just as much sworn enemies of *pan-Slavism* as we are of *pan-Germanism*, and in one of our future books we intend to devote a special article to this issue, which we consider extremely important. For now, let us say only that we consider it the sacred and inescapable obligation of Russia's revolutionary youth to oppose pan-Slav propaganda with all its might and all the resources at its disposal. This propaganda has been carried on in Russia and particularly in the Slavic lands by governmental and private Slavophiles or by official Russian agents. They try to convince the unhappy Slavs that the Slavic tsar in Petersburg, filled with burning paternal love for his Slavic brethren, and the despicable Russian Empire, which destroys its people and is hated by them, which has suppressed Ukraine and Poland and has even sold out the latter in part to the Germans, can and will liberate the Slavic countries from the German yoke – and this at the very time when the Petersburg cabinet is patently selling out and betraying all of Bohemia and Moravia to Bismarck in return for a promise of help in the East.

a Throughout the text Bakunin uses the term Little Russia instead of the modern term Ukraine. The latter came into common usage only toward the end of the nineteenth century.

powerful intervention of the Russian Empire, or, as others would have it, even the creation of a *great Slavic empire* under the scepter of the Russian tsar.

It is remarkable to what degree that accursed German civilization, intrinsically bourgeois and thereby statist, has succeeded in penetrating the souls even of Slavic patriots. They were born into a Germanized bourgeois society, they studied in German schools and universities, they grew accustomed to thinking, feeling, and aspiring in German, and they would have become perfect Germans had not the goal they are pursuing been anti-German: by German ways and means they want to liberate the Slavs from the German yoke. Prevented by their German education from comprehending any other method of liberation than the formation of Slavic states or of a single mighty Slavic state, they are setting themselves a thoroughly German objective, for the modern state of the centralized, bureaucratic, police and military type – the new German Empire, for example, or the Russian Empire – is a purely German creation. (In Russia it originally had an admixture of Tatar elements, but because of the Tatars' courtesy[a] that is not an issue in Germany today.)

By their very nature and in their very being the Slavs are absolutely not a political, that is, state-minded, people. In vain the Czechs invoke the memory of their Great Moravian Empire and the Serbs the empire of Dušan.[26] Those are either ephemeral phenomena or ancient myths. The truth is that no Slavic nation of its own accord ever created a state.

The Polish monarchy-republic arose under the dual influence of Germanism and Latinism after the total defeat of the peasants (the *chłopy*) and their enslavement to the gentry – who, according to the testimony of many Polish historians and writers (Mickiewicz,[27] among others), were not even of Slavic origin.

The Bohemian or Czech kingdom[28] was pasted together purely in the Germans' own image and likeness, and under their direct influence, as a result of which Bohemia so soon became an organic member, an inseparable part of the German Empire.

Everyone knows the history of the formation of the Russian Empire. The Tatar knout, Byzantine blessings, and German bureaucratic, military, and police enlightenment took part in it. The poor Great Russians, and then the other peoples who were annexed

---

[a] That is, in refraining from conquering Germany as well as Russia.

to the empire, the Ukrainians, Lithuanians, and Poles, participated in its creation only with their backs.

Thus it is unquestionable that the Slavs, on their own initiative, never formed a state. They did not do so because they were never a conquering nation. Only conquering peoples create states, and they create them purely for their own benefit, at the expense of the peoples they have subjugated.

The Slavs were preeminently peaceable and agricultural. Alien to the warlike spirit that animated the Germanic tribes, they were thereby alien to the statist aspirations the Germans manifested from early times. Living in their separate and independent communes, governed according to patriarchal custom by elders, but on an elective basis, and all making equal use of the commune's land, they did not have and did not recognize a nobility, nor did they even have a caste of priests. They were all equal and put into practice the idea of human brotherhood, though only in a patriarchal and consequently very imperfect form. There was no permanent political bond among the communes. When common danger threatened, such as an attack by an alien tribe, they would conclude a temporary defensive alliance, but as soon as the danger passed, this shadow of political unification disappeared. Hence, there was not and could not be a Slavic state. Instead, a social, fraternal bond existed among all the Slavic tribes, which were hospitable to the highest degree.

Organized in this way, the Slavs would naturally prove defenseless against attacks and encroachments by warlike tribes, especially the Germans, seeking to extend their sway everywhere... The Slavs were partly wiped out but were for the most part subjugated by the Turks, Tatars, Magyars, and particularly the Germans.

The second half of the tenth century marks the beginning of their tormented history of enslavement – not just tormented, however, but heroic as well. In the course of many centuries of stubborn and unremitting struggle against their conquerors, they shed a great deal of blood for the freedom of their land. In the eleventh century we encounter two events: a general uprising of the pagan Slavs who dwelt between the Oder, the Elbe, and the Baltic, against the German knights and priests; and an equally significant revolt of the Polish peasants against the sway of the gentry. Then, until the fifteenth century, a small-scale, inconspicuous, but unceasing struggle was carried on by the west Slavs against the Germans, the south

Slavs against the Turks, and the northeastern Slavs against the Tatars.

In the fifteenth century we encounter the great, and this time victorious as well as purely popular, revolution of the Czech Hussites.[29] Leaving their religious views aside (let us note in passing, however, that they were far closer to the principles of human brotherhood and popular liberty than those of the Catholics or the Protestants who came after them), we note the purely social and anti-state character of this revolution. It was an uprising of the Slavic commune against the German state.

In the seventeenth century, in consequence of a whole series of betrayals by the half-Germanized petty bourgeoisie of Prague, the Hussites were ultimately defeated. Almost half the Czech population was wiped out, and its lands were handed over to colonists from Germany. The Germans and Jesuits triumphed, and for more than two centuries after this bloody defeat the west Slavic world remained immobile, mute, held down by the Catholic Church and victorious Germanism. At the same time the south Slavs were dragging out their servile lot under Magyar dominance or the Turkish yoke. To make up for it, though, Slav rebellion in the name of popular and commercial principles flared up in the northeast.

Passing over the desperate struggle of Novgorod the Great, Pskov, and other territories against the Muscovite tsars in the sixteenth century, and the united militia of the Great Russian land against the king of Poland, the Jesuits, the Moscow boyars, and the general domination of Moscow at the beginning of the seventeenth century, let us recall the celebrated uprising of the Ukrainian and Lithuanian population against the Polish gentry, followed by the even more determined uprising of the peasantry of the Volga region under the leadership of Stepan Razin. Finally, a hundred years later, came the no less significant revolt of Pugachev.[30] In all these purely popular movements, insurrections, and revolts, we find the same hatred of the state, the same desire to create a peasant world of free communes.

Finally, the nineteenth century can be called the century of the general awakening of the Slavic nation. Nothing need be said about Poland. It had never gone to sleep, for ever since the rapacious theft of its liberty (true, not the people's liberty but that of the gentry and the state), ever since it was partitioned among the three predatory powers, it had not stopped struggling, and whatever the Muravevs[31] and the Bismarcks may do, it will keep on rebelling until it regains its liberty. Unfortunately for Poland, its leading parties, which are still drawn primarily from the gentry, have been unable to renounce their state-centered program. Instead of seeking the liberation and renewal of their homeland in social revolution, in obedience to ancient traditions they pursue those objectives now under the patronage of one Napoleon or the other, now in alliance with the Jesuits and the feudal lords of Austria.

But in our century the west and south Slavs have also awakened. In defiance of all the Germans' political, police, and civilizing efforts, Bohemia after three centuries of slumber took heart anew as a purely Slavic country and became the natural focal point for the entire west Slavic movement. Turkish Serbia has come to play the same role for the south Slavic movement.

With the Slavic revival, however, an extremely important, one might say fateful, question arises.

How is this Slavic revival to be accomplished? By taking the ancient path of state domination, or by means of the real liberation of all peoples, or at least those of Europe, liberation of the entire European proletariat from every kind of yoke, and first of all from the yoke of the state?

Can and should the Slavs extricate themselves from their foreign, primarily German yoke, the one they find most hateful, by resorting in their turn to the German method of conquest and usurpation, by forcing conquered masses to submit to a hated allegiance, formerly German but now Slavic? Or should they do so only by means of a joint uprising of the entire European proletariat, by means of a social revolution?

The entire future of the Slavs depends on which of these two paths they choose. Which one should they resolve to take?

We are convinced that to pose this question is to answer it. Despite the wise saying of King Solomon, the old never does repeat itself. The modern state, which merely brings to full realization the ancient idea of domination (just as Christianity is the realization of the latest form of theological belief or religious bondage), the bureaucratic, military, centralized police state, which strives by the intrinsic necessity of its very nature to usurp, subjugate, and stifle everything around it that lives, moves, and breathes – this state, which has found its ultimate expression in the pan-German empire, has outlived its time. Its days are numbered, and all peoples await their final deliverance from its downfall.

Are the Slavs fated to repeat the answer that already stands condemned by history, an answer abhorrent to men and nations alike? For what purpose? It would be not an honor but a crime and a disgrace, and they would be cursed by their contemporaries and their descendants. Have the Slavs come to envy the Germans for the hatred they have earned from all the other peoples of Europe? Or do they like the role of a universal God? The devil take all the Slavs and their whole military future if after their long years of bondage, torture, and silence they are to bring mankind new chains!

And what use would it be to the Slavs? What benefit would there be for the Slavic masses in the formation of a great Slavic state? Such states are unquestionably of benefit, not for the many millions of proletarians, however, but for a privileged minority, priestly, noble, bourgeois – or, perhaps, even intellectual, one which in the name of its licensed erudition and fancied intellectual superiority considers itself called upon to take charge of the masses. The benefit is for a few thousand oppressors, hangmen, and exploiters of the proletariat. For the proletariat itself, for the masses of common laborers, the more extensive the state the heavier their chains and the narrower their prison walls.

We have stated and demonstrated above that a society cannot be and cannot remain a state unless it becomes an aggressive one. The same competition which in the economic field destroys and swallows up small and even medium-size capital funds, industrial establishments, landholdings, and merchant houses for the benefit of big ones, destroys and swallows up small and medium-size states for the benefit of empires. Henceforth, any state that wants to exist not just on paper or by the grace of its neighbors for as long as they are pleased to tolerate it, but genuinely and independently, must without fail be aggressive.

Being an aggressive state, however, means having to keep many millions of alien people forcibly subjugated. That requires the development of massive military force. And where military force triumphs, goodbye freedom! Goodbye, especially, to the freedom and prosperity of the working people. Hence it follows that the formation of a great Slavic state would be nothing other than the massive enslavement of the Slavic people.

"But," the Slavic proponents of the state will reply, "we do not want one great Slavic state. We desire only the formation of several purely Slavic states of medium size, as the necessary guarantee of the Slavic peoples' independence." This sentiment is contrary to logic and to historical fact, to the very nature of things. No state of medium size can lead an independent existence today. Consequently, either there will be no Slavic state or there will be one huge and all-devouring pan-Slav, knouto-St. Petersburg state.

Moreover, would a Slavic state be able to combat the enormous power of the new pan-German empire without being equally enor-mous and powerful? Certainly one should never count on concerted action by a number of separate states bound together only by their interests. In the first place, a coalition of disparate organizations and forces, though in numbers it may equal or even exceed the forces of its opponents, is still weaker than the latter, for they are homogeneous and have a stronger and simpler organization, obedient to one thought and one will. In the second place, one should never count on con-certed action by a number of sovereign powers even when their own interests demand such an alliance. Rulers of states, just like ordinary mortals, are for the most part afflicted with blindness, which keeps them from discerning the essential requirements of their own situa-tion beyond the interests and passions of the moment.

In 1863 it was in the direct interest of France, England, Sweden, and even Austria to take Poland's part against Russia, but none did so. In 1864 it was even more directly in the interest of England, France, particularly Sweden, and even Russia to intervene on behalf of Denmark, which was threatened by Prusso-Austrian, essentially Prusso-German, aggression, and again none did so. Finally, in 1870, England, Russia, and Austria, not to mention the small northern states, in their own obvious interest should have stopped the vic-torious invasion of France by Prusso-German forces right up to Paris and almost to the south. Even this time none intervened, however, and only when a new German power that threatened everyone had been created did other states realize they should have intervened, but then it was too late.

Therefore one should not count on the governmental wisdom of neighboring states but rather on one's own forces, and these should at least equal the forces of one's opponent. Consequently, no one Slavic state, on its own, would be in a position to resist the pressure of the pan-German empire.

Would it not be possible, however, to oppose pan-German

centralization with a pan-Slav federation, a union of independent Slavic states or entities along the lines of North America or Switzerland? We must answer this question, too, in the negative.

First of all, for any such union to take place the Russian Empire would have to disintegrate. It would have to be broken up into a number of separate and independent states, themselves linked only by a federal bond, because the independence and freedom of the small or even medium-size Slavic states could not possibly be maintained in a federation with such a colossal empire.

Let us even assume that the Petersburg empire were broken up into a larger or smaller number of free entities, and that the independent states of Poland, Bohemia, Serbia, Bulgaria, and so forth, formed a great Slavic federation with them. Even in such a case, we maintain, this federation would be in no position to struggle against German centralization, for the simple reason that the preponderance of state and military power will always be on the side of centralization.

A federation of states can guarantee bourgeois freedom to some extent, but it cannot create state and military power, precisely because it is a federation; state power necessarily demands centralization. We will be offered the examples of Switzerland and the United States. But Switzerland, precisely in order to augment its state and military forces, is now patently moving in the direction of centralization, while a federation has remained possible in North America only because the great republic does not have as its neighbors on the American continent any powerful centralized states of the order of Russia, Germany, or France.

Thus, to counteract triumphant pan-Germanism by means of state or political power, only one method remains – to create a pan-Slav state. In all other respects this method is extremely disadvantageous for the Slavs, for it would inevitably entail their common bondage under the Russian knout. But is it at least a reliable method in respect to its objective of overthrowing German power and subjecting the Germans to a pan-Slav – that is, an imperial Petersburg – yoke?

No, not only is it unreliable, it is assuredly insufficient. True, there are only 50,500,000 Germans in Europe (including, of course, the 9,000,000 Austrian Germans). Let us assume that the dream of the German patriots finally came true and the German Empire came to include the Flemish part of Belgium, Holland, German Switzerland, the whole of Denmark, and even Sweden and Norway, all together adding up to a population of a little over 15 million. What of it? Even then there would be at most 66 million Germans, while the Slavs number approximately 90 million. Therefore the Slavs are stronger in numbers than the Germans. Yet, despite the fact that the Slavic population of Europe exceeds the German population by almost a third, we still maintain that a pan-Slav state would never equal the pan-German empire in terms of real state and military power. Why not? Because there is a passion for state order and state discipline in German blood, German instinct, and German tradition, while not only do the Slavs lack this passion, but wholly contrary passions dwell within them and act upon them. In order to discipline them, therefore, you have to keep them under the lash, whereas every German has swallowed the lash, freely and with conviction. His freedom consists of submitting to regimentation and gladly bowing down before authority of any kind.

In addition, the Germans are a serious and hard-working people. They are educated and economical, prudent, painstaking, and punctilious – which does not prevent them, when necessary (meaning, when the authorities wish it), from being excellent fighters. They demonstrated that in their recent wars. Their military and administrative organization, moreover, has been brought to the highest possible degree of perfection, a level no other nation will ever attain. Is it imaginable, then, that the Slavs can compete with them in terms of state power?

The Germans seek their life and liberty in the state, while to the Slavs the state is a coffin. The Slavs must seek their liberation outside of the state, not just in struggle against the German state but in an uprising of all nations against all states, in a social revolution.

The Slavs can liberate themselves, they can destroy the hated German state, not through futile efforts to subject the Germans to *their* domination and make them slaves of their own Slavic state, but only by summoning them to universal liberty and universal brotherhood on the ruins of all existing states. But states do not topple of their own accord; they can only be toppled by a multi-national, multi-racial, world-wide social revolution.

Organizing the popular forces to carry out such a revolution is the sole task of those people who sincerely desire the liberation of the Slavic race from its yoke of many years' duration. Those progressive individuals must understand that what constituted the weakness of the Slavic peoples in times past, their inability to form a state, today constitutes their strength, their right to the future, and lends meaning to all their current national movements. Despite the massive development of contemporary states – and as a consequence of it, for it has the thoroughly logical and inevitable effect of reducing the very principle of statehood to absurdity – it has become clear that the days of the state and of statism are numbered. The time is drawing near for the total liberation of the laboring masses and their free social organization from below upward, without governmental interference, from voluntary economic associations of the people, formed in disregard of all the old state boundaries and all national differences, on the sole basis of productive labor completely humanized and fully collective notwithstanding its great diversity.

Progressive Slavs must finally understand that the time has passed for naive games of Slavic philology, and that there is nothing more ridiculous as well as more harmful and lethal for the people than to set up the false principle of nationality as the ideal of all popular aspirations. Nationality is not a universal human principle but an historical, local fact which has an undeniable right to general recognition, like any other real and harmless fact. Every nation, even a very small one, has its own character, its own particular way of life and manner of speaking, feeling, thinking, and behaving. These distinctive features are the essence of nationality, the product of a nation's entire history and conditions of existence.

Every nation, like every individual, is of necessity what it is, and has an unquestionable right to be itself. So-called national rights consist precisely of this. But just because a nation or an individual has a certain identity and can have no other, it does not follow that they have a right, or would benefit by advancing such a right, to nationality or individuality as special principles, and that they should constantly preoccupy themselves with those principles. On the contrary, the less they think about themselves and the more they are filled with universal human content, the more the nationality of the one and the individuality of the other come to life and become meaningful.

This is precisely the case with the Slavs. They will remain extremely insignificant and poor as long as they preoccupy themselves with their narrow, self-centered, and abstract Slavism, which is extraneous, and therefore adverse, to the universal question and universal

46

cause of humanity. They will win their rightful place in history and in the free brotherhood of nations as Slavs only when they are imbued like others with a universal ideal.

A universal human ideal, prevailing over all other, more parochial or exclusively national interests, has existed in every period of history. The nation or nations that find a mission within themselves – that is, sufficient understanding, passion, and vigor to devote themselves exclusively to this universal ideal – are for the most part the ones that become historic nations. The prevailing ideal has differed from one period to another. Not too far back in history it was the highly aggressive ideal of the Catholic faith and the Catholic Church, not so much a human as a divine ideal and therefore contrary to popular freedom and well-being. The nations which then had the greatest inclination and capacity to devote themselves to it – the Germans, French, Spanish, to some degree the Poles – were, as a result, each in its own sphere, the preeminent nations.

That period was followed by one of intellectual revival and religious revolt. The universal human ideal of the Renaissance first drew the Italians to the forefront, then the French, and to a much weaker degree the English, Dutch, and Germans. But religious revolt, which earlier had aroused the south of France, thrust our Slavic Hussites into prominence in the fifteenth century. After prolonged heroic struggle the Hussites were crushed, just as the French Albigensians had been earlier. Then the Reformation revived the German, French, English, Dutch, Swiss, and Scandinavian peoples. In Germany it very quickly lost the character of a revolt, which was alien to the German temperament, and took on the aspect of a peaceful state reform, which forthwith became the basis for the most methodical, systematic, and scientific state despotism. In France, after a long and bloody struggle which to no small degree served the development of free thought in that country, it was overwhelmed by triumphant Catholicism. In Holland, England, and subsequently in the United States, however, it created a new civilization, essentially anti-state but economically bourgeois and liberal.

Thus the movement of religious reformation, which encompassed nearly the whole of Europe in the sixteenth century, generated within civilized mankind two main orientations: one bourgeois-liberal, headed chiefly by England and later by England and America; the other despotic-statist, in essence also bourgeois and Protestant (though combined with a Catholic noble element), but wholly subordinated to the state. The principal representatives of the latter orientation were France and Germany – first Austria, then Prussia.

The great revolution that marked the end of the eighteenth century again thrust France into the preeminent position. It created a new universal ideal, the ideal of absolute human liberty – but *exclusively on the political plane*. It is an ideal that contains an insoluble contradiction and is therefore unrealizable: political liberty without economic equality, and political liberty in general, that is, liberty within a state, are lies.

Thus the French Revolution in turn generated two principal orientations, mutually antagonistic and perpetually struggling with each other but at the same time inseparable, we would even say inexorably converging, in their identical pursuit of one and the same objective: the systematic exploitation of the laboring proletariat for the benefit of a propertied minority which is constantly diminishing in numbers but growing richer and richer.

One party wants to build a democratic republic on the exploitation of the people's labor. The other, which is more consistent, seeks to create a monarchical – that is, sincere – state despotism, a centralized, bureaucratic police state, a military dictatorship barely camouflaged with innocuous constitutional forms.

The first party, under Gambetta's leadership, is now trying to seize power in France. The second, led by Prince Bismarck, already holds sway in Prussian Germany.

It is difficult to decide which of these two orientations is more beneficial for the people – or, more accurately, which of them will inflict the least harm and evil on the laboring masses, the proletariat. Both seek with the same stubborn passion to establish or to consolidate a strong state, that is, the absolute bondage of the proletariat.

In opposition to these oppressive statist orientations, republican and neo-monarchist, both products of the great bourgeois revolution of 1789 and 1793, an entirely new orientation finally arose from the depths of the proletariat itself, first in France and Austria, then in the other countries of Europe. It proceeds directly to the abolition of all exploitation and all political or juridical as well as governmental and bureaucratic oppression, in other words, to the abolition of all classes through the equalization of economic conditions, and the abolition of their last buttress, the state.

That is the program of social revolution.

Thus at the present time all the countries of the civilized world face one universal question and share one universal ideal – the total and definitive liberation of the proletariat from economic exploitation and state oppression. Obviously, this question cannot be resolved without a fierce and bloody struggle, and the actual situation, and indeed the significance, of every nation will depend on the direction, nature, and degree of its participation in this struggle.

Is it not clear, then, that the Slavs must seek and can attain their rights and their place in history and in the fraternal alliance of nations only through social revolution?

But a social revolution cannot be a revolution of one nation alone. It is by nature an international revolution. Therefore the Slavs, in their quest for liberty and for the sake of their liberty, must join their aspirations and the organization of their national forces to the aspirations and national forces of all other countries: the Slavic proletariat must enter the International Working Men's Association en masse.

We have already had occasion to mention the splendid avowal of international brotherhood in 1868 by the workers of Vienna, who refused to raise the pan-German standard despite the efforts of the Austrian and Schwabian patriots to persuade them. They declared categorically that the workers of the entire world were their brothers and that they recognized no other camp than that of international proletarian solidarity. At the same time, they reasoned correctly in stating that as Austrian workers they could not raise any national standard because the Austrian proletariat consists of the most diverse nationalities: Magyars, Italians, Romanians, predominantly Slavs and Germans. Therefore they would have to seek the practical solution of their problems outside the framework of the so-called national state.

A few more steps in this direction and the Austrian workers would have understood that liberation of the proletariat is absolutely impossible within the framework of any state, and that the primary condition for achieving it is to destroy every state. That is possible, however, only through concerted action by the proletariat of all countries, whose organization first on an economic basis is precisely the object of the International Working Men's Association.

Once they had understood this, the German workers in Austria would have become the initiators not just of their own liberation but also of the liberation of the non-German masses in the empire, including, of course, all the Slavs. We would have been the first to urge the Slavs to form an alliance with them having as its objective the destruction of the state, the people's prison, and the creation of a new international workers' world based on the principle of complete equality and liberty.

But the Austrian workers did not take these necessary first steps because they were brought to an abrupt halt by the propaganda of Liebknecht and the other social democrats who came with him to Vienna, I believe in July of 1868. Their objective was to direct the true social instinct of the Austrian workers away from the path of international revolution and toward political agitation for the establishment of a unified state, which they term *popular* but which obviously means pan-German – in short, for the realization of Bismarck's patriotic ideal but on a social-democratic basis and by means of so-called legal popular agitation.

It is not just the Slavs who should refuse to take this path but the German workers as well, for the simple reason that the state, be it called popular ten times over and embellished with the most highly democratic forms, will necessarily be a prison for the proletariat. It is even more impossible for the Slavs to follow this course, however, because it would mean submitting voluntarily to the German yoke, and that is repugnant to every Slavic heart. Therefore we will refrain from urging our Slavic brothers to join the ranks of the Social-Democratic Party of the German workers, which is led first and foremost by Marx and Engels in a kind of duumvirate vested with dictatorial power, with Bebel,[32] Liebknecht, and a few Jewish *literati* behind them or under them. On the contrary, we must exert all our efforts to dissuade the Slavic proletariat from a suicidal alliance with this party, which is in no way a popular party but in its orientation, objective, and methods is purely bourgeois and, furthermore, exclusively German, that is, lethal to the Slavs.

The more energetically the Slavic proletariat, for its own salvation, must reject not just alliance but even rapprochement with this party – we do not mean with the workers who belong to it but with its organization and particularly its leadership, which is bourgeois through and through – the more closely, likewise for its own salvation, it must join forces with the International Working Men's Association. The German party of social democrats should by no means be confused with the International. The political and patriotic program of the former not only has almost nothing in common with the program of the latter but is even totally opposed to it. True, at the rigged Hague Congress the Marxists tried to foist their program on the whole International. This attempt, however, evoked such enormous protest by the delegates from Italy, Spain, part of Switzerland, France, Belgium, Holland, England, and in part the United States that the whole world could see that no one wanted the German program except the Germans themselves.[33] Indeed, there is no doubt that the time will come when the German proletariat itself, having better understood both its own interests (which are inseparable from the interests of the proletariat of all other countries) and the pernicious orientation of this program (which has been imposed on it but by no means created by it), will renounce it and will abandon along with it its bourgeois leaders, its *Führers*.

As for the Slavic proletariat, we reiterate that for the sake of its own liberation from its onerous yoke, it must enter the International en masse, form factory, artisan, and agrarian sections, and unite them into local federations – and, if it proves necessary, perhaps even into a general Slavic federation. Within the International, which liberates each and everyone from his statist fatherland, the Slavic workers can and should meet fraternally with the German workers, without the slightest danger to their independence; alliance with them on any other basis is absolutely impossible.

That is the sole path to the liberation of the Slavs. But the path which the great majority of the west and south Slavic youth are now taking under the leadership of their venerable and more or less time-honored patriots is exactly the opposite. It is exclusively the path of the state, and it is a disastrous one for the masses.

Take Turkish Serbia, for example, and specifically the principality of Serbia, the one spot outside of Russia, except for Montenegro, where the Slavic element has achieved a more or less independent political existence.[34]

The Serbian people shed a great deal of blood to liberate themselves from the Turkish yoke. Scarcely had they freed themselves from the Turks, however, than they were harnessed to a new, this time home-grown state called the principality of Serbia, a yoke which is in fact at least as heavy as that of the Turks. No sooner had this part of the Serbian land received the form, structure, laws, and institutions of a more or less regular state than the people's vitality and vigor, which had ignited the heroic struggle against the Turks and gained ultimate victory over them, seemed suddenly to die away. Granted, they are an uneducated and extremely poor nation, but they are energetic, passionate, and by nature freedom-loving – and all of a sudden they were transformed into a mute and seemingly immobile herd offered up as a sacrifice to bureaucratic plunder and despotism.

Turkish Serbia has neither a nobility nor very big landowners, neither industrialists nor extremely wealthy merchants. Instead, it has formed a new bureaucratic aristocracy consisting of young people educated, for the most part at state expense, in Odessa, Moscow, Petersburg, Vienna, Germany, Switzerland, and Paris. While they are young and not yet corrupted by state service, these individuals are for the most part distinguished by fervent patriotism, love for the people, a quite sincere liberalism, and lately even adherence to democracy and socialism. As soon as they enter state service, however, the iron logic of their position, the force of circumstances inherent in certain hierarchical and profitable political relationships, makes itself felt, and the young patriots become bureaucrats from head to toe, while continuing, perhaps, to be both patriots and liberals. Everyone knows, though, what a liberal bureaucrat is; he is incomparably worse than a simple and straightforward bureaucratic scourge.

The demands of a certain position always prove stronger than sentiments, intentions, or good impulses. When they return home, the young Serbs who have received an education abroad have to become bureaucrats – because of their education, but especially because of their obligations to the government, at whose expense they were for the most part supported while abroad, and also because they have absolutely no other way of earning a living. They have to become members of the bureaucratic class, the sole aristocracy in the country. Once they have joined this class, they become enemies of the people whether they want to or not. It is possible, and highly probable, especially at the outset, that they would like to liberate their people, or at least to improve their condition, but they are obliged to oppress and plunder them. Two or three years in such a situation are enough for them to get used to it and ultimately to reconcile themselves to it, with the help of some liberal or even democratic doctrinaire lie – our times are rich in lies of this sort. Once they have reconciled themselves to iron necessity, against which it is beyond their power to rebel, they become out and out scoundrels, all the more dangerous to the people the more liberal and democratic their public pronouncements.

Then, those among them who are a bit more skillful and a bit more cunning acquire a dominant influence in the microscopic government of the microscopic principality. No sooner have they done so than they begin to peddle themselves to all comers: at home, to the ruling prince or to a pretender to the throne (in Serbia, overthrowing one prince and replacing him with another is called a revolution); or instead (though sometimes at the same time), to the governments of the protecting powers, Russia, Austria, Turkey, now Germany (which in the East, as everywhere else, has taken France's place), and frequently even to all of them together.

One can imagine how free and easy life is for the people in a state like this – and do not forget that Serbia is a constitutional state, where the *Skupština*^a elected by the people is in charge of all the laws.

Some Serbs console themselves with the thought that this state of affairs is essentially transitory. It represents an unavoidable evil at present but will surely change as soon as the little principality has expanded its frontiers and incorporated all of the Serbian lands – some even say all of the south Slavic lands – and restored the empire of Dušan to its full extent. Then, they say, an era of complete freedom and broad opportunity for the people will begin.

Yes, among the Serbs there are people still naive enough to believe this!

Indeed, they imagine that when the state expands its frontiers and the number of its subjects doubles, triples, increases tenfold, it will become more of a popular state, and its institutions, the conditions of its existence, and its governmental actions will be less contrary to the people's interests and all of the people's instincts. On what do they base this hope, or supposition? On theory? From a theoretical point of view, however, it seems clear that the more extensive a state the more complex its structure and the more alien it is to the people. Consequently, the more contrary its interests are to those of the masses, the more overwhelming the oppression it imposes on them, the more impossible it becomes for the people to exercise any control over it, and the more remote the state administration becomes from popular self-government.

Or do they base their expectations on the practical experience of other countries? In reply we need only point to Russia, Austria,

<hr>

^a The parliament of Serbia.

expanded Prussia, France, England, Italy, or even the United States, where everything is run by a distinct, entirely bourgeois class of so-called political bosses, or politicians, while the life of the laboring masses is almost as constricted and miserable as it is in monarchical states.

Perhaps there are well-educated Serbs capable of objecting that the masses are beside the point: their task is and always will be to feed, clothe, and in general support with their crude physical labor the flower of their fatherland's civilization, the true representative of the nation. Therefore the educated, more or less propertied and privileged classes alone are relevant.

That is precisely where the problem lies: these so-called educated classes – the nobility, the bourgeoisie – which at one time really did flower and stand at the forefront of the vital and progressive civilization of Europe, have been rendered dull-witted and paltry by their obesity and their cowardice. If they represent anything nowadays, it is only the most pernicious and ignoble qualities of human nature. In a country as highly educated as France we see that these classes were not even capable of defending their country's independence against the Germans. In Germany itself we see that they are capable only of serving as loyal and faithful lackeys.

Finally, let us note that in Turkish Serbia these classes do not even exist – there is only a bureaucratic class. Thus, the Serbian state will crush the Serbian people for the sole purpose of enabling Serbian bureaucrats to live a fatter life.

Others, though they despise the existing structure of the principality of Serbia with all their hearts, tolerate it as a necessary means or instrument for liberating those Slavs still subject to the Turkish or even Austrian yoke. At some point, they say, the principality may become the basis and starting-point for a general revolt of the Slavs. This is another of those baneful illusions that must without fail be dispelled for the Slavs' own good.

Those who harbor it are misled by the example of the Kingdom of Piedmont, which is supposed to have liberated and united all of Italy. Italy liberated itself, by means of a countless number of heroic sacrifices which it endured for half a century. It owes its political independence mainly to the forty years of uninterrupted and irrepressible effort by its great citizen Giuseppe Mazzini, who was able, it may be said, to resurrect the youth of Italy and then train it in the perilous but valiant cause of patriotic conspiracy. In 1848, thanks to Mazzini's twenty years of work, when the rebellious people again summoned the entire European world to the festival of revolution, in all the towns of Italy, from the far south to the far north, a handful of bold young men raised the standard of revolt. The whole Italian bourgeoisie followed them. In the Kingdom of Lombardy–Venetia, which was still under Austrian rule, the people rose up en masse and drove the Austrian regiments out of Milan and Venice by themselves, without any military assistance.

And what did royal Piedmont do? What did Victor Emmanuel's father, King Charles Albert, do – the one who, in 1821, when he was still crown prince, handed over to the Austrian and Piedmontese executioners those who had conspired with him for the liberation of Italy? His paramount concern in 1848 was to paralyze the revolution throughout Italy with promises, machinations, and intrigues. He very much wanted to rule Italy, but he hated revolution as much as he feared it. He did in fact paralyze the revolution, the force and momentum of the Italian people, after which it was not difficult for the Austrian forces to deal with his army.

His son, Victor Emmanuel, is called the liberator and unifier of the Italian lands. This grossly slanders him! If anyone should be called the liberator of Italy, it is Louis Napoleon, the Emperor of the French. But Italy emancipated itself, and above all it unified itself, despite Victor Emmanuel and against the will of Napoleon III.

In 1860, when Garibaldi launched his celebrated expedition to Sicily, just as he was setting out from Genoa Count Cavour,[35] Victor Emmanuel's minister, warned the Neapolitan government of the impending attack. When Garibaldi liberated Sicily and the entire Kingdom of Naples, however, Victor Emmanuel accepted both of them from him, of course, and without very much gratitude.

And for thirteen years, what has his government done with this unfortunate Italy? He has ravaged it, simply looted it, and now, hated by everyone, his despotism almost makes people regret the expulsion of the Bourbons.

That is the way kings and states liberate their co-nationals. No one would find it more useful than the Serbs to learn the actual details of Italy's recent history.

One of the methods the Serbian government employs to calm the patriotic fervor of its young people is to make periodic promises to declare war on Turkey next spring – or sometimes in the autumn, when the farm work is done. The young people believe it, they get excited, and every summer and every winter they get ready, after which some unforeseen obstacle, some diplomatic note from one of the protecting powers, always bars the way to the promised declaration of war. It is postponed for six months or a year, and in this way the Serbian patriots spend their whole lives in an agonizing and futile wait for a fulfillment that never comes.

Not only is the principality of Serbia in no position to liberate the south Slavs, Serbian or non-Serbian, but with its machinations and intrigues it actually divides and weakens them. The Bulgarians, for example, are prepared to recognize the Serbs as brothers, but they do not want to hear about the Serbian empire of Dušan. The same goes for the Croats, the Montenegrins, and the Bosnian Serbs.

For all these countries the sole deliverance and the sole road to unification is social revolution, not a state war that can have only one outcome – their subjugation either by Russia or by Austria, or, what is more likely, at least initially, their partition between the two.

Czech Bohemia, thank heaven, has not yet managed to restore the orb and crown of Wenceslas in all their ancient grandeur and glory.[36] The central government in Vienna treats Bohemia as a mere province, which does not even enjoy the privileges of Galicia, yet there are as many political parties in Bohemia as there are in any Slavic state. Indeed, the accursed German spirit of political intrigue and statism has permeated the education of the Czech youth to such a degree that they run a serious risk of ultimately losing the ability to understand their own people.

The Czech peasants represent one of the most splendid Slavic types. Hussite blood flows in their veins, the hot blood of the Taborites, and the memory of Žižka lives within them.[37] In our own experience and recollections of 1848,[38] one of the most enviable advantages of the Czech students is their intimate, truly fraternal relationship with them. The Czech urban proletarian is in no way inferior in his energy and fervent devotion to the peasant; he too proved it in 1848.

To date, the proletariat and the peasantry love the students and trust in them. But the young Czech patriots should not count too much on that trust. It will necessarily weaken and ultimately disappear if they do not find within themselves a sufficient sense of justice, equality, liberty, and real love for the people to keep in step with them. And the Czech people, the Slavic proletariat of Bohemia (by the word people we always means particularly the proletariat), is striving naturally and ineluctably for the same objective as the proletariat of every country, for economic liberation, for social revolution.

They would have to be a nation highly unendowed by nature and downtrodden by history, or, to put it bluntly, extremely stupid and inert, to remain alien to this aspiration, which constitutes the sole substantive world issue of our time. The Czech youth do not want to pay their people such a compliment, and even if they did, the people would not deserve it. Indeed, we have incontrovertible evidence of the west Slavic proletariat's keen interest in the social question. In all the Austrian towns where the Slavic and German populations are intermingled, Slavic workers take the most energetic part in all the general declarations of the proletariat. But in these towns hardly any worker associations exist other than those that have accepted the program of the social democrats of Germany. In practice, therefore, Slavic workers, drawn by their social-revolutionary instinct, are recruited into a party which has the immediate and loudly proclaimed objective of establishing a pan-German state, that is, a vast German prison.

It is a very sad fact, but it is a very natural one as well. The Slavic workers are faced with two choices. Attracted by the example of the German workers, their brothers by virtue of social status, common fate, hunger, want, and oppression, they can join a party that promises them a state – a German one, granted, but still a thoroughly popular one, with all sorts of economic advantages to the detriment of the capitalists and property-owners and the benefit of the proletariat. Or, attracted by the patriotic propaganda of their venerable and illustrious leaders and their ardent but as yet undiscerning youth, they can join a party in whose ranks and leadership they encounter their everyday exploiters and oppressors – bourgeoisie, factory-owners, merchants, financial speculators, Jesuit priests, and feudal lords of vast hereditary or acquired estates. The latter party, however, with much greater consistency than the former, promises them a national prison – a Slavic state, the restoration in all its ancient splendor of the crown of Wenceslas, as though that splendor will make life easier for the Czech workers!

If the Slavic workers really had no other alternative than these two, then, admittedly, we would advise them to choose the first. Though mistaken, they would at least share a common fate with their brethren in toil, traditions, and life, whether Germans or non-Germans. In choosing the second, however, they would have to call brethren their direct executioners and bloodsuckers and would be compelled to bind themselves with the heaviest chains in the name of Slavic liberation. In the first instance they would deceive themselves, in the second they would be sold out.

There is a third recourse, however, one which will lead directly to deliverance – the formation and alliance of factory and agrarian worker associations on the basis of the International's program. We do not mean, of course, the program propagated under the name of the International by the almost exclusively patriotic and political party of the German social democrats, but the one now recognized by all the free federations of the International Working Men's Association, that is, by the workers of Italy, Spain, the Jura, France, Belgium, England, and in part America, and not recognized essentially by the Germans alone.*

We are convinced that this is the sole alternative, both for the Czechs and for all the other Slavic peoples seeking their complete liberation from oppression of every kind, German or non-German. Everything else is a fraud, bringing honors and bulging pockets to dishonorable and ambitious party leaders, but slavery to the laboring masses.

The question that stands before the Czech youth, and the educated Slavic youth in general, is now very clear: do they want to exploit their own people, to enrich themselves by their labor and achieve their base ambitions on their backs? If they do, they will go along with the old Slavophile parties, with the Palackýs, Riegers, Brauners, and company.[39] We hasten to add, however, that among the young adherents of those leaders are many who are blind or deceived, who are not out for anything for themselves but in the hands of adroit individuals serve to ensnare the people. In any event their role is a highly unenviable one.

Those who truly and sincerely want the total emancipation of the masses, however, will come with us along the road of social revolution, for no other leads to the conquest of the people's liberty.

---

* In Zurich a Slavic Section has formed which has become part of the Jura Federation. We enthusiastically recommend the program of this section, which is to be found at the end of the Introduction, to all the Slavs (see Appendix B).

Until now, however, the old politics, the narrowest kind of statism, has prevailed in all the west Slavic countries. A German comedy has been performed, but in Czech translation, and not just one comedy but two separate ones, Czech and Polish. Who is unfamiliar with the deplorable history of alternating alliances and ruptures between the statesmen of Bohemia and Galicia, and the series of hilarious statements made by the Czech and Galician deputies in the Austrian *Reichsrat*, sometimes jointly and sometimes separately? At the bottom of it all is Jesuit-feudal intrigue. And by such pitiful and, it may be said, ignoble methods, these gentlemen hope to liberate their compatriots! Strange statesmen, these – and how amused their close neighbor, Prince Bismarck, must be as he observes their political games!

Once, however, after the celebrated defeat inflicted on them in Vienna as a result of one of the countless betrayals by their Galician allies, the Czech political triumvirate, Palacký, Rieger, and Brauner, decided to stage a bold demonstration. On the occasion of the Slavic ethnographic exhibition which opened in Moscow in 1867 expressly for this purpose, they set out for Moscow with a great number of west and south Slavs in tow to pay homage to the "white tsar,"[a] the executioner of the Slavic Poles.[40] In Warsaw they were greeted by Russian generals, Russian officials, and Russian ladies of high rank, and in the Polish capital, amidst the deathly silence of the entire Polish population, these freedom-loving Slavs exchanged kisses and embraces with those Russian fratricides, drank with them, and cried "Hurrah for Slavic brotherhood!"

Everyone knows what kind of speeches they subsequently delivered in Moscow and Petersburg. In brief, more shameful obeisance to a brutal and merciless regime, and a more criminal betrayal of Slavic brotherhood, of truth, and of freedom on the part of venerable liberals, democrats, and defenders of the people had never before been seen. Then these gentlemen serenely returned to Prague with their whole synod, and no one told them that what they had done was not merely base but stupid.

And uselessly stupid, too, for it was of no service to them whatsoever in Vienna and did not improve matters for them there. That is

---

[a] A term for the ruler of Muscovy, used by subject tribes of the East in the sixteenth century.

clear now: they have not restored the crown of Wenceslas to its former independence, and they have had to watch a new parliamentary reform remove the last arena in which they had played their political game.

After its defeat in Italy the Austrian government, having been forced to give the Kingdom of Hungary a certain measure of liberty, pondered for a long time how it would structure its Cisleithan state. Its own instincts and the demands of the German liberals and democrats inclined it toward centralization, but the Slavs, especially Bohemia and Galicia, relying on the feudal-clerical party, loudly demanded a federal system. The government's hesitation lasted until this year. It finally decided, to the horror of the Slavs and the immense joy of the German liberals and democrats, to put the old German bureaucratic garb back on all the lands comprising the Cisleithan state.[41]

It should be noted, however, that the Austrian Empire has not thereby made itself stronger. It has lost its real focal point. All the Germans and Yids in the empire will henceforth gravitate toward Berlin. At the same time some of the Slavs look to Russia, while others, guided by a surer instinct, seek deliverance in the formation of a popular federation. No one expects anything from Vienna any more. Is it not clear that the Austrian Empire, strictly speaking, is finished, and that if it still maintains the façade of existence it is only thanks to the calculated forbearance of Russia and Prussia, which hesitate to partition it just yet because each one secretly hopes to seize the lion's share when it has the opportunity?

Obviously, therefore, Austria is unable to compete with the new Prusso-German Empire. Let us see if Russia is in any position to do so.

III

Is it not true, reader, that Russia has made unprecedented progress in every respect since the now happily reigning Emperor Alexander II came to the throne?[42]

If we want to measure the progress Russia has made in the last twenty years, let us compare the distance that separated it in all areas from Europe in, say, 1856, with the distance between them now: the progress indeed has been astonishing. Russia has not risen so high, it is true, but rather Western Europe, official and semi-official, bureaucratic and bourgeois, has declined considerably, so that the gap between them has decidedly diminished. What German or Frenchman, for example, will dare speak of Russian barbarism or butchery after the horrors perpetrated by the Germans in France in 1870 and by the French forces against their own Paris in 1871? What Frenchman will dare talk about the baseness and venality of Russian officials and statesmen after all the dirt that has come to light and practically buried the French bureaucratic and political world? No, when they look at the French and the Germans, Russia's scoundrels, boors, thieves, and butchers have no cause at all to blush. In respect to morality, throughout official and semi-official Europe brutishness, or at least an astonishingly brute-like form of behavior, has firmly established itself.

It is a different matter in regard to political power, although even here, at least in comparison with the French state, our *kvass* patriots can plume themselves, for politically Russia is without doubt more independent than France and ranks higher. Bismarck himself pays court to Russia, while vanquished France pays court to Bismarck. The question is, what is the power of the All-Russian Empire in relation to the power of the pan-German empire, which is unquestionably predominant, at least on the European continent?

We Russians, every last one of us, it may be said, know what our dear Russian Empire is like as far as its domestic life is concerned. For a small number of people, perhaps a few thousand, headed by the emperor with his most august house and his distinguished flunkeys, it is an inexhaustible source of all blessings (except for those of an intellectual and moral nature). For a more extensive, though still limited minority, consisting of some tens of thousands of people – high military, civil, and ecclesiastical officials, rich landowners, merchants, capitalists, and parasites – it is an amiable, beneficent, and indulgent patron of legalized and highly lucrative thievery. For the great mass of petty officials, still insignificant in number compared to the people, it is a stingy wet-nurse. And for the countless millions of laborers it is a wicked stepmother, a pitiless robber, and a torturer driving them to the grave.

That is what the empire was before the peasant reform, and that is what it has remained and will always be. There is no need to prove it to the Russians. What adult does not know it, cannot help but know it?

Russian educated society is divided into three categories: those who know it but find it too unprofitable to acknowledge its truth, which they find as unquestionable as everyone else does; those who do not acknowledge it and do not speak of it out of fear; and, finally, those who, for lack of any other kind of audacity, at least dare to talk about it. There is yet a fourth category, unfortunately too few in number, consisting of people earnestly devoted to the people's cause and not content with mere talk.

Perhaps there is a fifth category, and not so few in number, of people who see nothing and understand nothing. But there is no use talking to them.

Any Russian who is the least bit thoughtful and scrupulous must understand that our empire cannot alter its relationship to the people. By its very nature it is condemned to be the destroyer and blood-sucker of the people. The people hate it instinctively, and it cannot avoid oppressing them, since its entire existence and its power are built on the people's poverty. To maintain internal order, to preserve its forcibly imposed unity, and to maintain its external strength, not even for aggressive purposes but merely for self-preservation, the empire needs a vast army and police force, a countless number of bureaucrats, a state-supported clergy . . . in short, an official world of colossal size, with whose upkeep – not to mention its thievery – the people are inevitably saddled.

One would have to be an ass, an ignoramus, or a madman to imagine that any kind of constitution, even the most liberal and democratic, could change this relationship of the state to the people for the better. It might worsen it, it might make it even more onerous and ruinous, perhaps, though that would be difficult, since the evil has been taken to such an extreme. That it might liberate the people and improve their situation – that is just nonsense! As long as the empire exists, it will victimize our people. The only kind of constitution that would be useful for the people is the destruction of the empire.

So, we will not talk about its domestic circumstances, convinced as we are that they could not be any worse. Let us see, however, whether it is in fact achieving the external objective that gives meaning to its existence – not human meaning, of course, but political meaning. At the cost of huge and countless sacrifices by the people (involuntary ones, to be sure, but all the more cruel for that), has it at least been able to create a military force capable of competing, for example, with that of the new German Empire?

Strictly speaking, that question sums up the entire *political* issue facing Russia today. The only domestic question, as we know, remains the question of social revolution. But we are dwelling for the moment on the external issue, and we ask, is Russia capable of fighting Germany?

The mutual compliments, vows, kisses, and tears which the two imperial courts, that of the Berlin uncle and that of the Petersburg nephew, are currently lavishing on each other mean nothing. It is well known that in politics none of this is worth a cent. The question we have broached is the one posed of necessity by the new position of Germany, which grew overnight into a vast and all-powerful state. All of history bears witness, and logic itself confirms, that two states of equal strength cannot exist side by side. That is contrary to their nature, which invariably and necessarily consists of and manifests itself in supremacy – and supremacy cannot tolerate equivalence. One force must inevitably be shattered and subordinated to the other.

Indeed, that is now a vital necessity for Germany. After its long, long political humiliation it suddenly became the mightiest power on the continent of Europe. Can it now bear to have a power next door to it, under its very nose, so to speak, that is completely independent of it, that it has not yet defeated, and that dares to regard itself as an equal? Especially when that power is Russia, the one it hates most!

We believe that few Russians are unaware of how much the Germans hate Russia – all the Germans, but particularly the German bourgeois, and under their influence, alas, the German people, too. They also hate the French, but that is nothing compared to the hatred they harbor toward Russia. It constitutes one of the strongest national passions of the Germans.

How did this nation-wide passion come into being? Its origins were quite respectable: it was the protest of an incomparably more humane (even though German) civilization against our Tatar barbarism. Then, in the 1820s, it took on a more specific character, the protest of political liberalism against political despotism. It is well known that in the 1820s the Germans called themselves liberals and earnestly believed in their liberalism. They hated Russia as the representative of despotism. True, in all fairness they should at least have divided their hatred equally among Russia, Prussia, and Austria. But that would have been contrary to their patriotism, so they heaped all responsibility for the policies of the Holy Alliance on Russia.

At the beginning of the 1830s the Polish revolution elicited the liveliest sympathy throughout Germany, and its bloody suppression intensified the indignation of German liberals against Russia. That was perfectly natural and legitimate, though here, too, justice would have demanded that at least some share of this indignation fall upon Prussia, which blatantly assisted Russia in the loathsome deed of suppressing the Poles. Nor did it do so out of magnanimity, but because its own interests demanded it: the liberation of the Kingdom of Poland and of Lithuania would have had as a direct consequence the insurrection of all of Prussian Poland, which would have destroyed the burgeoning power of the Prussian monarchy.

In the second half of the 1830s, however, a new reason arose for the Germans' hatred of Russia and gave it a whole new character, no longer liberal but political and national: the Slavic question emerged, and soon a whole party formed among the Austrian and Turkish Slavs which began to hope for and expect help from Russia. Back in the 1820s a secret society of democrats, specifically the southern branch of this society, led by Pestel, Muravev-Apostol, and Bestuzhev-Riumin, had first conceived the idea of a free federation of all the Slavs.[43] Emperor Nicholas seized upon this idea but recast it in his own image. In his mind the free federation of all the Slavs turned into a single, autocratic pan-Slav state – under his iron scepter, of course.

In the 1830s and 1840s Russian agents set out from Petersburg and Moscow for the Slavic lands, some official, others unpaid volunteers. The latter belonged to the not at all secret Moscow circle of Slavophiles. Pan-Slav propaganda began to be carried on among the west and south Slavs. A number of pamphlets appeared, some written in German, some translated into German, and they gave the pan-German public a real fright. An uproar arose among the Germans.

The idea that Bohemia, an ancient imperial land penetrating to the very heart of Germany, might secede and become an independent Slavic country, or, God forbid, a Russian province, deprived them of appetite and of sleep. Curses have rained down on Russia ever since, and the Germans' hatred of Russia has grown to this very hour. Now it manifests itself on a vast scale. The Russians, for their part, do not look very kindly on the Germans, either. Is it possible, given the existence of such a touching relationship, that these two neighboring empires, the All-Russian and the pan-German, can remain at peace for very long?

So far, there have been enough reasons for them to maintain peace, and indeed those reasons still exist. The first is Poland. There were three sovereign plunderers who partitioned Poland among themselves like real bandits, Austria, Prussia, and Russia. At the very moment of partition, however, and whenever the Polish question came up again subsequently, Austria was and remained the least interested. Everyone knows that the Austrian court initially protested even against partition, and only at the insistence of Frederick the Great and Catherine the Great did Empress Maria Theresa agree to take the share that fell to her. She even shed virtuous tears over it, tears which became historic, but all the same she took it.[44] And how could she not have taken it? That is what she was a crowned head for – to grab. Laws are not written for emperors, and their appetites have no bounds. In his memoirs Frederick remarks that once the Austrian government decided to take part in the joint plunder of Poland, in a search for some non-existent river it hastened to occupy with its troops much more territory than it was supposed to under the agreement.

It is remarkable nonetheless that Austria prayed and wept as it plundered, while Russia and Prussia carried out their banditry joking and laughing. (It is well known that at this very time Catherine and Frederick were conducting a most witty and philanthropic correspondence with the French philosophes.) It is even more remarkable that subsequently, right up to our own day, whenever unhappy Poland made a desperate attempt to liberate and reestablish itself, the Russian and Prussian courts trembled with rage and openly or covertly hastened to join forces to put down the insurrection. Meanwhile, Austria, like an unwilling accomplice, not only refused to get excited and join in their undertaking, but, on the contrary, at the start of every new Polish insurrection acted as though it were prepared to help the Poles, and to a certain degree actually did help them. Such was the case in 1831, and even more patently in 1862, when Bismarck openly assumed the role of Russia's policeman. By contrast, Austria allowed the Poles (secretly, of course) to transport arms into Poland.

What is the explanation for this difference in behavior? Is it Austria's nobility, philanthropy, and sense of justice? No, quite simply it is Austria's interest. Maria Theresa had good reason to weep. She sensed that in joining the others in violating Poland's political existence she was digging the Austrian Empire's grave. What could be more advantageous for her than to have as a neighbor on her northeastern frontier this gentry state – not an intelligent one, true, but strictly conservative and not at all aggressive. It not only freed her from having Russia as an unpleasant neighbor but also separated her from Prussia, serving as a precious safeguard against both aggressive powers.

To fail to understand this, one had to have the inveterate stupidity and especially the venality of Maria Theresa's ministers, and then the arrogant petty-mindedness and spitefully reactionary stubbornness of old Metternich – who, moreover, as everyone knows, was also in the pay of the Petersburg and Berlin courts. One had to have been condemned to death by history.

The Russian Empire and the Kingdom of Prussia understood their own mutual advantage very well. The partition of Poland gave the former the status of a great *European* power; the latter embarked on the road to its current incontestable preeminence. At the same time, having thrown a bloody chunk of dismembered Poland to Austria, which is gluttonous by nature, they prepared it for slaughter, condemning it to be sacrificed eventually to their own insatiable appetite. Until such time as they satisfy that appetite and divide Austria's possessions between them, they will remain, and are compelled to remain, allies and friends, even though they hate each other wholeheartedly. Of course, they will quarrel over the actual division of Austria, but until then nothing will cause them to fall out.

It is not to their advantage to fall out. The new Prusso-German Empire at the present time does not have a single ally in Europe or the world as a whole except Russia and perhaps the United States. Everyone fears it, everyone hates it, and everyone will rejoice at its downfall because it oppresses and plunders everyone. Meanwhile, it still needs to carry out a number of annexations in order to realize fully the plan and idea of a pan-German empire. It must seize not just part but all of Lorraine from the French; it must annex Belgium, Holland, Switzerland, Denmark, and the whole of the Scandinavian peninsula; it must also lay hands on our Baltic provinces in order to be sole master of the Baltic Sea. In short, except for the Kingdom of Hungary, which it will leave to the Magyars, and Galicia, which it will cede to Russia along with Austrian Bukovina, it will assuredly be compelled to try to seize all of Austria, up to and including Trieste and, of course, Bohemia, too, which the Petersburg cabinet will not even think of disputing.

We are certain, we know for a fact, that secret negotiations have long been taking place between the Petersburg and German courts concerning a more or less private partition of the Austrian Empire – in which, of course, as is always the case in friendly relations between two great powers, they keep trying to swindle each other.

However great the power of the Prusso-German Empire, it is clear nonetheless that by itself it is not strong enough to carry out such vast undertakings against the will of all Europe. Therefore alliance with Russia is a vital necessity and will be for a long time.

Does the same necessity exist for Russia?

Let us begin with the fact that our empire, more than any other, is preeminently a military state. That is not just because, from the very day it was created, it has sacrificed everything that constitutes the life and well-being of the people so as to form as great a military force as possible. It is because, as a military state, it pursues a single objective, a single mission that gives meaning to its existence: conquest. Apart from that objective it is simply an absurdity. Hence, conquests in every direction and at whatever cost – there you have the normal life of our empire. Now the question is, in which direction should it point this aggressive force?

Two paths are open to it, one western, the other eastern. The western path is aimed straight at Germany. It is the pan-Slav path as well as the path of alliance with France against the joint forces of Prussian Germany and the Austrian Empire, with the probable neutrality of England and the United States.

The other path leads directly to India, Persia, and Constantinople. The enemies here are Austria, England, and probably France, the allies Prussian Germany and the United States.

Which of these two paths will our bellicose empire choose to take? It is said that the heir to the throne[45] is a passionate pan-Slav, hates the Germans and is an inveterate friend of the French, and stands for taking the first path, while the emperor is a friend of the Germans, a loving nephew of his uncle, and stands for taking the second one. However, it is not a matter of where the sentiments of one or the other will draw him; the question is, where can the empire go with hope of success and without running the risk of destroying itself?

Can it take the first path? True, that would entail alliance with France, an alliance not nearly as advantageous now in terms of material and moral force as it promised to be three or four years ago. France's national unity has been shattered irrevocably. Within the frontiers of an ostensibly unified France there now exist three or perhaps even four different and mutually antagonistic Frances: aristocratic-clerical France, consisting of nobles, rich bourgeois, and priests; purely bourgeois France, encompassing the middle and petty bourgeoisie; worker France, including the whole urban factory proletariat; and, finally, peasant France. Except for the last two, which can reach accord and, in the south of France, for example, are already starting to do so, the possibility of these classes reaching unanimity on any point whatsoever has vanished, even when it is a matter of defending the fatherland.

We saw this just the other day. The Germans are still in France, occupying Belfort while awaiting their last billion francs. Some three or four weeks remained until they would evacuate the country. But no, the majority of the assembly at Versailles, consisting of legitimists, Orleanists, and Bonapartists, insane, rabid reactionaries, did not want to wait that long. They brought down Thiers and replaced him with Marshal MacMahon, who promises to restore moral order in France at the point of a bayonet . . .[46] Statist France has ceased to be the country of life, intellect, and magnanimous impulses. It has suddenly degenerated, as it were, and become the leading country of vileness, baseness, venality, brutality, treachery, vulgarity, and utter and amazing stupidity. Boundless obscurantism holds sway over it. It consigns itself to the pope, the priests, the inquisition, the Jesuits, the Virgin, and the monastery. It earnestly seeks its rebirth in the Catholic Church, its mission in the defense of Catholic interests. Religious processions cover the land and with their solemn litanies drown out the protests and complaints of the vanquished proletariat. Deputies, ministers, prefects, generals, professors, and judges march in these processions holding candles in their hands, without blushing, not with faith in their own hearts but only because "the people need faith." In addition, a whole throng of religious nobles, ultramontanes, and legitimists, educated by the Jesuits, loudly demands that France solemnly consecrate itself to Christ and his immaculate mother. While the nation's wealth, or, more accurately, the people's labor, the producer of all wealth, is being looted by stock-market speculators, swindlers, rich property-owners and capitalists, while all the statesmen, government ministers, deputies, civil and military officials of every stripe, lawyers, and especially all those hypocritical Jesuits, are stuffing their pockets in the most unscrupulous fashion – all of France is actually being handed over to the government of priests. They have taken into their hands the whole educational system, the universities, gymnasia, and popular schools. They have again become the confessors and spiritual guides of the valiant French army, which will soon lose its capacity to fight external enemies but will become all the more dangerous an enemy of its own people.

That is the real condition of statist France! In a very short time it has outdone Schwarzenberg's post-1849 Austria – and we know how Austria ended up: defeated in Spain, defeated in Bohemia, and in a general state of ruin.

France is rich, to be sure, even in spite of its recent defeat, unquestionably richer than Germany, which has derived little industrial and commercial advantage from the 5 billion francs France has paid it. This wealth allowed the French people to restore in a very short time all the outward signs of strength and regular organization. Without even looking very deeply, however, we need only glance beneath the falsely glittering surface to become convinced that everything within has rotted, and it has rotted because the whole vast body of the state no longer contains so much as a spark of a living soul.

Statist France is irrevocably finished, and anyone who counts on an alliance with it will be cruelly deceived. He will find nothing within it but impotence and fear. It has dedicated itself to the pope, Christ, the Mother of God, divine reason and human folly. It has been sacrificed to thieves and priests, and if it still has any military strength left, it will go entirely into subduing and suppressing its own proletariat. What use can there be in an alliance with it?

But there is a more important reason that will never permit our government, be it headed by Alexander II or Alexander III, to follow the path of western or pan-Slav conquest. This is a revolutionary path, in the sense that it leads directly to the revolt of nations, primarily Slavs, against their *legitimate* sovereigns, Austrian and Prusso-German. It was suggested to Emperor Nicholas by Prince Paskevich.[47]

Nicholas's situation was perilous. He had two of the strongest powers, England and France, opposing him. Grateful Austria threatened him. Only Prussia, which he had offended, remained faithful, but even Prussia, yielding to pressure from the other three states, was beginning to waver and along with the Austrian government was making imposing representations to him.[48] Nicholas, who believed that his glory lay chiefly in his reputation for inflexibility, had either to yield or to die. To yield was shameful, but to die, of course, was undesirable. At that critical moment it was suggested to him that he raise the standard of pan-Slavism, and, moreover, that he place the Phrygian cap[a] atop his imperial crown and summon not just the Slavs but the Magyars, Romanians, and Italians[*] to revolt.

Nicholas thought it over, but, to do him justice, he did not hesitate for long. He realized that he ought not end his long career of purest despotism by taking up the career of a revolutionary. He preferred to die.

He was right. One could not plume oneself on one's despotism within the state while stirring up revolution outside it. It would have been particularly impossible for Nicholas, because the moment he set foot on this path he would have come face to face with Poland. How could he call on the Slavs and other nations to revolt while continuing to stifle Poland? But what was to be done with Poland? Liberate it? No, even aside from the fact that this was contrary to all of Nicholas's instincts, he could not help but realize that the liberation of Poland was absolutely incompatible with the idea of the Russian state.

A struggle between two forms of statehood had gone on for centuries. The question was, which would prevail, the Polish gentry's freedom or the Russian tsar's knout? (Nothing was said about the people in either camp; in both, they were in equal measure slaves and toilers, the breadwinners and mute pedestals of the state.) It seemed at first that the Poles would win out. They had education, military skill, and bravery on their side, and since their army consisted predominantly of petty gentry they fought as free men, while the Russians fought as slaves. All the odds seemed to be in their favor. In fact, for a very long period of time they emerged the victors in every war, ravaged Russian provinces, and once even subjugated Moscow and installed the son of their own king on the tsar's throne.

[a] The symbol of liberty in the French Revolution.
[*] We have heard from Mazzini himself that at this very time official Russian agents in London asked to meet with him and made proposals to him.

The force that drove them out of Moscow was not that of the tsar or even of the boyars but of the people. Until the masses intervened in the struggle, fortune favored the Poles. As soon as the people themselves came onstage, however, once in 1612, again in the form of the unanimous uprising of the Ukrainian and Lithuanian peasantry under the leadership of Bohdan Khmelnytsky,[49] fortune utterly abandoned them. From then on, the Polish gentry free state began to wither and decline, until it finally perished.

The Russian knout was victorious thanks to the people and together with them – to the great detriment of the people themselves, of course, who as a mark of the state's sincere gratitude were handed over as hereditary slaves to the tsar's servants, the noble landowners. The now reigning emperor, Alexander II, is said to have emancipated the peasants. We know what kind of an emancipation it was.

Meanwhile, the knouto-Russian empire was being founded on the very ruins of the Polish gentry state. Deprive it of that foundation, take away the provinces that until 1772 were part of the Polish state, and the Russian Empire will disappear.

It will disappear because with the loss of those provinces – its richest, most fruitful, and most populous – its wealth (which is not exceptional to begin with) and its power will diminish by half. This loss will immediately be followed by the loss of the Baltic territories. Assuming also that a Polish state is restored not just on paper but in actuality, and will begin a new and vigorous life, the empire will very soon lose all of Ukraine, which will become either a Polish province or an independent state; thereby it will also lose its Black Sea frontier and will be cut off from Europe on all sides and driven back into Asia.

Some people believe that the empire can at least give Lithuania back to Poland. No, it cannot, for the very same reasons. A united Lithuania and Poland would surely, and, one might say, inexorably, serve Polish state patriotism as a broad point of departure for conquest of the Baltic provinces and Ukraine. It would be enough just to liberate the Kingdom of Poland: Warsaw would immediately unite with Vilna, Grodno, Minsk, and perhaps Kiev, not to mention Podolia and Volhynia.[50]

How could that happen? The Poles are such an unruly people that not a single free town can be left to them: they will immediately start to conspire in it and to establish secret ties with all their lost provinces with the aim of restoring the Polish state. In 1841, for example,

71

Cracow was the one free city they had left, and Cracow became the center of all Polish revolutionary activity.[51]

Is it not clear that the Russian Empire can prolong its existence only on the condition that it stifle Poland in accordance with the Muravev system? We are speaking of the empire, not of the Russian people, who, we are convinced, have nothing in common with it and whose interests and instinctive aspirations are completely contrary to the empire's interests and conscious aspirations.

Once the empire collapses and the Great Russian, Ukrainian, White Russian, and other peoples regain their freedom, the ambitious plans of the Polish state patriots will hold no terror for them; they are deadly only for the empire.

That is why no Russian emperor, assuming he is in his right mind and is not compelled by iron necessity, will ever consent to liberate even the smallest portion of Poland. And if he does not liberate the Poles, can he call on the Slavs to revolt?

The reasons that prevented Nicholas from raising the pan-Slav standard of revolt still apply in full, the difference being that this path promised more rewards in his time than it does today. Then one could still count on an insurrection of the Magyars and of Italy, which were under the hated Austrian yoke. Now Italy would doubtless remain neutral, since Austria would probably hand over without argument those few scraps of Italian land still in its possession, just to have done with it. As for the Magyars, it can be said for sure that with all the passion inspired by their own domination of the Slavs, they would take the Germans' side against Russia.

So, in the event of a pan-Slav war instigated by the Russian emperor against Germany, he could count on the more or less active assistance only of the Slavs, and at that only of the Austrian Slavs, for if he took it into his head to stir up the Turkish Slavs, too, he would create a new enemy, England, the jealous defender of the Ottoman state's sovereignty. But in Austria the Slavs number approximately 17 million. Subtract the 5 million inhabitants of Galicia, where the more or less sympathetic Ruthenians would be paralyzed by the hostile Poles, and that leaves 12 million on whose revolt the Russian emperor *might* be able to count – excluding, of course, those drafted into the Austrian army, who, following the custom of any army, would fight whomever their commanders ordered them to fight.

Let us add that these 12 million Slavs are not even concentrated in one locality or in several but are scattered across the whole expanse of

the Austrian Empire, speak totally different dialects, and are intermingled with the German, Magyar, Romanian, and Italian population. They are numerous enough to keep the Austrian government
and the Germans in general in a constant state of anxiety, but too few
to afford a Russian army serious support against the combined forces
of Prussian Germany and Austria.

Alas! The Russian government knows this and has always understood it very well. Therefore it has never had, and will never have, any
intention of conducting a pan-Slav war against Austria, which would
necessarily turn into a war against all of Germany. If our government
has no such intention, however, then why does it carry on real pan-
Slav propaganda through its agents in Austria's possessions? For a
very simple reason, one we just indicated: because the Russian
government finds it very agreeable and useful to have a multitude of
fervent but blind, not to say stupid, adherents in all the Austrian
provinces. It paralyzes, constrains, and worries the Austrian government, and it increases Russia's influence not just on Austria but on
Germany as a whole. Imperial Russia incites the Austrian Slavs
against the Magyars and the Germans, knowing full well that in the
end it will betray them to those same Magyars and Germans. It is a
despicable but thoroughly statist game.

Thus, the Russian Empire will find few allies and little real support in the West in the event of a pan-Slav war against the Germans.
Let us look now at whom it will have to fight: first, all the Germans,
both Prussian and Austrian, second, the Magyars, and third, the
Poles.

Leaving aside the Poles and even the Magyars, let us ask whether
imperial Russia is capable of conducting an offensive war against the
combined forces of Prussia and Austria, or even Prussia alone. We say
an offensive war because we assume Russia would initiate it under the
pretense of liberating the Austrian Slavs, though with the actual
intention of annexing them.

First of all, it is indisputable that in Russia no offensive war will be
a national war. It is almost a general rule: nations rarely take an active
part in wars undertaken and conducted by their governments beyond
the frontiers of their fatherland. Such wars are in most cases
exclusively political, except when they are combined with a religious
or revolutionary ideal. For the Germans, French, Dutch, English, and
even the Swedes, the wars of the sixteenth century between the
reformers and the Catholics contained such an ideal, as did the

revolutionary wars at the end of the eighteenth century for the French. In recent history, however, we know of only two exceptional examples of the masses regarding with real sympathy political wars undertaken by their governments for the purpose of expanding the boundaries of their states, or for the sake of other exclusively political interests.

The first example is that of the French people under Napoleon I. It is not sufficiently indicative, however, because the imperial armies were a direct continuation, a natural result, as it were, of the revolutionary armies, so that the French people, even after the fall of Napoleon, continued to view them as an expression of the same revolutionary ideal.

Much more telling is the second example, that of the ardent rapture experienced by the entire German people in the absurd, colossal war undertaken by the newly formed Prusso-German state against the second French Empire. Yes, at that significant moment, which has just gone by, the entire German nation, all strata of German society, with the possible exception of a small handful of workers, were motivated by an exclusively political interest, to found and expand the boundaries of a pan-German state. And that interest still prevails over every other in the minds and hearts of all the Germans, whatever their estate, and it is what constitutes Germany's special strength today.

To anyone who knows and understands anything about Russia, however, it should be clear that no offensive war undertaken by our government will be a national war. In the first place, our people are not only alien to any political interest but are even instinctively opposed to it. The state is their prison, why should they make it stronger? In the second place, no bond exists between government and people, not a single vital thread that might unite them even for a moment in any cause whatsoever – there is not even any capability, any possibility of mutual understanding. What is white to the government is black to the people, and, conversely, what seems very white to the people, what constitutes their life and liberty, is death to the government.

It might be asked, perhaps, with Pushkin: "Or is the word of the Russian tsar already powerless?"[52]

Yes, powerless, when it demands of the people what is repugnant to them. Just let the tsar wink and call out to the people, "tie up and slaughter the landowners, officials, and merchants, seize their property and divide it up among yourselves." In an instant all the Russian people would rise up, and by the next day not even a trace of merchants, officials, or landowners would remain in the Russian land. But as long as he orders the people to pay taxes and provide soldiers for the state, and to work for the benefit of the landowners and merchants, the people will obey unwillingly, under the lash, as they do today, and will refuse to obey whenever they can. Where, then, is the magical and wonder-working effect of the tsar's word?

And what can the tsar say to the people that would stir their hearts and kindle their imaginations? In 1828, when he declared war on the Ottoman Porte on the pretext of offenses suffered by our Greek and Slavic coreligionists in Turkey, Emperor Nicholas tried to incite religious fanaticism in the people with his manifesto, which was read to them in the churches. The attempt was a complete failure. If a fierce and stubborn piety exists anywhere in Russia, it is only among the Old Believers, who least of all recognize the state or even the emperor himself.[53] In the Orthodox and official Church, however, routine and lifeless ritual reigns alongside the most profound indifference.

At the beginning of the Crimean campaign, when England and France declared war, Nicholas again tried to incite religious fanaticism in the people, and just as unsuccessfully. Remember what was said among the people during that war: "The Frenchman is demanding that we be set free." There were popular militias, but everyone knows how they were formed: for the most part by order of the tsar and at the command of the authorities. It was army recruitment, but in a different form and for a fixed period of time. In many places the peasants were promised that when the war ended they would be emancipated.

That is the kind of political interest our peasants have! Among the merchants and gentry, patriotism was expressed in a highly original form: in foolish speeches, in loud declarations of loyalty to the tsar, and particularly in banquets and drinking parties. But when the time came for some to provide funds and others to lead their peasants off to war themselves, there turned out to be very few enthusiasts. Everyone tried to find someone else to take his place. The militia made a lot of noise but proved of no use. And the Crimean War was not even an offensive war; it was defensive, meaning that it could have and should have become a national war. Why did it not? Because our upper classes are corrupt, paltry, and base, and the people are the natural enemies of the state.

And they hope to stir the people up over the Slavic question! Among our Slavophiles there are some honest individuals who seriously believe that the Russian people are burning with impatience to fly to the aid of their "Slavic brethren," of whose existence they are not even aware. They would be highly astonished to be told that they themselves are a Slavic nation. Duchiński and his Polish and French followers, of course, deny that Slavic blood flows in the veins of the Great Russian people, thereby sinning against historical and ethnographic truth.[54] But Duchiński, who knows our people so little, probably does not even suspect that they are not at all concerned with their Slavic origin. What does it matter to them, when they are exhausted, starving, and oppressed by a supposedly Slavic but actually Tatar-Germanic empire?

We should not deceive the Slavs. Those who speak to them of any participation whatsoever by the Russian people in the Slavic question are either cruelly deluding themselves or are lying shamelessly (and, of course, with dishonest intentions). And if we Russian socialists and revolutionaries summon the Slavic proletariat and Slavic youth to a common cause, let us not offer them our more or less Slavic origin as the common ground for that cause. The only common ground we can recognize is social revolution, without which we see no deliverance either for their nations or for our own. We believe that on this ground they can unite fraternally, thanks to the many identical features in the character, historic destiny, and past and present aspirations of all the Slavic peoples, and their identical attitude toward the statist pretensions of the Germans. Their objective will not be to form a common state but to destroy all states, and not to isolate themselves but to enter a world-wide sphere of activity, beginning perforce with a close alliance with the Latin nations, who, like the Slavs, are now threatened by the aggressive policy of the Germans.

Even that alliance should last only until the Germans realize from their own experience what calamities the existence even of a pseudo-popular state entails for the people, cast off the yoke of the state, and renounce forever their unfortunate passion for state supremacy. Then, and only then, will the three principal nationalities of Europe, the Latin, Slavic, and German, form a free alliance, as brothers.

Until then, however, an alliance of the Slavic and Latin nations against the German aggression that threatens all of them will remain a bitter necessity.

The Germans have a strange mission! By provoking a common sense of danger and a common hatred, they bring nations together. Thus they have united the Slavs, for there is no doubt that the hatred of the Germans which is deeply rooted in the hearts of all the Slavic peoples has furthered the success of pan-Slav propaganda more than all the preaching and intrigue of Moscow's and Petersburg's agents. Now the same hatred will probably draw the Slavs into alliance with the Latins.

In this sense the Russians, too, are a wholly Slavic people, in that they have no love for the Germans. But we should not deceive ourselves: their antipathy does not go so far that they will of their own accord make war on them. That will happen only when the Germans themselves invade Russia and try to establish their sway over it. Anyone who counts on any participation by our people in an offensive action against Germany will prove deeply mistaken.

Hence it follows that if our government ever takes it into its head to make such a move it will have to do it without any popular assistance, with the financial and military resources of the state alone. Are those resources sufficient to fight Germany, much less to conduct a successful offensive war against it?

One would have to be an exceptional ignoramus or a blind *kvass* patriot not to realize that all our military resources and our illustrious, seemingly numberless army are nothing compared to the resources and army of Germany.

The Russian soldier is undeniably brave, but German soldiers are certainly no cowards; they proved that in three successive campaigns. Moreover, in any offensive war on Russia's part the German forces will be fighting on home ground and will be supported by a patriotic – and this time really universal – uprising of all classes and the whole population of Germany, as well as by their own patriotic fanaticism, while the Russian troops will be fighting without purpose and without passion, merely in obedience to their commanders.

As far as a comparison of Russian and German officers is concerned, from a purely human point of view we would give the advantage to our officers, not because they are ours but on grounds of strict fairness. Despite all the efforts of our minister of war Miliutin,[55] the great mass of our officer corps has remained just as it was before – crude, ignorant, and in almost every respect completely mindless.

Military exercises, carousing, card-playing, drunkenness, and, whenever there is a profit to be made, systematic, almost legalized thievery in the upper ranks, starting with the company or squadron or battery commander – these are still the daily indulgences of officer life in Russia. It is a thoroughly vacuous and uncivilized world, even when French is spoken in it. Amidst the crude and absurd slovenliness with which it is filled, however, a human heart can still be found, an instinctive capacity to love and understand mankind, and in the right conditions, under a good influence, the ability to become a fully conscious friend of the people.

In the world of the German officers there is nothing but form, military regulations, and a repugnant arrogance peculiar to officers. This last consists of two elements: servile obedience to anyone who is hierarchically superior, and insolent contempt for anyone who, in their opinion, is inferior – first of all, the people, then anyone who does not wear a military uniform, with the exception of the highest civilian officials and nobles.

In relation to his sovereign – be he a duke, a king, or now the all-German emperor – the German officer is a slave by conviction, by passion. At a nod from him the officer is prepared at any time and any place to commit the most terrible atrocities, to burn down, wipe out, and slaughter dozens or hundreds of towns and villages, not just foreign ones but even his own.

He feels not only contempt for the people but hatred, because (doing them too much honor) he assumes that they are always in revolt, or on the brink of revolt. He is not the only one, however; all the privileged classes make the same assumption these days, and the German officer, in fact any officer of a regular army, can be termed the privileged guard dog of the privileged classes. The whole world of exploiters, in Germany and outside of Germany, views the people with fear and distrust, which are not always justified, unfortunately, but which nonetheless prove beyond doubt that within the masses the conscious force that will destroy this world is beginning to arise.

So, at the very thought of popular crowds, the German officer's hair bristles, like that of a good guard dog. His conception of the people's rights and duties is highly patriarchal. In his opinion the people should work so their masters may be clothed and fed; they should obey the authorities without question, and pay their state taxes and communal obligations; they should take their turn as soldiers,

78

clean the officer's boots, bring him his horse, and shoot, slash, and cut down anybody and everybody whenever he gives the command and brandishes his saber, and go to their death for *Kaiser* and *Vaterland* when ordered to do so. When their term of active duty is over, they should live on charity if they have been wounded or crippled, but if they remain whole and unharmed they should enter the reserves and serve there till they die, always obeying the authorities, bowing down before any superior, and ready to die on demand.

Any development among the people that contradicts this ideal is capable of sending the German officer into a rage. It is not difficult to imagine how he must hate revolutionaries. But under this general term he includes all democrats and even liberals, in other words, anyone who in any manner or form dares to do, will, or think anything contrary to the inviolable thought and will of His Imperial Majesty, the Sovereign of all the Germanies . . .

One can imagine the special hatred with which he must regard his country's revolutionary socialists or even social democrats. The very thought of them drives him into a frenzy, and he considers it unseemly to speak of them without foaming at the mouth. Woe to those who fall into his clutches – and unfortunately it must be said that a number of social democrats in Germany have passed through an officer's hands of late. He does not have the right to tear them to pieces or summarily shoot them, and he does not dare to give free rein to his fists, so he employs the grossest insults, harassments, gestures, and words in the effort to vent his furious, mean-spirited spite. But if he were allowed, if the authorities gave the order, he would take on the role of torturer, hangman, and butcher with ferocious zeal and, above all, with an officer's pride.

Just take a look at this civilized brute, this lackey by conviction and executioner by calling. If he is young, you will be surprised to see not a monster but a blond youth, fresh-faced and downy-cheeked, modest, quiet and even bashful, proud – the arrogance shows through – and unfailingly sentimental. He knows Schiller and Goethe by heart, and all the humanistic literature of the great eighteenth century has passed through his head – without leaving a single humane thought in it or a single humane emotion in his heart.

It was left to the Germans, and particularly German officials and officers, to solve a seemingly insoluble problem: how to combine education and barbarism, learning and servility. It makes them repulsive and at the same time highly comical in a social sense, systematic and merciless villains in relation to the masses, but valued individuals in respect to state service.

The German burghers know this and patriotically endure all the insults they receive from them, partly because they recognize their own character in them but chiefly because they regard these privileged imperial guard dogs, who so often nip them out of boredom, as the most reliable bulwark of the pan-German state.

For a regular army, it is really hard to imagine anything better than the German officer. He is a man who combines learning with doltishness, doltishness with valor, strict fulfillment of orders with a capacity for initiative, discipline with brutality, brutality with a peculiar kind of honesty, and a certain exaltation (albeit one-sided and even disagreeable) with uncommon obedience to the will of the authorities. Ever capable of slashing or hacking apart dozens, hundreds, thousands of people at the least sign from his commanders, he is quiet, modest, submissive, obedient, always at attention before his superiors, and arrogant, disdainfully cold, and, when necessary, even cruel in relation to the ordinary soldier. His whole life is expressed in two words: obey, and command. A man like that is irreplaceable for an army and a state.

As far as the training of the soldiers is concerned, one of the chief concerns in the organization of a good army, it has been brought to a systematic, carefully planned, and empirically tested degree of perfection in the German army. The main principle underlying this discipline is contained in the following aphorism, which we still heard repeated not long ago by the many Prussian, Saxon, Bavarian, and other German officers who have been traipsing around Switzerland in droves since the French campaign (probably to study the terrain and draw maps – they might come in handy in the future): "To master the soldier's soul, you must first master his body."

And how do you master his body? By means of incessant exercises. Do not get the idea that German officers scorn drilling – not at all, they view it as one of the best ways to condition the limbs and master the soldier's body. Then there is rifle practice, weapons maintenance, cleaning uniforms; the soldier has to be kept occupied from morning till night and feel the stern, coldly magnetizing eye of his commanders upon him at every step. In winter, when there is a little more time available, the soldiers are sent to school, where they are taught reading, writing, and arithmetic but above all are forced to learn by heart the military regulations, which are imbued with deification of the emperor and contempt for the people: present arms to the emperor but shoot at the people, that is the quintessence of the soldiers' moral and political education.

Having spent three, four, or five years in this maelstrom, the soldier can emerge from it only as a monster. The same is true of the officer, though in a different form. The soldier is meant to become an unconscious weapon; the officer, however, is supposed to be a conscious one, a weapon by conviction, thought, interest, and passion. His world is the officer corps; he does not set foot beyond it, and the whole corps, permeated with the spirit described above, watches over each of its members. Woe to the unfortunate individual who gets carried away by inexperience or by some humane sentiment and allows himself to become friendly with some other circle. If it is a politically harmless one, he will merely be laughed at. But if it has a political orientation not in accord with the general orientation of the officers, if it is liberal or democratic (let alone social-revolutionary), then the poor fellow is done for. Each of his comrades will become an informer on him.

In general, the higher authorities prefer the officers to keep to themselves for the most part, and they try to leave them, as well as the soldiers, as little free time as possible. Drilling the soldiers and constantly supervising them takes up three-quarters of the officer's day; the remaining quarter is supposed to be devoted to improving his proficiency in military science. Before rising to the rank of major, the officer has to pass several examinations. In addition, he is given periodic assignments on various subjects, and these are used to judge his aptitude for promotion.

As we see, the German military, just like the French, is a completely self-contained world, which serves as a reliable guarantee that it will be the enemy of the people.

But the German military has an enormous advantage over that of the French and indeed of the rest of Europe: German officers surpass all others in the extent and scientific quality of their knowledge, their theoretical and practical grasp of military matters, their zealous and quite scholarly dedication to the military profession, their exactitude, thoroughness, endurance, stubborn perseverance, and also their relative honesty.

As a result of all these qualities, the organization and armament of the German forces exists in reality and not just on paper, as was the case in France under Napoleon III and is nearly always the case in Russia. Moreover, thanks to those same German advantages, administrative, civil, and especially military audits are carried out in such a way that protracted fraud is impossible. In Russia, by contrast, from top to bottom and bottom to top "one hand washes the other," so that it becomes almost impossible to find out the truth.

Keep all this in mind and ask yourself whether a Russian army could possibly hope for success in an offensive war against Germany. You will say that Russia can raise a million troops. Well, perhaps not a million well-organized and well-armed troops, but let us suppose that there are a million. Half of them will have to remain dispersed across the vast expanse of the empire to maintain order among the happy people, who might grow finicky from good living if you do not keep an eye on them. How many troops would be needed for Ukraine, Lithuania, and Poland alone! A lot, if you are going to send a 500,000-man army against Germany. Russia has never yet raised such an army.

In Germany, you will encounter an army that really does number a million, the foremost army in the world in terms of organization, training, science, spirit, and armament. Behind it, as a huge militia, will stand the entire German nation, which possibly, and even probably, would not have risen up against the French had the victor in the recent war been Napoleon III instead of the Prussian Fritz,[a] but which, we reiterate, will rise up unanimously against a Russian invasion.

You will say that in case of need Russia (meaning the Russian Empire) is capable of raising another million troops. And why not, if only on paper: all it takes is to issue a decree for a new levy of recruits, so many per thousand men, and there you have your million. But how are they to be mustered? Who will muster them? Your reserve generals, adjutant-generals, aides-de-camp, commanders of paper reserve and garrison battalions, your governors and bureaucrats? My Lord, how many tens or even hundreds of thousands of men they will starve to death before they get them assembled. And finally, where will you find a sufficient number of officers to organize a million new troops, and what will you arm them with? Sticks? You do not have the

---

[a] It was actually Frederick William IV who had been known familiarly as "Fritz."

funds to arm one million properly, and you are threatening to arm another million. No banker will loan you the money, and even if he does, it will take years to equip a million men.

Let us compare your poverty and feebleness with the Germans' wealth and strength. Germany received 5 billion francs from France. Let us assume that 3 billion were spent to offset various expenses, to reward princes, statesmen, generals, colonels, and other officers (not the soldiers, of course), and also for various domestic and foreign junkets. That leaves 2 billion, which are being used exclusively to arm Germany, to build new fortresses or strengthen a countless number of old ones, to order new cannon, rifles, and so forth. Indeed, the whole of Germany has been turned into a formidable arsenal, bristling with weapons on all sides. And you, with your haphazard training and armament, hope to defeat it.

At your first step, the moment you poke your nose onto German soil, you will get your head severely battered, and your offensive war will turn straightaway into a defensive one. German troops will cross the frontiers of the Russian Empire.

But then, at least, will they not provoke a general uprising of the Russian people against them? Yes, if the Germans penetrate into the Russian provinces and head straight for Moscow, for example. But if, instead of doing anything that stupid, they proceed north to Petersburg through the Baltic provinces, they will find a great many friends, not only among the petty bourgeoisie, the Protestant pastors, and the Yids, but also among the discontented German barons and their children, the students, and through them among our countless Baltic generals, officers, and higher and lower officials who fill Petersburg and are scattered throughout Russia. Moreover, they will stir up Poland and Ukraine against the Russian Empire.

It is true that of all Poland's enemies and oppressors, from the day it was partitioned Prussia proved to be the most persistent, the most systematic, and therefore the most dangerous. Russia behaved like a barbarian, like a savage force, slaughtering, hanging, torturing, exiling thousands to Siberia, and still could not Russify the part of Poland that fell to it, nor can it even to this day, despite Muravev's methods. Austria, for its part, has not Germanized Galicia at all, nor has it even tried. Prussia, as the true representative of the German spirit and the great German mission of forcibly and artificially Germanizing non-German countries, immediately set to work to Germanize at whatever cost the province of Danzig and the Duchy of Poznan, not to mention the Königsberg region which it had obtained much earlier.

It would take too long to describe the methods Prussia used to achieve this objective; among them, extensive colonization of Polish land by German peasants occupied a prominent place. Full emancipation of the peasants in 1807, with the right to purchase land and with every possible assistance in making such purchases, greatly enhanced the popularity of the Prussian government, even among the Polish peasants. Then village schools were established, and in them and through them the German language was introduced. As a result of these measures, by 1848 more than a third of the Duchy of Poznan had been Germanized. There is no need even to mention the towns. From the very beginning of Polish history German was spoken there, thanks to the throngs of German burghers, artisans, and especially Yids, to whom they offered broad hospitality. It is well known that since ancient times the majority of the towns in this part of Poland were governed according to the so-called Magdeburg Law.[56]

That is how Prussia pursued its objective in times of peace. Whenever Polish patriotism provoked or tried to provoke a popular movement, however, Prussia did not hesitate to adopt the most drastic and barbaric measures. We have already had occasion to remark that in the task of quelling Polish uprisings, not only within its own frontiers but also in the Kingdom of Poland, Prussia always displayed unfailing loyalty to the Russian government and the most fervent readiness to assist it. Prussian police, indeed, magnanimous Prussian officers of both the Guards and the army, with a certain special zeal hunted down Poles hiding in Prussian territory and with malicious pleasure handed them over to the Russian police, often expressing the hope that the Russians would hang them. In this regard Muravev the Hangman could not speak highly enough of Prince Bismarck!

Until Bismarck's ministry, Prussia always acted in this manner but did it shamefacedly, on the quiet, and whenever possible disavowed its own actions. Bismarck was the first to throw off the mask. Loudly and cynically he not only acknowledged but boasted in the Prussian parliament and to European diplomats that the Prussian government was using all its influence on the government of Russia to persuade it to suppress Poland completely, to stop at nothing in the use of bloody measures, and that in this regard Prussia would always render Russia the most active assistance.

Finally, not long ago, Bismarck bluntly declared in parliament the government's firm resolve to eradicate all vestiges of Polish nationality in the Polish provinces that currently enjoy Prusso-German administration. Unfortunately, as we mentioned earlier, the Poles of Poznan, like those of Galicia, have now bound the Polish national cause more closely than ever to the issue of the supremacy of papal power. Their advocates are Jesuits, ultramontanes, monastic orders, and bishops. A lot of good this alliance and this friendship will do them – as much good as it did them in the seventeenth century. But that is the Poles' business, not ours.

We have mentioned all this in order to show that the Poles have no enemy more dangerous and vicious than Bismarck. He seems to have made it his life's work to wipe them off the face of the earth. All the same, it will not prevent him from calling on the Poles to rebel against Russia when Germany's interests demand it. And even though the Poles detest him and Prussia, not to mention the whole of Germany, even if they do not care to admit it; even though a historic hatred of the Germans dwells deep in their hearts as it does in all the other Slavic peoples; and even though they cannot forget the mortal insults they have endured at the hands of the Prussian Germans – the Poles will without doubt rise up at Bismarck's call.

In Germany, and in Prussia itself, a large and serious political party has long existed – actually three parties, one liberal-progressive, one purely democratic, and one social-democratic,[57] which together form an indisputable majority in the German and Prussian parliaments and an even more decisive majority in the society itself – parties which, foreseeing, to some degree desiring, and in a sense calling for a war by Germany against Russia, understood that the insurrection and *within certain boundaries* the reestablishment of Poland would be a necessary condition for such a war.

It goes without saying that neither Bismarck nor any of those parties will ever agree to give Poland back all of the provinces Prussia took from it. Nothing in the world will induce them to give up Danzig or even the merest scrap of West Prussia, not to mention Königsberg. They will even detach a considerable part of the Duchy of Poznan for themselves, claiming that it is now completely Germanized. Of the segment of Poland that fell to the Prussians, they will leave the Poles essentially very little. To make up for it they will give them all of Galicia, including Lwow and Cracow, since it now belongs to Austria, and even more gladly will give them as much territory far inside Russia as they have the power to seize and hold. In addition, they will offer the Poles the funds they need (in the form, of course, of a Polish loan guaranteed by Germany), arms, and military assistance.

Who can doubt that the Poles will not only agree to the Germans' offer but will jump at it? Their situation is so desperate that if they were made an offer a hundred times worse, they would accept it.

It has now been a century since the partition of Poland, and in those hundred years scarcely a single one has passed without Polish patriots shedding their blood as martyrs. A hundred years of uninterrupted struggle, of desperate revolts! Is there any other nation that can boast of such valor?

What have the Poles not tried? Gentry conspiracies, petty-bourgeois plots, armed bands, national insurrections, and finally all the tricks of diplomacy and even the aid of the Church. They have tried everything, they have grasped at every straw, and everything has crumbled in their hands, everything has betrayed them. How can they refuse when Germany itself, their most dangerous enemy, offers to assist them on certain conditions?

Perhaps there are Slavophiles who will accuse them of betrayal. Betrayal of what? Of the Slavic cause, the Slavic alliance? But what does that cause consist of, and how has that alliance manifested itself? Was it not in the trip Palacký and Rieger made to Moscow for the pan-Slav exhibition, and their obeisance to the tsar? How and when, by what deed, have the Slavs, as Slavs, expressed their fraternal sympathy for the Poles? Was it not when the same Palacký and Rieger and their multitudinous retinue of west and south Slavs exchanged kisses in Warsaw with Russian generals who had scarcely washed the Poles' blood from their hands, and toasted Slavic brotherhood and the health of the tsar-hangman?

The Poles are martyrs and heroes, and they have great glory in their past; the Slavs are still children, and their entire significance lies in the future. The Slavic world, the Slavic question, is not a reality but a hope, and a hope which can be fulfilled only by means of a social revolution. So far, however, the Poles have shown little enthusiasm for such a revolution – meaning, of course, the Polish patriots, who for the most part belong to the educated class and predominantly to the gentry.

What can the Slavic world, which does not yet exist, and the world of the Polish patriots, which has more or less outlived its day, have in common? In fact, except for a very few individuals who are trying to raise the Slavic question in a Polish spirit and on Polish soil, the Poles are generally not interested in it. They find it much easier to understand the Magyars and feel closer to them. They have some similarity to them and share a number of historical memories with them, while they are divided from the south and west Slavs particularly – and categorically, one may say – by the latter's sympathies for Russia, the Poles' most hated enemy.

In Poland and in the Polish emigration, as in any other country, the political world was formerly divided into a number of parties. There was an aristocratic party, a clerical party, and a party of constitutional monarchists; there was a party in support of military dictatorship; a party of moderate republicans, admirers of the United States; a party of red republicans along French lines; finally, even a small party of social democrats, not to mention the mystical-sect parties, or, more accurately, church parties. One only needed to look into each of them a little more deeply, however, to be convinced that essentially they all had the same basis: a passionate desire to reestablish the Polish state within the frontiers of 1772. Aside from the mutual antagonism of their leaders, what chiefly distinguished them from one another was each party's conviction that this common objective, restoration of the old Poland, could be achieved only by the particular means it recommended.

Until 1850, it can be said, the vast majority of the Polish emigration was revolutionary, for it was confident that the restoration of an independent Poland would inevitably result from the triumph of revolution in Europe. It can also be said that in 1848 there was not a single movement in the whole of Europe in which the Poles did not participate, often even assuming the leadership. We recall how one Saxon German expressed his astonishment on this score: "wherever there is so much as a disturbance, there are sure to be Poles!"

In 1850, with revolution defeated everywhere, faith in it declined, Napoleon's star rose, and a great many Polish émigrés, the vast majority of them, became fierce and thorough-going Bonapartists. My Lord, what did they not hope to achieve with Napoleon III's help! Even his flagrant, despicable treason in 1862–63 was not enough to destroy their faith.[58] It was extinguished only at Sedan.

After that catastrophe the only remaining refuge for the Poles' hopes was the Jesuits and ultramontanes. The Austrian and most other Polish patriots scurried to Galicia in desperation. But imagine Bismarck, their inveterate enemy, forced by Germany's situation to call on them to revolt against Russia. He will not offer them far-fetched hopes, no, he will give them money, arms, and military aid. Is there any possibility of their rejecting it?

It is true that in return for that aid they will be required to make a formal renunciation of the greater part of the old Polish lands now in the possession of Prussia. They will find it a very bitter pill, but forced by circumstances and certain of triumphing over Russia, consoling themselves in the end with the thought that if only Poland be restored they will get back what belongs to them afterward, they will unques-tionably rise up – and from their point of view they will be right ten thousand times over.

True, Poland restored with the aid of German troops and under the patronage of Prince Bismarck will be a strange Poland. But better a strange Poland than none at all. And eventually, ultimately, the Poles will surely reckon, they will be able to liberate themselves from Bismarck's patronage, too.

In short, the Poles will agree to everything; Poland will rise up, Lithuania will rise up, and a little later Ukraine will rise up, too. The Polish patriots are bad socialists, to be sure, and at home they will not occupy themselves with revolutionary socialist propaganda. Even if they wanted to, their protector, Prince Bismarck, would not allow it – it is too close to Germany, and who knows, such propaganda might even make its way into Prussian Poland. But what cannot be done in Poland can be done in Russia and against Russia. It would be highly useful for both the Germans and the Poles to stir up a peasant rebellion there, and it would not be hard to do – just think how many Poles and Germans are scattered around Russia. Most if not all of them would be natural allies of Bismarck and the Poles. Imagine the situation: our troops, their heads battered, will flee; on their heels in the north the Germans will march on Petersburg, and in the west and south the Poles will march on Smolensk and Ukraine – while at the same time, in Russia and in Ukraine, a universal, triumphant peasant rebellion is taking place, incited by external and domestic propaganda.

That is why it can be said with assurance that no Russian govern-ment and no Russian tsar, unless he is demented, will ever raise the standard of pan-Slavism and make war on Germany.

Having conclusively defeated first Austria and then France, the great new German Empire will permanently reduce to the level of second-rank powers and German dependencies not only those two states but eventually our Russian Empire as well, which it has cut off from Europe for good. (We are referring, of course, to the empire, not to the Russian people, who will break a path for themselves wherever they need to go.)

For the Russian Empire, however, the gates of Europe now are locked. Prince Bismarck holds the keys to them, and not for anything in the world will he give them to Prince Gorchakov.[59]

But if the gates to the northwest are barred to the empire forever, are not the gates to the south and southeast still open, and perhaps more dependably and more widely: Bukhara, Persia, Afghanistan and the frontiers of India, and, finally, the ultimate object of all imperial schemes and desires, Constantinople? For a long time now, Russian politicians, zealous proponents of the grandeur and glory of our dear empire, have been discussing whether it would not be better to transfer the empire's capital, and along with it the center of gravity of its forces, of its whole life, from the north to the south, from the bleak shores of the Baltic to the ever verdant shores of the Black Sea and the Mediterranean – in a word, from Petersburg to Constantinople.

To be sure, there are patriots so insatiable as to want to keep Petersburg and supremacy on the Baltic and to seize Constantinople, too. But this desire is so unattainable that even they are beginning to abandon any hope of fulfilling it, for all their faith in the omnipotence of the Russian Empire. Moreover, in recent years an event took place which must have been an eye-opener for them: the annexation of Holstein, Schleswig, and Hanover to the Kingdom of Prussia, which immediately thereby became a North Sea power.

It is a well-known axiom that no state can be counted as a first-rank power unless it has an extensive seacoast guaranteeing it direct communications with the whole world and permitting it to take a direct part in the world's progress, social, political, and moral, as well as material. This truth is so obvious as to require no proof. Let us assume the strongest, best-educated, and happiest state – to the extent that happiness is possible in a state – and imagine that circumstances have cut it off from the rest of the world. You can be certain that within fifty years or so, two generations, everything in it will come to a standstill: its strength will have been sapped, its educational level will verge on stupidity, and its happiness will give off the smell of Limburger cheese.

Look at China. It seems to have been intelligent, learned, and probably, in its own way, happy, too. Why did it become so decrepit that the most paltry efforts of the European maritime powers were sufficient to subject it to their intellect and, if not to their suzerainty, then at least to their will? Because for centuries China had stagnated, thanks in part to its domestic institutions but also to the fact that it was so remote from the current of world life that for a long time it had no contact with it.

There are a number of different conditions that enable a nation shut up within a state to take part in world progress: native wit and innate energy, education, capacity for productive labor, and the broadest domestic freedom (impossible as the latter is for the masses within a state). But those conditions necessarily include seafaring and sea-borne trade, for maritime communications, with their relative cheapness, speed, and freedom (in the sense that the seas do not belong to anyone), are superior to all others, including railroads. Perhaps aviation will someday prove even more convenient in every respect and will be particularly important in that it will finally equalize the conditions of existence and development in all countries. For now, however, it cannot be regarded as a serious alternative, and seafaring remains the principal method by which nations attain prosperity.

The time will come when states will exist no more – and all the efforts of the social-revolutionary party in Europe are being bent to their destruction. The time will come when on the ruins of political states there will be created, in complete freedom and organized from below upwards, a voluntary fraternal union of voluntary productive associations, communes, and provincial federations, embracing without distinction, because they embrace freely, people of every language and nationality. Then all will have equal access to the sea – coastal dwellers directly, and those who live far from the sea via railroads free of all state supervisors, taxes, tariffs, restrictions, regulations, prohibitions, permissions, and applications. Even then, however, coastal inhabitants will have a number of natural advantages, not only of a material nature but intellectual and moral, too. Direct contact with the world market and with the progress of world life in general is developing to an extraordinary degree, and however much relations may be equalized, inhabitants of the interior, deprived of those advantages, will live and develop at a slower and lazier pace than those on the coasts.

That is why aviation will be so important. The atmosphere is a boundless ocean, its shores are everywhere, so that all individuals, even those living in the most out-of-the-way places, are without exception coastal dwellers. Until aviation replaces seafaring, however, coastal inhabitants will be advanced in every respect and will constitute a kind of aristocracy of the human race.

All history, and particularly the greater part of progress in history, has been made by coastal nations. The first nation, the creators of civilization, were the Greeks – and it can be said that the whole of Greece is nothing but a coastline. Ancient Rome became a mighty, world state only when it became a maritime state. In modern history, to whom do we owe the resurrection of political liberty, social life, commerce, the arts, science, free thought – in a word, the renaissance of humanity? To Italy, which, like Greece, is almost entirely a coastline. After Italy, who inherited the position of the leader of world progress? Holland, England, France, and finally America.

On the other hand, let us take a look at Germany. Its people are endowed with many undeniable qualities: exceptional industry, a capacity for thought and science, an esthetic sensibility which has produced great artists and poets, and a profound transcendentalism which has produced philosophers no less great. Why, we ask, did Germany lag so far behind France and England in all respects other than the one in which it outstripped everyone else, the development of a bureaucratic, police, and military state order? Why is it still inferior to Holland in trade, to Belgium in industry?

Because, it will be said, Germany never had liberty, a love of liberty, a demand for liberty. That would be justified in part, but it is not the sole reason. Another, just as important, is the absence of a long coastline. Back in the thirteenth century, when the Hanseatic League originated, Germany had no lack of a seacoast, at least in the west. Holland and Belgium still belonged to it, and Germany's trade seemed to hold the promise of fairly extensive development. In the fourteenth century, however, the towns of the low countries, animated by a bold entrepreneurial spirit and a love of liberty, began manifestly to separate themselves from Germany and to become estranged from it. This separation was completed in the sixteenth century, and the great empire, the ungainly heir of the Roman Empire, became an almost entirely landlocked state. It retained only a narrow window on the sea between Holland and Denmark, far from sufficient to allow such a vast country to breathe freely. As a result, a somnolence very similar to China's stagnation descended upon Germany.

From that time on, all *progressive* political development in Germany, in the sense of the formation of a strong new state, was concentrated in the small Electorate of Brandenburg. In fact, the electors of Brandenburg, through their constant efforts to gain control of the shores of the Baltic, rendered Germany a great service. They can be said to have created the conditions for its greatness today, first seizing Königsberg and then, in the first partition of Poland, taking Danzig. But that was not enough: Kiel had to be seized, and all of Schleswig and Holstein as well.

Prussia carried out these new conquests to the applause of all Germany. We all witnessed the passion with which Germans of every separate state *Vaterland*, in the north, south, west, east, and center of the country, followed the development of the Schleswig-Holstein question after 1848. Those who accounted for this passion on the grounds of sympathy for their German blood brothers supposedly suffocating under Danish despotism were profoundly mistaken. An entirely different interest was involved here, a political interest, a pan-German interest, an interest in conquering seacoasts and maritime routes, an interest in creating a powerful German navy.

The question of a German navy had already been raised in 1840 or 1841, and we recall the enthusiasm with which all Germany greeted Herwegh's poem "The German Navy."[60]

The Germans, we reiterate, are such a state-minded people that their passion for the state prevails over all their other passions and completely overwhelms their instinct for liberty. At the present time, however, it is also what constitutes their special greatness: it serves, and for some time will continue to serve, as a direct and unfailing source of support for all the ambitious designs of their Berlin sovereign. Prince Bismarck relies upon it greatly.

The Germans are a learned people, and they know that no great state can exist without maritime frontiers.[a] That is why they per-

---

[a] The text reads "without unstable (*neprochnykh*) maritime frontiers." I have omitted the word "unstable," which makes no sense here.

sistently maintain, in defiance of historical, ethnographic, and geographical truth, that Trieste was, is, and will be a German city, that the whole of the Danube is a German river. They strain toward the sea. And if social revolution does not stop them one can rest assured that in twenty years, or ten, or maybe even less – events nowadays follow one another so quickly – in any case, in a short time they will conquer the whole of *German* Denmark, *German* Holland, and *German* Belgium. It lies within the natural logic, so to speak, of their political situation and their instinctive desires.

They have already covered one stretch of this road.

Prussia, the present-day embodiment of Germany, its head and its hands, has firmly established itself on the Baltic and on the North Sea. The autonomy of Bremen, Hamburg, Lübeck, Mecklenburg, and Oldenburg is a hollow and harmless joke. Along with Holstein, Schleswig, and Hanover, they have all become part of Prussia, and Prussia, flush with French money, is building two strong navies, one on the Baltic and the other on the North Sea. Thanks to the shipping canal that is now being dug to connect the two seas, these two navies will soon be one. And before many years have passed, this navy, which already surpasses both the Danish and the Swedish, will become much stronger than the Russian Baltic Fleet. Then, Russian hegemony on the Baltic will sink into . . . the Baltic. Goodbye Riga, goodbye Revel, goodbye Finland, and goodbye Petersburg, with its impregnable Kronstadt![61]

To our *kvass* patriots, who are wont to exaggerate Russia's power, this will seem nonsense, an evil fairy-tale, but it is nothing other than an entirely accurate conclusion drawn from accomplished facts. It is based on a fair assessment of the character and capabilities of the Germans and the Russians, not to mention their financial resources and relative numbers of conscientious, dedicated, and knowledgeable officials of every sort, and not to mention scientific learning, either, which gives all the Germans' undertakings a decided advantage over those of the Russians.

German state service produces results that are unattractive, unpleasant, one might say loathsome, but nonetheless practical and serious.

Russian state service produces results that are equally unpleasant and unattractive but frequently even more primitive in form and at the same time futile. Let us take an example. Suppose the governments of

Germany and Russia simultaneously appropriated a certain sum, say a million, to carry out some purpose, such as building a new ship. In Germany, do you think it would be stolen? Perhaps a hundred thousand, maybe even two hundred thousand, but at least eight hundred thousand would go directly to the purpose at hand, which would be accomplished with all the efficiency and competence for which the Germans are noted. And in Russia? First of all, half of it would be embezzled, and a quarter of it would be wasted as a result of negligence and ignorance, so that at most the remaining quarter would be used to knock together something that was falling to pieces, good for show but unfit for its purpose.

How, then, is the Russian navy to resist the German navy, and Russian coastal fortifications like Kronstadt to withstand bombardment by the Germans, who can fire not just iron but golden shells?

Goodbye dominance on the Baltic! Goodbye the political significance and power of the northern capital that Peter the Great raised up on the Finnish swamps! If our great and venerable chancellor, Prince Gorchakov, was still in possession of his faculties, he must have said that to himself when our ally Prussia, with impunity and, as it were, with our consent, was pillaging Denmark, which was no less our ally. He must have understood that Petersburg Russia's supremacy on the Baltic came to an end on the very day Prussia, relying now on the whole of Germany and constituting in indissoluble unity with it the strongest of the continental powers – in short, on the very day the new German Empire, formed under the scepter of Prussia, took up its present position on the Baltic, a position so menacing to all the other Baltic powers. Peter's great political creation had been destroyed, and along with it the very power of the Russian state, unless a new route were opened in the south to compensate for the loss of a free maritime route in the north.

It is clear that the Germans will now come to hold sway on the Baltic. True, the entrance to it is still in the hands of Denmark. But who is blind to the fact that this poor little state has almost no other choice but first, perhaps, to become voluntarily federated with Germany, then to be fully swallowed up by pan-German state centralization. Hence the Baltic in a very short time will turn into an exclusively German sea, and Petersburg will necessarily lose all political significance.

Gorchakov must have known this when he agreed to the dismemberment of the Kingdom of Denmark and the annexation of Holstein and Schleswig by Prussia. These events logically pose the following dilemma: either he betrayed Russia, or, in return for the Russian state's sacrifice of its supremacy in the northwest, he received a formal commitment from Bismarck to help Russia gain new power in the southeast.

We have no doubt as to the existence of such a treaty, a defensive and offensive alliance concluded between Russia and Prussia almost immediately after the Peace of Paris, or at least at the time of the Polish insurrection in 1863, when almost all the European powers except Prussia followed the example of France and England and publicly and officially protested against Russian barbarism. We have no doubt that Prussia and Russia made a formal and mutually binding agreement, for such an alliance alone can explain the calm, one might say carefree, assurance with which Bismarck undertook the war against Austria and a large part of Germany despite the danger of French intervention, and then the still more decisive war against France. The least demonstration of hostility on Russia's part, such as the movement of Russian forces toward the Prussian frontier, would have been sufficient in both cases, and particularly the latter, to stop any further advance by the victorious Prussian army. Remember that at the end of the last war the whole of Germany, and especially the northern part of it, was completely stripped of troops, that Austria's non-intervention on France's behalf had no other cause than Russia's declaration that if Austria moved its forces Russia would move its army against them, and that Italy and England failed to intervene only because Russia did not wish it. Had Russia not declared itself such a resolute ally of the Prusso-German emperor, the Germans would never have taken Paris.

Bismarck evidently was confident that Russia would not betray him. What were the grounds for that confidence? The family ties and personal friendship of the two emperors? Bismarck is too clever and experienced a man to count on sentiment in politics. Let us even suppose that our emperor, who, as everyone knows, is endowed with a sensitive heart and sheds tears very easily, might be carried away by such feelings, which he has more than once expressed at imperial drinking parties. He is surrounded by an entire government, a court, an heir to the throne who supposedly hates the Germans, and, finally, our venerable state patriot, Prince Gorchakov. All of them together,

95

along with public opinion and the very force of circumstances, would remind him that states are guided not by feelings but by interests.

Nor could Bismarck have counted on the identity of Russian and Prussian interests. There is no such identity, nor can there be. It exists only on one point, the Polish question. That question has long since been settled, however, and in all other respects nothing could be more contrary to the interests of the all-Russian state than the formation next door to it of a great and powerful all-German Empire. The existence of two massive empires side by side entails war, which can have no other conclusion than the destruction of one or the other of them.

War is unavoidable, but it can be postponed if the two empires realize that they have not adequately strengthened and stabilized themselves domestically to initiate a decisive encounter, a life and death struggle. Then, even though they hate one another, they continue to offer each other support and do each other good turns, each one hoping to make better use than the other of this involuntary alliance and to amass greater strength and resources for the inevitable future conflict. That is precisely the situation of both Russia and Prussian Germany.

The German Empire has by no means consolidated its power either internally or externally. Internally, it is a peculiar conglomeration of many autonomous small and medium-size states, which are doomed to extinction but have not yet been extinguished and seek to preserve at all costs the vestiges of their visibly dwindling autonomy. Externally, a humbled but not yet completely crushed Austria and a defeated and consequently irreconcilable France scowl upon the new empire. Furthermore, the neo-German empire has not yet adequately rounded out its frontiers. Succumbing to a necessity intrinsic to military states, it plans new acquisitions, new wars. Setting itself the objective of reestablishing the medieval German empire within its primordial frontiers – and pan-German patriotism, which has seized the whole of German society, draws it inexorably toward that objective – it dreams of annexing all of Austria except Hungary, including Trieste but not Bohemia, all of German Switzerland, part of Belgium, and all of Holland and Denmark, which are essential for establishing its sea power. There are gigantic plans, the implementation of which will arouse a considerable part of western and southern Europe against it and is therefore categorically impossible without Russia's consent. Hence the neo-German empire still needs a Russian alliance.

For its part, the Russian Empire cannot do without a Prusso-German alliance. Having renounced any expansion or new acquisitions in the northwest, it has to go southeastward. Having ceded supremacy on the Baltic to Prussia, it has to win and secure power on the Black Sea. Otherwise it will be cut off from Europe. For its dominion on the Black Sea to be real and useful, however, it must gain possession of Constantinople. Without it, not only can its access to the Mediterranean be blocked at any time, but entry into the Black Sea will always be open to hostile armies and navies, as was the case during the Crimean campaign.

Hence the one objective for which the annexationist policy of our state is striving more than ever is Constantinople. The realization of this objective is contrary to the interests of all of southern Europe, including, of course, France. It is contrary to England's interests and also to the interests of Germany, since Russia's unlimited sway over the Black Sea would make the banks of the Danube directly dependent on Russia.

Nevertheless, it cannot be doubted that Prussia, forced to rely on a Russian alliance to carry out its plans of conquest in the west, formally obligated itself to aid Russia in its southeastern policy. Nor can it be doubted that it will take the first opportunity to betray its promise.

Violation of the accord should not be expected just yet, when it has only begun to be carried out. We have seen how zealously the Prusso-German Empire supported Russia over the issue of abrogating the constraints imposed by the Treaty of Paris, and there is no doubt that it is continuing to support Russia just as zealously over Khiva. Furthermore, it is to the Germans' advantage that the Russians withdraw as deeply as possible to the east.

But what impelled the Russian government to undertake the campaign against Khiva? We cannot suppose that it was to defend the interests of Russian merchants and Russian commerce. If that were the case, one might ask why the government does not undertake similar campaigns inside Russia, against itself – against the governor-general of Moscow, for example, and against all the provincial and town governors, who, as everyone knows, oppress and plunder both Russian commerce and Russian merchants in the most impudent manner and by every conceivable means.

Of what use can it be to our state to conquer desert sands? Some, perhaps, are prepared to answer that our government undertook this campaign in order to fulfill Russia's great mission of bringing the West's civilization to the East. This explanation may be suitable for academic or official speeches, or for doctrinaire books, pamphlets, and journals, which are always filled with elevated nonsense and always say the opposite of what is actually the case. It cannot satisfy us. Imagine the Petersburg government being guided in its undertakings and actions by its recognition of Russia's civilizing mission! The very idea is enough to make anyone who is the least bit familiar with the nature and motives of our rulers die laughing.

Nor will we bother referring to the opening of new trade routes to India. Trade politics is England's politics, it has never been Russia's. The Russian state is primarily, one can say exclusively, a military state. It subordinates everything solely to the interests of coercive power. The sovereign, the state – that is what counts. Everything else – the people, even class interests, the flourishing of industry, trade, and so-called civilization – is but a means to the attainment of that one objective. Without a certain degree of civilization, without industry and trade, no state can exist, especially a modern one, because so-called national wealth (not the people's wealth, but the wealth of the privileged classes) is its strength. In Russia the state devours it all and in turn feeds a huge class of military, civil, and ecclesiastical officials. Universal graft, embezzlement of public funds and robbery of the people – that is the truest expression of the Russian state's civilization.

It is not surprising, therefore, that among other, more important reasons motivating the Russian government to undertake the campaign against Khiva there were also so-called commercial reasons. New opportunities had to be opened up for the growing number of officials (among whom we count our merchants), they had to be given new provinces to loot. But no appreciable increase in the state's wealth and strength can be expected to result. On the contrary, one can be sure that financially the enterprise will produce much greater losses than profits.

Why march to Khiva, then? To give the army something to do? For many decades the Caucasus served as a military school, but now the Caucasus has been pacified; a new school had to be opened, so the Khiva campaign was thought up. This explanation does not withstand criticism either, even if we assume appalling incompetence and stupidity on the part of the Russian government. The experience gained by our troops in the Khiva desert is in no way applicable to a war against the West, and it is also too costly, so the advantages gained cannot compare with the losses and expense.

Can the Russian government have thought seriously of conquering India? We are not guilty of excessive confidence in the wisdom of our Petersburg rulers, but we cannot believe that they set themselves such a preposterous objective. Conquer India! For whom, why, and how? It would require moving at least a quarter, if not half, of the Russian population to the East. And why conquer India anyway, which can be reached only by first subduing the numerous and warlike tribes of Afghanistan? Conquering Afghanistan, however, which is armed and in part trained by the English, would be at least three or four times harder than overcoming Khiva.

If it is a matter of conquests, why not begin with China? China is very rich and in every respect more accessible to us than India, since there is nothing and nobody between China and Russia. Go take it, if you can.

Indeed, by taking advantage of the disorders and civil wars which are the chronic malady of China one could extend one's conquests very far into the country, and the Russian government seems to be venturing something along these lines. It is making manifest efforts to detach Mongolia and Manchuria; one fine day, perhaps, we will hear that Russian forces have crossed China's western frontier. It is an extremely risky business, reminding us very much of the famous victories of the ancient Romans over the Germanic peoples – victories which ended, of course, with the Roman Empire being sacked and conquered by the savage Germanic tribes.

In China alone there are, by some estimates, 400 million inhabitants, by others 600 million, who evidently have become too crowded within the boundaries of the empire and in an inexorable flow are emigrating on a mass scale, some to Australia, some across the Pacific to California. Others may ultimately move to the north and the northwest. And then? Then, in the twinkling of an eye, Siberia, the whole region from the Tatar Strait to the Urals and the Caspian Sea, will cease to be Russian.

Consider that this vast region (12,220,000 square kilometers), which is more than twenty times the size of France (528,600 square kilometers), contains no more than 6 million inhabitants, only about 2,600,000 of whom are Russians while the rest are indigenous peoples of Tatar or Finnish origin, and a negligible number of troops. Will there be any possibility of stopping an invasion by the Chinese masses, who will not only inundate the whole of Siberia, including our new possessions in Central Asia, but will pour across the Urals right up to the Volga River?

That is the danger all but inevitably facing us from the East. It is a mistake to scorn the Chinese masses. They are a threat by virtue of their numbers alone, because their inordinate increase makes their future existence within China's boundaries almost impossible. They are a threat also because they should not be judged by the Chinese merchants with whom the Europeans do business in Shanghai, Canton, or Maimachin.[62] Within China live masses much less debased by Chinese civilization, incomparably more energetic, certainly warlike, and habituated to military ways by their endless civil wars in which tens and hundreds of thousands of people perish. It should be noted too that of late they have begun to familiarize themselves with the use of modern weapons and with European training – the flower and last official word of Europe's state civilization. Combine that training, and that familiarity with new weapons and tactics, with the primitive barbarism of the Chinese masses, their lack of any conception of human protest or instinct for liberty, and with their habit of servile obedience (and they are now being combined, under the influence of the multitude of military adventurers, American and European, who flooded into China after the last Franco-English campaign in 1860); take into consideration, too, the monstrous size of the population, which has to find an outlet, and you will understand the magnitude of the danger threatening us from the East.

That is the danger with which our Russian government is toying, naive as a child. It is impelled by the absurd desire to expand its frontiers, failing to take into account the fact that Russia is so sparsely populated, so poor, and so weak that to this day it has been unable, and always will be unable, to populate its newly acquired Amur region, which contains only 65,000 inhabitants, including the army and navy, in an area of 2,100,000 square kilometers (nearly four times the size of France).[63] Notwithstanding this impotence, notwithstanding the universal poverty of the Russian people, who have been reduced by their fatherland's government to such desperate straits that they have no other recourse or deliverance than the most destructive rebellion – yes, notwithstanding these conditions, the Russian government hopes to establish its power over the whole Asiatic East.

To proceed any further with even the slightest chance of success, it would not only have to turn its back on Europe and renounce any interference in European affairs – and Bismarck would like nothing better – it would have to move absolutely all of its military forces into Siberia and Central Asia and undertake the conquest of the East, like Tamerlane with his whole nation. Tamerlane's people followed him, however; the Russian people will not follow the Russian government.

Let us turn again to India. However ridiculous the Russian government may be, it cannot entertain the hope of conquering India and consolidating its power over it. England conquered India initially with its trading companies; we have no such companies, or, if they exist at all, they are merely pocket-size, for show. England conducts its massive exploitation of India, or its forced trade with it, by sea, by means of its great merchant and military fleets. We have no such fleets, and we are separated from India not by the sea but by endless desert – so there can be no talk of conquering India.

If we cannot conquer it, however, we can destroy or at least seriously weaken England's dominion over it by stirring up and assisting native rebellions, even supporting them, when necessary, with military intervention.

Yes, we can, though with enormous losses of men and money, and we are not rich in either one. Why would we bear these losses, however? For no other purpose than to give ourselves the naive satisfaction of playing dirty tricks on the English with no benefit to ourselves – and, in fact, to our actual detriment? No, it is because the English obstruct us. And where do they obstruct us? *In Constantinople.* As long as England maintains its power it will never, not for anything in the world, allow Constantinople to become in our hands the new capital either of the Russian Empire or of a Slavic or Eastern empire.

That is why the Russian government undertook the war in Khiva, and why from time immemorial it has sought to draw closer to India. It seeks a point at which it can do harm to England, and finding no other it threatens India. It hopes in this way to make the English accept the idea that Constantinople must become a Russian city, to compel them to consent to this conquest, which more than ever is a necessity for statist Russia.

Russia's supremacy on the Baltic is irretrievably lost. To contend with the awesome and magnificently organized power of the newly risen German Empire is beyond the capacity of the Russian state, unified by bayonet and knout, hated by all the nations imprisoned and enchained within it (starting with the Great Russians), demoralized, disorganized, and despoiled by its native despotism, native stupidity, and native thievery; and it is beyond its military strength, which exists more on paper than in reality and is of use only against the unarmed (and even then only so long as we lack resoluteness). Therefore it must give up the Baltic and await the moment when the entire Baltic region becomes a German province. Only a popular revolution can prevent it. But for the state such a revolution means death, and our government will not seek its salvation there.

No other salvation remains to it than alliance with Germany. Forced to give up the Baltic to the Germans, the Russian state must now seek a new arena on the Black Sea, a new basis for its grandeur and simply for its political existence and significance. It cannot obtain it, however, without the permission and assistance of the Germans.

The Germans have promised their assistance. Indeed, we are certain that Bismarck and Gorchakov concluded a formal treaty in which the Germans obligated themselves to render that assistance to the Russian state – but they never will, of that we are equally certain. They will not do so because they can never subject the banks of the Danube and their Danube trade to Russia's whim. Also, because it cannot be in their interest to foster an increase in Russian power, the rise of a great pan-Slav empire in the south of Europe. That would simply be a form of suicide by the pan-German empire. But to nudge Russian troops into Central Asia, toward Khiva, under the pretext that this is the most direct route to Constantinople – that is something else again.

It seems to us beyond doubt that our venerable state patriot and diplomat, Prince Gorchakov, and his imperial patron Alexander II played an extremely stupid role in this deplorable affair, and that the celebrated German patriot and state swindler, Prince Bismarck, duped them even more adroitly than he duped Napoleon III.

The deed is done, however, and it cannot be undone. A new German Empire has arisen, majestic and menacing, laughing both at its enviers and its enemies. It will not be brought down by Russia's flabby forces – that can be accomplished only by a revolution. Until revolution triumphs in Russia or in Europe, statist Germany will triumph and will hold sway over all, and the Russian state, like the other continental states of Europe, will exist only by its leave and by its grace.

That, it goes without saying, sorely grieves the heart of every Russian state patriot, but a threatening fact is a fact nonetheless. The Germans more than ever have become our masters, and it is no wonder that all the Germans in Russia so noisily and enthusiastically celebrated the victory of the German army in France, no wonder that all the Petersburg Germans so jubilantly welcomed their new pan-German emperor.

IV

Today there is only one truly sovereign state left on the entire continent of Europe, and that is Germany. Indeed, of all the continental powers – we are referring, of course, only to the great powers, since it is obvious that the small and medium-size states are inescapably doomed first to utter dependence, and then, after a short time, to extinction – of all the first-rank states, the German Empire alone fulfills all the conditions of complete independence, while the others are reduced to dependence on it. That is not only because it won brilliant victories in recent years over Denmark, Austria, and France; because it seized all of the latter's arms and military supplies and forced it to pay 5 billion francs; and because with the annexation of Alsace and Lorraine it assumed a superb military position, defensive as well as offensive, vis-à-vis France. It is not only because the German army now unquestionably surpasses all the armies of Europe in numbers, weaponry, discipline, organization, and the efficiency and military knowledge not only of its officers but of its non-commissioned officers and soldiers, not to mention the undeniable superiority of its general staff. It is not only because the mass of the German population consists of literate, industrious, productive, and relatively well-educated, not to say learned, individuals, who are also submissive and obedient to the authorities and the law. Nor is it only because the German administration and bureaucracy have all but realized the ideal which the administration and bureaucracy of every other state strive in vain to achieve . . .

All these advantages, of course, have furthered and are furthering the astounding success of the new pan-German state, but they are not the main cause of its current overwhelming power. It may even be said that they are themselves nothing more than effects of a deeper and more general cause lying at the basis of all of German social life. That is the *social instinct* which forms the characteristic trait of the German people.

This instinct consists of two elements, seemingly antithetical but always inseparable: a servile instinct for obedience at any price, for docile and prudent submission to superior force under the pretext of obedience to so-called legitimate authority; and at the same time a domineering instinct for systematic subjugation of anything that is weaker, an instinct for command, conquest, and systematic oppression. Both of these instincts have attained a considerable degree of development in almost every German, except, of course, for the proletariat, whose circumstances preclude the possibility of satisfying at least the second of the two. Always inseparable, complementing and explaining each other, both lie at the very basis of patriotic German society.

The entire history of Germany attests to the classic obedience of Germans of every class and rank to the authorities, especially modern German history, which is an uninterrupted series of feats of submissiveness and patience. A veritable cult of state power developed in the German heart over the centuries, a cult which gradually created a bureaucratic theory and practice. Thanks to the efforts of German scholars, it subsequently formed the basis of all the political science now taught in the universities of Germany.

History likewise attests forcefully to the aggressive and tyrannical aspirations of the German nation, from the German crusader-knights and barons of the Middle Ages to the last philistine burgher of modern times.

No one has experienced those aspirations as bitterly as the Slavs. It may be said that the entire historical mission of the Germans, at least in the north and the east, and, of course, as the Germans themselves understand it, consisted – and still does, by and large – of exterminating, enslaving, and forcibly Germanizing the Slavs.

It is a long, sad story, the memory of which is preserved deep in the hearts of the Slavs and will without doubt take its toll in the final, inevitable struggle of the Slavs against the Germans, unless social revolution reconciles them first.

For an accurate assessment of the aggressive aspirations of German society as a whole, a brief glance at the development of German patriotism since 1815 will suffice.

From 1525, the time of the bloody suppression of the peasant rebellion, to the literary renaissance of the second half of the eighteenth century, Germany remained sunk in a deep sleep, interrupted at times by cannon fire and terrible scenes and experiences of merciless war, of which it was for the most part both theater and victim. At such times it would wake up in fright but would soon go back to sleep again, lulled by Lutheran sermons.

In this period of almost two and a half centuries, under the influence of those sermons, its obedience and servile patience developed to the utmost, attaining virtually heroic proportions. A system of unconditional obedience to and blessing of authority formed at this time and was absorbed into the entire life, flesh, and blood of every German. A science of administration and a pedantically systematic, inhuman, and impersonal bureaucratic practice developed along with it. Every German official became a priest of the state, prepared to sacrifice his most beloved son on the altar of state service, not with a knife but with a clerk's pen. At the same time the German nobility, incapable of anything other than military activity and servile intrigue, was offering its mercenary sword and its unscrupulous services as courtiers and diplomats to better-paying European courts. The German burgher, obedient unto death, endured, toiled, paid heavy taxes without complaint, lived in squalid and cramped conditions, and consoled himself with the idea of the immortality of the soul. The power of the countless princes who divided up Germany among themselves was unlimited. Professors slapped each other's faces and then denounced each other to the authorities. The students, dividing their time between dead knowledge and beer, were fully deserving of them. As far as the laboring people were concerned, nobody spoke of them or gave them a thought.

That was still Germany's situation in the second half of the eighteenth century, when suddenly, by some miracle, from this bottomless abyss of vileness and vulgarity, a magnificent literature arose, created by Lessing and culminating in Goethe, Schiller, Kant, Fichte, and Hegel. As is well known, this literature took shape at first under the direct influence of the great French literature of the seventeenth and eighteenth centuries, first the classical and then the philosophical literature. From the very start, however, in the works of its progenitor,

Lessing, it took on a fully independent character, content, and form, drawn, it may be said, from the very depths of German contemplative life.

In our opinion, this literature constitutes the greatest, and virtually the only, service of modern Germany. With its boldness and its broad scope it significantly advanced the human intellect and opened new horizons to thought. Its principal merit consists of the fact that while on the one hand it was a thoroughly national literature, at the same time it was to the highest degree humanistic and universal, which is the characteristic feature of all, or nearly all, of the European literature of the eighteenth century.

But whereas French literature, for example in the works of Voltaire, Rousseau, Diderot and the other encyclopedists, strove to transpose all human problems from the realm of theory to practice, German literature chastely and rigorously preserved its theoretical and largely pantheistic character. It was the literature of an abstractly poetic and metaphysical humanism, from the heights of which its devotees looked upon real life with scorn – a scorn fully merited, however, since everyday German life was vulgar and repellent.

Thus German life was divided into two opposed spheres, which negated but also complemented each other. One was a world of broad and lofty but wholly abstract humanism, the other a world of historically inherited submissive vileness and vulgarity. The French Revolution found Germany in this bifurcated condition.

As we know, the revolution was welcomed with great approval and, it may be said, with real sympathy by almost the whole of literary Germany. Goethe frowned a bit and grumbled that the noise of those unprecedented events was disturbing him and breaking the thread of his learned and artistic pursuits and poetic meditations. The majority of the representatives and adherents of the latest literature, metaphysics, and science, however, greeted the revolution with joy, in the expectation that it would realize all their ideals. Freemasonry, which still played a very serious role at the end of the eighteenth century and united progressive individuals of all the countries of Europe in an invisible but quite real brotherhood, formed a vital bond between the French revolutionaries and the noble dreamers of Germany. When the republican forces, having heroically rebuffed Brunswick[64] and put him to disgraceful flight, first crossed the Rhine, they were met by the Germans as deliverers.

Their sympathetic attitude toward the French did not last long. The French soldiers, as was befitting of Frenchmen, were of course very polite, and as republicans were deserving of every sympathy, but they were soldiers all the same, that is, unceremonious representatives and servants of force. The presence of such liberators soon became onerous for the Germans, and their enthusiasm cooled considerably. The revolution itself, moreover, assumed such an energetic character that it could no longer be reconciled in any way with the abstract ideas and the philistine and contemplative temperament of the Germans. Heine[65] relates that in the end, in the whole of Germany only the Königsberg philosopher Kant retained his sympathy for the French Revolution, despite the September Massacres, the execution of Louis XVI and Marie Antoinette, and Robespierre's Terror.[66]

Then the republic was replaced, first by the Directory, then by the Consulate, and finally by the empire. The republican army became a blind and for a long time victorious instrument of Napoleon's ambition, which was colossal to the point of madness, and at the end of 1806, after the battle of Jena, Germany was completely enslaved.

Its new life began in 1807. Who does not know the amazing story of the rapid rebirth of the Kingdom of Prussia, and through it of the whole of Germany? In 1806 the state power created by Frederick the Great and his father and grandfather lay completely in ruins. The army, which had been organized and trained by the great commander, had been destroyed. All of Germany and all of Prussia, except for the outlying territory of Königsberg, had been subjugated by French troops and was actually governed by French prefects, while the political existence of the Kingdom of Prussia had been spared only thanks to the entreaties of Alexander I, the emperor of Russia.

In this critical situation a group of people, ardent Prussian or, even more, German patriots, came forward. Intelligent, bold, and resolute, having learned the lessons and profited by the example of the French Revolution, they conceived the idea of saving Prussia and Germany by means of broad liberal reforms. At another time, before the battle of Jena, for instance, or perhaps after 1815, when noble and bureaucratic reaction came into its own once again, they would not have dared even to think about such reforms. The court and military party would have crushed them, and their very virtuous and very stupid King Frederick William III, who knew nothing except his unlimited divine right, would have locked them up in Spandau Prison as soon as they had uttered one word on the subject.

In 1807, however, the situation was entirely different. The military, bureaucratic, and aristocratic party had been destroyed, put to shame and humiliated to such a degree that it had lost its voice, while the king had received a lesson that could have made even a fool wise, at least for a short time. Baron Stein[67] became prime minister and with a bold hand began to break up the old order and build a new one in Prussia.

His first task was to emancipate the peasants from serfdom, with not only the right but the real possibility of acquiring land as personal property. His second task was to abolish the privileges of the nobility and to make all estates equal before the law in respect to military and civil service. His third task was to create a provincial and municipal administration on an elective basis. But his principal task was to reform the army completely, or, rather, to turn the whole Prussian nation into an army, divided into three categories: the active army, the *Landwehr*, and the *Sturmwehr*.[a] Finally, Stein gave broad access and refuge in the Prussian universities to all that was intelligent, ardent, and vital in Germany. He took into the University of Berlin the renowned Fichte, who had just been expelled from Jena by the Duke of Weimar (the friend and protector of Goethe) for advocating atheism.

Fichte began his lectures with a fiery speech directed primarily at German youth but published subsequently under the title *Addresses to the German Nation*.[68] In it he predicted very well and clearly the future political greatness of Germany and expressed the proud patriotic conviction that the German nation was predestined to be the highest representative, the agent, the culmination of humanity. To be sure, this was a delusion into which other nations had fallen before the Germans, and with greater justification – the ancient Greeks, the Romans, in modern times the French – but it became deeply rooted in the consciousness of every German and has assumed crude and grotesque proportions in Germany today. In Fichte, at least, it bore a truly heroic character. He voiced it under the French bayonets, at a time when Berlin was governed by a Napoleonic general and French drums sounded in the streets. Moreover, the world-view which this idealist philosopher brought to German patriotic pride in fact

[a] I.e., the Territorial Reserve and the Home Guard.

breathed humanism, the broad, somewhat pantheistic humanism with which the great German literature of the eighteenth century was stamped. But contemporary Germans have retained the vast pretensions of their philosopher-patriot while rejecting his humanism. They simply do not understand it and are even prepared to laugh at it as a degenerate product of abstract, utterly impractical thought. The patriotism of a Bismarck or a Marx is more intelligible to them.

Everyone knows how the Germans finally rose up, taking advantage of Napoleon's total defeat in Russia and his hapless retreat, or, rather, flight with the remnants of his army. Of course, they praise themselves to the skies for this uprising, and completely in vain. There never was any independent popular uprising, strictly speaking. Once Napoleon had been beaten and ceased to be dangerous and fearsome, the German army corps, first the Prussians and then the Austrians, which had previously been directed against Russia, now turned against him and joined the victorious Russian army pursuing him. The legitimate but till now hapless Prussian King Frederick William III, with tears of emotion and gratitude, embraced his deliverer the Russian emperor in Berlin and then issued a proclamation summoning his loyal subjects to a legitimate uprising against the illegitimate and impertinent Napoleon. Obeying the voice of their king and father, the German (primarily Prussian) youth rose up and formed legions, which were incorporated into the regular army. The Prussian privy councillor, well-known spy, and official informer was not very far wrong when in 1815 he published a pamphlet that aroused the indignation of all the patriots. In it he denied that there had been any independent activity on the part of the people in the liberation, stating "that the Prussian citizenry took up arms only when the king ordered them to, and that there was nothing heroic in this, nothing extraordinary, merely the fulfillment of any loyal subject's duty."[69]

Be that as it may, Germany was liberated from the French yoke, and when the war finally ended it took up the work of internal reform under the supreme leadership of Austria and Prussia. The first task was to mediatize the multitude of petty principalities, which were thus transformed from independent states into honored and (with the billion francs taken from the French) richly indemnified subjects. A total of thirty-nine states and rulers remained in Germany.

The second task was to establish mutual relations between the princes and their subjects.

During the period of struggle, when Napoleon's sword still hung over everyone and the princes great and small needed the *loyal* assistance of their people, they had made a number of promises. The Prussian government, and all the others after it, promised a constitution. Now that the calamity was past, however, the governments became convinced that a constitution was no longer useful. The Austrian government, led by Prince Metternich, bluntly declared its determination to return to the old patriarchal order. The good Emperor Francis,[70] who enjoyed enormous popularity among the Viennese burghers, expressed it forthrightly in an audience he gave to the professors of the Laibach Lyceum: "There is a vogue at present for new ideas," he said, "which I cannot and will never approve. Abide by the old ideas; our forebears prospered with them, why should we not also? I do not need scholars, only honest and obedient citizens. To educate them is your obligation. He who serves me must teach what I command. Anyone who cannot or will not do this should take himself away, or I will dismiss him . . ."[71]

Francis[a] kept his word. In Austria, unlimited arbitrariness reigned until 1848. In the most rigorous fashion a system of government was introduced whose main objective was to lull its subjects to sleep and turn them into blockheads. Thought slumbered and remained stagnant even in the universities, where instead of living knowledge there was rote learning. There was no literature except for crude novels of a scandalous character, and very bad poetry. The natural sciences were fifty years behind the rest of Europe. There was no political life. Agriculture, industry, and trade were afflicted with a Chinese immobility. The people, the laboring masses, were in total bondage. Had it not been for Italy, and to some degree Hungary, which disturbed the happy slumber of Austria's subjects with their seditious unrest, the whole empire could have been taken for a vast kingdom of the dead.

Relying on this realm, Metternich tried for thirty-three years to reduce the rest of Europe to the same condition. He became the cornerstone, the soul, the leader of European reaction, and of course his principal concern necessarily was to stifle any liberal impulse in Germany.

Prussia troubled him most of all. This new, young state had joined

---

[a] The text has Francis Joseph, who came to the throne in 1848.

the ranks of the great powers only at the end of the previous century, thanks to the genius of Frederick the Great, thanks to Silesia (which he had taken from Austria) and the partitions of Poland, and thanks to the bold liberalism of Baron Stein, Scharnhorst,[72] and their associates in Prussia's rebirth, as a result of which Prussia had taken the lead in Germany's liberation. It seemed that circumstances, recent events, the experiences, successes, and victories, and the very interests of Prussia should have impelled its government to advance boldly along the new path which had proved so fortunate and so salutary for it. That was precisely what Metternich feared so greatly, and ought to have feared.

From the time of Frederick the Great, when all the rest of Germany was reduced to the utmost degree of intellectual and moral bondage and was being sacrificed to unceremonious, brazen, and cynical governments, to the intrigues and thievery of corrupt courts, Prussia had realized the ideal of orderly, honest, and, insofar as possible, just administration. Prussia had only one despot, though an implacable and fearsome one – reason of state, or the logic of state interest, to which everything else was sacrificed and before which every right had to bow down. On the other hand, there was much less personal, depraved arbitrariness in Prussia than in any of the other German states. The Prussian subject was a slave of the state, which was personified by the king, but not a plaything of his court, his mistresses, or his favorites, as in the rest of Germany. Therefore all of Germany already regarded Prussia with particular respect.

That respect increased greatly and turned into positive sympathy after 1807. At that time the Prussian state, having been reduced almost to complete extinction, began to seek its salvation and the salvation of Germany in liberal reforms, and after a whole series of felicitous reorganizations the Prussian king called on the whole of Germany as well as his own people to rise up against the French conqueror, while promising to grant his subjects the most broadly liberal constitution upon the conclusion of the war. A date was even set for the fulfillment of this promise, September 1, 1815. This solemn royal promise was issued on May 22, 1815, after Napoleon's return from the island of Elba and before the battle of Waterloo. It was merely a reiteration of the collective promise that had been made by all the rulers of Europe gathered at the Congress of Vienna, in panic-stricken terror at the news of Napoleon's landing. It was included as one of the most essential points in the statutes of the newly created *German Confederation*.[73]

Some of the petty princes of central and south Germany kept their promise quite honorably. In north Germany, however, where the military, bureaucratic, and noble element decisively predominated, the old aristocratic order was maintained under the direct and forceful protection of Austria.

From 1815 to May of 1819 all of Germany hoped that Prussia, in opposition to Austria, would take the common aspiration for liberal reforms under its powerful patronage. All the circumstances and the obvious interest of the Prussian government seemed to incline it in this direction. Even apart from Frederick William III's solemn promise of May 1815, all the ordeals Prussia had undergone since 1807 and its amazing restoration, which it owed chiefly to the liberalism of its government, should have reinforced this inclination. Finally, there was an even more important consideration impelling the Prussian government to declare itself the open and resolute patron of liberal reforms: the historic rivalry between the young Prussian monarchy and the ancient Austrian Empire.

Who would head Germany, Austria or Prussia? That was the question posed by previous events and by the logic of their respective positions. Germany, like a slave grown accustomed to obedience, did not know how to live freely and did not wish to do so. It sought a powerful master, a supreme commander to whom it could completely subordinate itself and who would unite it into an undivided state and give it an honored place among the great powers of Europe. Either the Austrian emperor or the Prussian king could serve as such a master. Both together could not occupy this position without paralyzing each other and thereby condemning Germany to its former helplessness and powerlessness.

Austria would naturally have tried to pull Germany back. It could not have acted otherwise. Obsolete and reduced to the stage of senile debility at which movement of any sort becomes fatal and immobility a necessary condition for maintaining a decrepit existence, to save itself it had to defend immobility as a principle not just in Germany but throughout Europe. Any manifestation of national vitality, any progressive impulse in any corner of the European continent, was an offense and a threat to Austria. It was dying, and it wanted everyone to die with it. In politics, as in any other aspect of life, to go backwards or merely to remain in one place means death. It is understandable, therefore, that Austria would use its last strength, still formidable in a material sense, to stifle ruthlessly and resolutely all movement in Europe generally and in Germany in particular.

Because that was necessarily Austria's policy, Prussia's policy should have been exactly the opposite. After the Napoleonic Wars; after the Congress of Vienna, which significantly rounded out its territory at the expense of Saxony, from which it took an entire province; especially after the fateful battle of Waterloo, which was won by the joint armies of Prussia, under the command of Blücher, and England, under the command of Wellington; and after the second triumphal entry of Prussian forces into Paris, Prussia occupied fifth place among the paramount powers of Europe. But in respect to real power – state wealth, population, and even geographical position – it was as yet by no means able to compete with them. Stettin, Danzig, and Königsberg on the Baltic were insufficient for the formation not just of a strong navy but even of a significant merchant marine. Sprawling misshapenly and separated from its newly acquired Rhineland province by the possessions of other states, Prussia had extremely inconvenient frontiers from a military point of view, making attacks on it from the direction of south Germany, Hanover, Holland, Belgium, and France very easy and defense very difficult. Finally, its population in 1815 was barely 15 million.

Despite this material weakness, which had been much greater under Frederick II, the great king's administrative and military genius succeeded in establishing Prussia's political significance and military power. Napoleon reduced his achievement to dust, however. After the battle of Jena everything had to be created anew, and we have seen that only a series of the boldest and most liberal reforms enabled the enlightened and intelligent state patriots not merely to restore Prussia's former significance and power but considerably to increase them. In fact, they increased them to the degree that Prussia no longer ranked last among the great powers. They were insufficient, however, for Prussia to maintain that position for long without continued and determined efforts to enhance its political significance and moral influence, and also to round out and expand its frontiers.

To achieve these results, two different paths were open to Prussia. One, at least in appearance, was a more popular path, the other purely a state and military path. Taking the first one, Prussia would have stood boldly at the head of the constitutional movement in Germany. Frederick William III, following the great example of the celebrated William of Orange in 1688, would have inscribed on his standard: "For the Protestant faith and the liberty of Germany," thus becoming the open opponent of Austrian Catholicism and despotism. Taking the second path, having broken his solemn royal word and categorically renounced any further liberal reforms in Prussia, he would have stood just as openly on the side of reaction in Germany, while concentrating all his attention and efforts on improving his domestic administration and his army with a view to potential conquests in the future.

There was yet a third path, taken long ago, in truth, by the Roman Emperor Augustus and his successors, but abandoned after them, rediscovered only in recent times by Napoleon III and widened and improved by his pupil, Prince Bismarck. That is the path of state, military, and political despotism, camouflaged and embellished with the broadest, and most innocuous, forms of popular representation.

In 1815, however, that path was as yet completely unknown. At that time no one even suspected the truth which has now become obvious even to the most stupid despots, that so-called constitutional forms, or forms of popular representation, do not impede state, military, political, and financial despotism. Instead, they have the effect of legitimizing it and giving it a false appearance of popular government, and they can significantly enhance its internal strength and vigor.

No one knew it then, or indeed could have known it, because the full extent of the breach between the exploiting class and the exploited proletariat was by no means as clear either to the bourgeoisie or to the proletariat itself as it is today. Every government, and the bourgeoisie itself, believed that the people would stand behind the bourgeoisie; the latter had only to bestir itself, to give a sign, and all the people would rise up with it against the government. Now it is a different matter altogether: the bourgeoisie in every European country fears social revolution more than anything else and knows that the state is its only refuge from this threat. Therefore it always wants and demands as *strong* a state as possible, or, to put it simply, a military dictatorship. To spare its vanity, and also to deceive the masses more easily, it wants that dictatorship to be arrayed in forms of popular representation, which will enable it to exploit the people *in the people's own name.*

In 1815, however, neither this fear nor this artful policy existed yet in any of the states of Europe. On the contrary, the bourgeoisie everywhere was sincerely and naively liberal. It still believed that in working for itself it worked for everyone, and therefore it was not afraid of the people, it was not afraid of inciting them against the government. Hence, all governments, relying as much as possible on the nobility, regarded the bourgeoisie with hostility, as a revolutionary class.

There is no doubt that in 1815, or even much later, if Prussia had made the slightest declaration of liberalism, if the Prussian king had granted his subjects even the shadow of a bourgeois constitution, it would have been enough for the whole of Germany to recognize him as its leader. The non-Prussian Germans had not yet conceived the strong antipathy for Prussia that manifested itself much later, especially in 1848. On the contrary, all the Germanic countries looked to it with hope, expecting from it the word of liberation. Just half of those *liberal and representative institutions* which the Prussian government recently bestowed so generously not just on the Prussians but on all the non-Prussian Germans except the Austrians (without any detriment to its despotic power, however), would have sufficed for the whole of non-Austrian Germany, at least, to recognize Prussia's hegemony.

That was precisely what Austria feared so much, because it would have been enough to put it right then and there in the unfortunate and hopeless position in which it finds itself today. Had it lost its position of primacy in the German Confederation, it would have ceased to be a German power. We have seen that Germans make up only one-quarter of the population of the Austrian Empire. As long as Austria's German provinces, as well as certain of its Slavic provinces, such as Bohemia, Moravia, Silesia, and Styria, taken together formed one of the members of the German Confederation, the Austrian Germans, relying on the numerous inhabitants of Germany, could to a certain degree regard their whole empire as a German one. Once the empire had been detached from the German Confederation, however, as it has been now, its 9 million Germans (at that time even fewer) would have proved too weak to maintain their historical predominance. The Austrian Germans would have had no choice but to renounce their allegiance to the House of Habsburg and unite with the rest of Germany. That is exactly what they are aiming to do now, some consciously, others unconsciously, thereby condemning the Austrian Empire to imminent death.

Once Prussian hegemony within Germany had been confirmed, the Austrian government would have been compelled to remove its German provinces from inclusion in the Confederation. In the first place, leaving them in the Confederation would in effect have meant subordinating them – and through them the Austrian government itself – to the suzerainty of the king of Prussia. Secondly, the Austrian Empire in such case would have been divided into two parts, one German, recognizing Prussian hegemony, the other not recognizing it, and that would also have been fatal to the empire.

True, there was another method, which Prince Schwarzenberg wanted to try in 1850 but did not succeed (and indeed could not have succeeded) in doing so: to include in the German Confederation the whole of the Austrian Empire, with Hungary, Transylvania, and all its Slavic and Italian provinces. This attempt could not have succeeded because it would have been resisted desperately by Prussia and by most of the rest of Germany along with it, as it was in 1850,[74] and by all the other great powers, especially Russia and France. Finally, it would have aroused the indignation of the three-quarters of the Austrian population that hates the Germans – the Slavs, Magyars, Romanians, and Italians – to whom the very idea of becoming Germans seems ignominious.

Prussia and the whole of Germany would naturally have opposed such an attempt, the realization of which would have destroyed the former and deprived it of its special German character. As for the latter, Germany would have ceased to be the fatherland of the Germans and become a conglomeration of the most heterogeneous nationalities, chaotic and held together by force. Russia and France would not have consented because Austria, with the rest of Germany now subordinated to it, would suddenly have become the mightiest power on the European continent.

Therefore Austria had only one recourse: not to smother Germany by joining it in entirety, but at the same time not to allow Prussia to become the leader of the German Confederation. In pursuing this policy, Austria could count on the active assistance of France and Russia. The latter's policy until very recently – that is, until the Crimean War – consisted of systematically encouraging the mutual rivalry between Austria and Prussia so that neither one might prevail over the other, while at the same time provoking mistrust and fear in the small and medium-size states of Germany and protecting them against Austria and Prussia.

Prussia's influence on the rest of Germany was chiefly of a moral nature, based primarily on the expectation that the Prussian government, which not long ago had given so much proof of its patriotic and enlightened liberal orientation, would soon keep its promise and grant its subjects a constitution, thereby assuming leadership of the progressive movement throughout Germany. Metternich's chief concern, therefore, was to keep the Prussian king from granting his subjects a constitution while getting him to join the Austrian emperor in assuming leadership of the reactionary movement in Germany. He found very enthusiastic support for this endeavor both in France, which was ruled by the Bourbons, and in Emperor Alexander I, who was ruled by Arakcheev.[75]

Metternich found equally enthusiastic support within Prussia itself, from (with very minor exceptions) the entire Prussian nobility, the upper bureaucracy, military as well as civil, and, finally, from the king.

Frederick William III was a very nice man, but he was a king, and well and truly a king: a despot by nature, upbringing, and habit. Furthermore, he was a devout and faithful son of the evangelical church, the cardinal dogma of which is that "all power is of God." He sincerely believed in his divine anointment, in his right, or, rather, his duty, to command, and in the obligation of each of his subjects to obey his orders and execute them without question. Such a cast of mind was incompatible with liberalism. To be sure, when misfortune struck the state he made a number of very liberal promises to his faithful subjects. He did so, however, in obedience to state necessity, to which even the sovereign must pay homage as the highest law. Now the crisis had passed, meaning that the promises, which would have been harmful to the people themselves if they were fulfilled, did not have to be kept.

Bishop Eylert explained it very well in a contemporary sermon. "The king," he said, "has acted like a wise father. On his birthday or his recovery from an illness, touched by the love of his children, he made them all sorts of promises. Then, with appropriate serenity, he modified them and restored his natural and salutary authority."[76] Around him the entire court, the military chiefs, and the upper bureaucracy were imbued with the same spirit. During the period of misfortune which they had brought down on Prussia they kept quiet, suffering in silence the unavoidable reforms of Baron Stein and his principal associates. Now they began to intrigue and to make more trouble than ever.

They were sincere reactionaries, no less than the king himself, perhaps even more. German patriotism was something they not only did not understand but hated with all their hearts. The German flag was repugnant to them and seemed the flag of revolt. All they knew was their dear Prussia – which, however, they were prepared to ruin once again if only to avoid making the least concession to the hated liberals. The idea of recognizing any political rights for the bourgeoisie, especially the rights of criticism and financial control, the idea of possible equality with them, simply horrified them and made them indescribably indignant. They wanted to expand and round out Prussia's frontiers, but only by means of conquest. From the very beginning their objective was clear: in contrast to the liberal party, which strove to Germanize Prussia, they wanted to Prussify Germany.

Moreover, beginning with their leader, the king's friend Prince Wittgenstein, who soon became prime minister, almost all of them were in the pay of Metternich.[77] Against them stood a small group of men, friends and associates of Baron Stein (who had already been dismissed). This handful of state patriots continued to make incredible efforts to keep the king on the path of liberal reforms. Finding no support anywhere except in public opinion, which was scorned equally by the king, the court, the bureaucracy, and the army, they were soon overthrown. Metternich's gold and the reactionary orientation of the highest circles in Germany proved much stronger.

To implement purely liberal plans, therefore, only one course remained open to Prussia: to refine and gradually augment its administrative and financial resources, as well as its military power, with a view to future annexations within Germany, that is, the gradual conquest of Germany as a whole. This course, moreover, conformed fully to the traditions and the very character of the Prussian monarchy, which was a military, bureaucratic, police regime – in other words, a state, exercising legalized force in all of its external and domestic actions. From that time the ideal of *rational and enlightened despotism* began to form in German official circles, and it governed Prussia until 1848. It was as contrary to the liberal aspirations of pan-German patriotism as was Metternich's despotic obscurantism.

Quite naturally, a struggle by the liberal-patriotic party against the reaction which found powerful expression in the domestic and foreign policies of Austria and Prussia arose more or less throughout Germany, but primarily in the south. It was a duel of sorts, which lasted exactly fifty-five years, from 1815 to 1870. It took various forms, but with results that were almost always identical and always highly lamentable for the German liberals. It can be divided into several periods:

1. The period of liberalism and Francophobia of the Teutonic romantics, from 1815 to 1830.

2. The period of overt imitation of French liberalism, from 1830 to 1840.

3. The period of economic liberalism and radicalism, from 1840 to 1848.

4. The period, albeit very brief, of decisive crisis, from 1848 to 1850, ending with the death of German liberalism. And lastly,

5. The period from 1850 to 1870, which began with the stubborn and, it can be said, final struggle of dying liberalism against statism in the Prussian parliament and ended with the definitive triumph of the Prussian monarchy throughout Germany.

German liberalism of the first period, from 1815 to 1830, was not an isolated phenomenon. It was only a national, though highly distinctive, offshoot of European liberalism, which almost everywhere, from Madrid to Petersburg and from Germany to Greece, began a very energetic struggle against pan-European monarchical and aristocratic-clerical reaction. The latter had triumphed with the restoration of the Bourbons to the thrones of France, Spain, Naples, Parma, and Lucca, the return of the pope and the Jesuits to Rome and the Piedmontese king to Turin, and the establishment of the Austrians in Italy.

The principal and official representative of this truly international reaction was the Holy Alliance (*la sainte alliance*), first concluded by Russia, Prussia, and Austria but later adhered to by all the European powers, great and small, except for England, Rome, and Turkey. It had its origins in romanticism. The idea first ripened in the mystical imagination of the celebrated Baroness Krüdener, who enjoyed the favors of the womanizing Alexander I, still quite young and not entirely past his prime.[78] She convinced him that he was a "white angel" sent down from heaven to save unhappy Europe from the clutches of the "black angel," Napoleon, and to establish God's order on earth. Alexander readily came to believe in his mission and proposed to Prussia and Austria the conclusion of a *Holy Alliance*. The three divinely anointed monarchs, appropriately invoking the Holy Trinity as witnesses, pledged their unconditional and indissoluble brotherhood and proclaimed as the objective of the alliance the triumph of God's will, morality, justice, and peace on earth. They promised always to act in concert, assisting each other in counsel and deed in any struggle that might be incited against them by the spirit of darkness, meaning the desire of nations for liberty. In actuality, this promise meant that they would wage collective and relentless war on all manifestations of liberalism in Europe, supporting to the end and at any cost the feudal institutions overthrown and destroyed by the revolution but reestablished by the restoration.

If Alexander was the bombastic and melodramatic spokesman for the Holy Alliance, its real leader was Metternich. Germany at that time was the cornerstone of European reaction, as it had been during the Great Revolution and as it is today.

Thanks to the Holy Alliance, reaction was internationalized, and, in consequence, uprisings against it also took on an international character. The period from 1815 to 1830 was the last heroic period of the bourgeoisie in Western Europe.

The forcible restoration of monarchical absolutism and feudal-clerical institutions, which deprived this respectable class of all the benefits it had won during the revolution, naturally had the effect of turning it once again into a more or less revolutionary class. In France, Italy, Spain, Belgium, and Germany, bourgeois secret societies were formed with the objective of overthrowing the order that had just triumphed. In England, in accordance with the customs of that country, the only one where constitutionalism had put down deep and vital roots, the ubiquitous struggle of bourgeois liberalism against resurrected feudalism assumed the character of legal agitation and parliamentary upheavals. In France, Belgium, Italy, and Spain it was obliged to take a decidedly revolutionary turn, which was echoed even in Russia and Poland. In all these countries each secret society uncovered and destroyed by the government was immediately replaced by another, and all had a single objective – armed insurrection, the organization of an uprising. The entire history of France from 1815 to 1830 was a series of attempts to topple the Bourbon throne, and after a number of failures the French finally achieved their goal in 1830. Everyone knows the history of the Spanish, Neapolitan, Piedmontese, Belgian, and Polish revolutions of 1830–31, and the Decembrist uprising in Russia. In all these countries, with success in some, without success in others, the insurrections were extremely serious. A great deal of blood was shed, a great many precious sacrifices were exacted – in short, it was a grave and often heroic struggle. Now let us take a look at what was happening in Germany at this time.

Throughout this first period we encounter only two expressions of the liberal spirit in Germany that are at all noteworthy. The first was the famous Wartburg gathering of 1817. At Wartburg Castle, which had once served as the secret refuge of Luther, some 500 students gathered from all parts of Germany bearing the tricolor German national flag[a] and with tricolor sashes across their chests.

They were the spiritual children of Arndt, the patriotic professor and bard who composed the famous national anthem, "Wo ist das deutsche Vaterland?," and of Jahn, the equally patriotic father of all German gymnasts, who in the four words "fresh, joyful, godly, free" expressed the ideal of the blond, long-haired German youth.[79] Students from north and south Germany found it necessary to come together and declare loudly to the whole of Europe, and especially to all the governments of Germany, the demands of the German people. What exactly were they declaring and demanding?

Throughout Europe at that time, constitutional monarchy was in fashion. The imaginations of the bourgeois youth of France, Spain, Poland, and even Italy went no further than that. Only in Russia, the branch of the Decembrists known as the Southern Society under the leadership of Pestel and Muravev-Apostol, demanded the destruction of the Russian Empire and the establishment of a Slavic federal republic with all land to be distributed to the people.

The Germans had no such thought. They did not want to destroy anything. They had as little inclination then as they do now for an act of that kind, the primary and indispensable condition for any serious revolution. They did not even dream of raising a seditious, sacrilegious hand against any of their numerous father-sovereigns. All they wanted, all they asked, was that each of those father-sovereigns grant

[a] Black, red, and gold.

a constitution of some kind. In addition, they wanted an all-German parliament set above the local parliaments, and an all-German emperor set above the local princes as the representative of national unity. It was an extremely moderate demand, as we see, and also highly ridiculous. They wanted a monarchical federation and at the same time dreamed of the power of a unified German state – a patent absurdity. One need only subject the Germans' program to closer scrutiny, however, to become convinced that its seeming absurdity stems from a misunderstanding. The misunderstanding is the mistaken assumption that the Germans, in addition to national power and unity, also demanded liberty.

The Germans have never needed liberty. To them life is simply inconceivable without government, that is, without a supreme will and thought and an iron hand to order them about. The stronger the hand the prouder they are and the more cheerful life becomes for them. What distressed them was not the absence of liberty, which they could not have made use of, but the absence of a unified and indivisible national power instead of the multitude of petty tyrannies. Their secret passion, their sole objective, was to create a huge, pan-German, all-devouring state before which all other nations would tremble.

Therefore it is perfectly natural that they never wanted a popular revolution. In this respect the Germans proved eminently logical. State power cannot in fact be the product of popular revolution. It may perhaps be the product of a victory gained by a certain class over a popular uprising, as it was in France. Even in France, however, the final construction of a strong state required the strong and despotic hand of Napoleon. The German liberals hated Napoleon's despotism, but they were prepared to worship state power, Prussian or Austrian, as long as it agreed to become pan-German power.

Arndt's famous song, "Wo ist das deutsche Vaterland?," which to this day has remained the national anthem of Germany, fully expresses the passionate desire to create a powerful state. It asks, "where is the German's fatherland? Prussia? Austria? north or south Germany? western or eastern Germany?" Then it answers, "no, no, his fatherland must be much broader." It extends everywhere: "wherever the German language is heard and sings hymns to God in heaven."

Since the Germans are one of the most prolific nations in the world and send out colonies everywhere, filling all the capitals of Europe,

America, and even Siberia, soon the entire globe will have to submit to the authority of the pan-German emperor.

That was the real significance of the Wartburg student gathering. They sought and demanded a pan-German master who would rule them with an iron hand, and on the strength of their passionate and voluntary submission would make all of Europe tremble.

Now let us see how they declared their discontent. At the Wartburg Festival they first sang Luther's famous hymn, "A Mighty Fortress is Our God," then "Wo ist das deutsche Vaterland?" They shouted "vivat" to some German patriots and cursed the reactionaries. Finally, they made bonfires of a few reactionary pamphlets. That was all.

Of greater significance were two other events that occurred in 1819: the assassination of the Russian spy Kotzebue by a student, Sand, and the attempted assassination of a petty state dignitary of the petty Duchy of Nassau, von Ibell, by a young pharmacist, Karl Löning.[80] Both acts were thoroughly ridiculous, since they could have brought no benefit whatsoever. But at least they manifested the sincere passion, the heroism of self-sacrifice, and the unity of thought, word, and deed without which revolutionism inevitably degenerates into rhetoric and becomes a disgusting lie.

Except for those two events, none of the other expressions of German liberalism went beyond the realm of the most naive and highly ludicrous rhetoric. It was a period of wild Teutonism. The German students, children of philistines and future philistines themselves, fancied themselves Germans of ancient times as described by Tacitus and Julius Caesar – warlike descendants of Arminius, innocent inhabitants of the dense forests. As a result, they conceived a profound scorn not for their own petty-bourgeois world, as logic would have demanded, but for France, for the French, in general for anything that bore the mark of French civilization. Francophobia became an epidemic disease in Germany. The university students began to dress up in ancient German garb, just like our Slavophiles of the 1840s and 1850s, and quenched their youthful ardor with inordinate quantities of beer, while displaying their warlike valor in incessant duelling, which usually ended with facial scars. Patriotism and pseudo-liberalism found their fullest expression and satisfaction in the bellowing of militantly patriotic songs, with the national anthem, "Where is the German's fatherland?" – the prophetic hymn to the pan-German empire now achieved, or in the process of being achieved – of course occupying pride of place.

Anyone who compares these expressions of liberalism with what was occurring at the time in Italy, Spain, France, Belgium, Poland, Russia, and Greece, will agree that there was nothing more naive and ridiculous than German liberalism. Its most vehement manifestations were permeated with that doltish sense of obedience and loyalty to the sovereign, or, to put it more politely, that pious reverence for power and authority, the spectacle of which wrenched from Börne the painful exclamation (it is well known and we have cited it elsewhere): "Other nations are often slaves, but we Germans are always lackeys."*[81]

In fact, German liberalism, except for a very small number of individuals and cases, was merely a special form of German lackeyism, of a nation-wide ambition to be lackeys. It was merely an expression, disapproved by the censorship, of the general desire for a firm imperial hand. But this demand on the part of loyal subjects seemed an insurrection to the various governments, and they persecuted it like an insurrection.

The explanation lies in the rivalry between Austria and Prussia. Each would gladly have seated itself on the abolished throne of Barbarossa, but neither could consent to that throne being occupied by its rival. As a result, supported simultaneously by Russia and France and acting in concert with them, though for entirely different reasons, Austria and Prussia began to persecute as a manifestation of the most extreme liberalism the common desire of all the Germans for the creation of a unified and powerful pan-German empire.

Kotzebue's assassination was the signal for the most ferocious reaction. German princes and ministers began to hold meetings and conferences, and there were international congresses in which Alexander I and a French envoy took part. A series of measures prescribed by the German Confederation bound the poor German liberal lackeys hand and foot. They were forbidden to engage in gymnastic exercises or sing patriotic songs; all they had left was beer. Censorship was established everywhere – and what was the result? Germany suddenly

---

* Lackeyism is voluntary slavery. A strange thing! It would seem that no slavery could be worse than that of the Russians. Among Russian students, however, there has never existed such a servile attitude toward professors and the authorities as exists to this day among all the German students.

grew calm, the *Burschen*[a] submitted without a word of protest, and in the eleven years from 1819 to 1830 there was not the slightest manifestation of political life anywhere on German soil.

This fact is so striking that the German professor Müller, who wrote a fairly detailed and truthful history of the fifty years from 1816 to 1865, in recounting the circumstances of this sudden and truly marvelous pacification, exclaims: "is any further proof needed that there is no basis for revolution in Germany?"[82]

The second period of German liberalism began in 1830 and ended around 1840. It was a period of almost blind imitation of the French. The Germans stopped baiting the Gauls and instead turned all their hatred against Russia.

German liberalism awoke from its eleven-year sleep not of its own accord but as a result of the three June Days in Paris, which delivered the first blow to the Holy Alliance by driving out a legitimate king.[83] Revolution then flared up in Belgium and Poland. Italy also roused itself but, betrayed to the Austrians by Louis-Philippe, was subjected to an even heavier yoke. In Spain a civil war broke out between the Cristinists and the Carlists.[84] In these circumstances even Germany could not help but awaken.

Its awakening was made easier by the fact that the July Revolution scared all the German governments to death, including those of Austria and Prussia. Until the advent of Bismarck, with his king-emperor on the German throne, all the German governments, despite their external appearance of military, political, and bourgeois strength, morally were very weak and lacked confidence in themselves.

That undeniable fact seems very strange in view of the German people's innate sentiments of affection and loyalty. What would have made the governments anxious and frightened? They sensed, they knew, that though the Germans obeyed their governments as good subjects should, they could not abide them. What had they done to arouse the hatred of a people so disposed to worship its rulers? What were the reasons for that hatred?

There were two. The first was the predominance of the noble element in the bureaucracy and the army. The July Revolution abolished the vestiges of feudal and clerical domination in France; in

---

[a] University students.

England, too, bourgeois-liberal reform triumphed after the July Revolution.[85] In general, 1830 marked the beginning of the complete triumph of the bourgeoisie in Europe – except in Germany. There, until very recently, that is, until the installation of the aristocrat Bismarck, the feudal party continued to reign. All the highest government posts and a large share of the lower ones, both in the bureaucracy and in the army, were in its hands. Everyone knows how contemptuously, how haughtily German aristocrats, princes, counts, barons, and even mere "von"s treat a burgher. According to the famous dictum of Prince Windischgrätz,[86] the Austrian general who shelled Prague in 1848 and Vienna in 1849, "human beings start only with barons."

The nobility's predominance was all the more offensive to the German burghers in that the nobility in every respect, in wealth as well as in intellectual development, is incomparably inferior to the bourgeois class. Nevertheless, it commanded everyone and everywhere. The burghers were granted only the right to pay and obey. That was exceedingly disagreeable to them. Despite their readiness to worship their legitimate sovereigns, they could not abide governments that were almost exclusively in the hands of the nobility.

It is remarkable, however, that several times they tried but were unable to throw off the nobility's yoke. It even survived the stormy years of 1848 and 1849 and is only now beginning to undergo systematic destruction – at the hands of the Pomeranian nobleman, Prince Bismarck.

We have already explained the second, and principal, reason for the Germans' antipathy toward their governments. The latter were opposed to Germany's unification into a strong state. Thus they offended all the bourgeois political instincts of the German patriots. The governments knew it and therefore distrusted their subjects. They were truly afraid of them, despite their subjects' constant efforts to demonstrate their boundless obedience, their utter innocuousness.

As a result of these misunderstandings, the governments very much feared the consequences of the July Revolution. They feared them so much that the most harmless and bloodless riot in the streets, a *Putsch*, as the Germans call it, was enough to impel the kings of Saxony and Hanover and the dukes of Hesse-Darmstadt and Brunswick to grant their subjects a constitution. Moreover, Prussia and Austria, even Metternich himself, hitherto the soul of reaction throughout Germany, now advised the German Confederation not to oppose the *legitimate* demands of their loyal subjects. In the parliaments of south Germany the leaders of the so-called liberal parties began to speak very loudly of renewing their demands for an all-German parliament and the election of an all-German emperor.

Everything hinged on the outcome of the Polish revolution. Had it triumphed, the Prussian monarchy, torn from its northeastern moorings and forced to make restitution of at least a considerable part if not all of its Polish provinces, would have had to seek a new point of support in Germany itself. Since it could not yet have done so by means of conquest, it would have had to win the indulgence and love of the rest of Germany by means of liberal reforms, boldly rallying all the Germans under the imperial flag . . . In short, what has been done now would have been accomplished then, though by different methods, and perhaps would have been accomplished from the start in more liberal forms. Instead of Prussia swallowing Germany, as it has today, Germany would have seemed to be swallowing Prussia. (It would only have seemed to do so, however, because in fact Germany would still have been enslaved by the power of Prussia's state organization.)

The Poles, however, were betrayed and abandoned by all of Europe and were finally defeated despite their heroic resistance. Warsaw fell, and with it all the hopes of German patriotism. King Frederick William III, who had rendered such significant services to his son-in-law, Emperor Nicholas, was emboldened by the latter's victory to throw off his mask and begin persecuting the pan-German patriots more than ever. The latter, rallying all their forces, then made a final solemn declaration – if not a powerful one then at least a very noisy one, preserved in modern German history under the name of the Hambach Festival of May 1832.

At Hambach, in the Bavarian Palatinate, some 30,000 men and women gathered on this occasion. The men wore tricolor sashes across their chests, the women tricolor scarves, all of them, of course, standing beneath tricolor German flags. What was spoken of at this meeting was no longer a federation of Germanic lands and Germanic peoples but pan-German centralization. Some of the orators, such as Dr. Wirth,[87] referred to a German republic and even a European federal republic, a United States of Europe.

These were only words, however, words of anger, spite, and

despair aroused in German hearts by the manifest unwillingness or inability of the German princes to create a pan-German empire. They were very eloquent words but were backed neither by will nor by organization and therefore had no force.

The Hambach meeting did not pass without leaving a trace, however. The peasants of the Bavarian Palatinate did not content themselves with words. Armed with scythes and pitchforks, they proceeded to destroy the castles of the nobility, the custom-houses, and government offices, consigning all documents to the flames, refusing to pay taxes, and demanding land for themselves and complete freedom on the land. This peasant rebellion, in its origins very similar to the general uprising of the German peasants in 1525, terribly frightened not only the conservatives but even the liberals and the republicans, whose bourgeois liberalism is in no way compatible with a real popular uprising. To the satisfaction of all, this renewed attempt at a peasant insurrection was put down by Bavarian troops.

Another consequence of the Hambach Festival was an attack by seventy armed students on the main sentry-post guarding the building of the German Confederation in Frankfurt. It was a ridiculous enterprise but a very bold one, and from that point of view worthy of respect. It was ridiculous because the German Confederation had to be fought not in Frankfurt but in Berlin or Vienna, and because seventy students were hardly sufficient to break the power of reaction in Germany. True, they hoped that the whole population of Frankfurt would rise up behind them and with them, not suspecting that the government had been warned several days beforehand of this senseless attempt. The government did not feel it necessary to forestall it, however, but allowed it to be carried out so as to have a good pretext for finally annihilating *revolutionaries and revolutionary aspirations* in Germany.

The fiercest reaction did in fact ensue in all the countries of Germany in the wake of the Frankfurt incident. In Frankfurt a central commission was set up, under the direction of which special commissions operated in all the big and small states. Austrian and Prussian state inquisitors, of course, sat on the central commission. It was a veritable festival for the officials and paper factories of Germany, for an immeasurable quantity of paper was consumed. More than 1,800 people were arrested throughout Germany, including a number of respectable individuals, such as professors, doctors, and lawyers – the whole flower of liberal Germany. Many fled, but many remained imprisoned until 1840, some until 1848.

We saw a considerable number of these desperate liberals in March 1848 in the pre-parliament and then in the National Assembly.[88] Without exception they all turned out to be desperate reactionaries.

All political movement came to an end in Germany with the Hambach Festival, the peasant uprising in the Palatinate, and the Frankfurt incident and the huge trial that followed it. A stillness of the grave descended, lasting without the slightest interruption right up to 1848. Literary movement took the place of political movement.

As we have already said, in contrast to the first period of German liberalism (1815–30), a period of frenzied Francophobia, the second period (1830–40) as well as the third (to 1848) can be called purely French, at least in respect to belles-lettres and political literature. Heading this new orientation were two Jews: one a poet of genius, Heine, the other the remarkable pamphleteer, Börne. Both moved to Paris almost in the first days of the July Revolution, and from there they began to advocate French theories, French institutions, and Parisian life to the Germans, the first in his poems, the second in his *Letters from Paris*.[89]

It can be said that they effected a revolution in German literature. Bookstores and libraries overflowed with translations and poor imitations of French plays, melodramas, comedies, stories, and novels. The bourgeois youth began to think, feel, talk, dress, and comb their hair in the French manner. That did not make them any more refined, however, just more ridiculous.

V

At the same time another orientation was taking root in Berlin, one more serious, more firmly grounded, and incomparably more characteristic of the German spirit. As often happens in history, Hegel's death, which occurred shortly after the July Revolution, confirmed the domination of his metaphysical thought, the reign of Hegelianism, in Berlin, in Prussia, and then throughout Germany. Prussia, at least for the time being and for the reasons set forth above, had renounced the unification of Germany by means of liberal reforms. It could not and would not, however, completely renounce moral and material hegemony over all the other German states and lands.

On the contrary, it constantly strove to become the intellectual and economic focal point of all Germany. To this end it employed two methods: the development of the University of Berlin, and a Customs Union.

In the last years of the reign of Frederick William III, the minister of culture was Privy Councillor von Altenstein, a statesman of the old liberal school of Baron Stein, Wilhelm von Humboldt, and the others.[90] In opposition to all of his ministerial colleagues and to Metternich, who, by systematically extinguishing all intellectual light hoped to consolidate the reign of reaction in Austria and throughout Germany, Altenstein remained true to the old liberal traditions insofar as it was possible in that reactionary period. He tried to gather all the progressive figures, all the luminaries of German scholarship, at the University of Berlin. Thus, at the very time that the Prussian government, in concert with Metternich and encouraged by Emperor Nicholas, was sparing no effort to stifle liberalism and the liberals, Berlin became the center, the brilliant focal point, of the scientific and spiritual life of Germany.

Hegel, whom the Prussian government had invited in 1818 to occupy Fichte's chair, died at the end of 1831. But he left behind him at the Universities of Berlin, Königsberg, and Halle a whole school of young professors, editors of his works, and ardent adherents and interpreters of his doctrines. Thanks to their tireless efforts, those doctrines were rapidly disseminated not only throughout Germany but in many other European countries, even in France, where they were introduced in thoroughly mutilated form by Victor Cousin.[91] They attracted a multitude of German and non-German intellects to Berlin as to a vital source of new light, not to say a new revelation. Unless you lived in those times, you will never understand how powerful the fascination of this philosophical system was in the 1830s and 1840s. It was believed that the eternally sought Absolute had finally been found and understood, and that it could be bought wholesale or retail in Berlin.

In the history of the development of human thought, Hegel's philosophy was in fact a significant phenomenon. It was the last and definitive word of the pantheistic and abstractly humanistic movement of the German spirit which began with the works of Lessing and achieved comprehensive development in the works of Goethe. This movement created a world that was infinitely broad, rich, lofty, and ostensibly perfectly rational, but that remained as alien to earthly life and reality as it was to the heaven of Christian theology. As a result, this world, like Fata Morgana neither reaching heaven nor touching the earth but suspended between them, turned the life of its adherents, its introspective and poetizing inhabitants, into an uninterrupted series of somnambulistic ideas and experiences. It rendered them totally unfit for life, or, even worse, condemned them to do in the real world exactly the opposite of what they worshipped in their poetic or metaphysical ideal.

This explains the amazing and quite common phenomenon that is still so striking in Germany today, that the fervent adherents of Lessing, Schiller, Goethe, Kant, Fichte, and Hegel could, and still can, serve as obedient and even willing agents of the inhumane and illiberal measures prescribed by their governments. It can even be said that in general the more elevated a German's ideal world, the uglier and more vulgar his life and actions in the real world.

Hegel's philosophy was the consummation of this world of lofty ideals. It fully expressed and explained this world in its metaphysical constructs and categories, and thereby destroyed it, attaining, by means of iron logic, complete awareness of it and of its own infinite groundlessness, unreality, and, to put it more simply, emptiness.

Hegel's school, as is well known, divided into two opposing parties. (Naturally, a third, middle party formed between them, which is not worth mentioning here.) One of them, the conservative party, found in the new philosophy the justification and legitimization of everything that exists, seizing upon Hegel's famous dictum "all that is real is rational." This party created the so-called official philosophy of the Prussian monarchy, which had been upheld by Hegel himself as the ideal political organization.

The other party, the so-called *revolutionary* Hegelians, proved more consistent than Hegel himself, and incomparably bolder. It tore away the conservative mask from his doctrines and revealed in all its nakedness the merciless negation that constitutes their essence. At the head of this party stood the illustrious Feuerbach, who pressed logical consistency not only to the utter negation of the whole divine world but to the negation of metaphysics itself. He could go no further. A metaphysician himself, he was obliged to yield his place to his legitimate heirs, the representatives of the school of materialists, or realists, most of whom, however, such as Büchner,[92] Marx, and

238

others, could not and cannot free themselves from the sway of abstract, metaphysical thought.

In the 1830s and 1840s the prevailing opinion was that a revolution which followed the dissemination of a Hegelianism developed in the direction of utter negation would be incomparably more radical, profound, merciless, and sweeping in its destructiveness than the revolution of 1793. That was because the philosophy worked out by Hegel and taken to its most extreme conclusions by his students was actually more complete, more comprehensive, and more profound than the thinking of Voltaire and Rousseau. They, as is well known, had had a direct and not always beneficial influence on the development and particularly the outcome of the first French Revolution. (It is undeniable, for example, that the admirers of Voltaire, who had instinctive contempt for the masses, the *stupid crowd*, were statesmen like Mirabeau, and that the most fanatical adherent of Jean-Jacques Rousseau, Maximilien Robespierre, reestablished divine and reactionary civic rites in France.)

In the 1830s and 1840s it was assumed that when the time for revolutionary action came again, the doctors of philosophy of the school of Hegel would leave the boldest figures of the 1790s far behind them and would amaze the world with their rigorously logical and relentless revolutionism. The poet Heine wrote many eloquent words on this subject. "All your revolutions are as nothing," he said to the French, "compared to our future German revolution. We, who had the audacity to destroy the entire divine world in a systematic, scientific fashion, will not hesitate before any idols on earth and will not rest until, on the ruins of privilege and power, we have won total equality and total liberty for the entire world." In much the same terms Heine proclaimed to the French the future marvels of the German revolution. And many people believed him. Alas, the experience of 1848 and 1849 was enough to shatter that belief. Not only did the German revolutionaries not outdo the heroes of the first French Revolution, they could not even compare with the French revolutionaries of the 1830s.

What was the reason for this lamentable bankruptcy? The explanation lies chiefly, of course, in the special historical character of the Germans, which disposes them much more to loyal obedience than to rebellion, but it lies also in the abstract method by which they approached revolution. Again in conformity with their nature, they proceeded not from life to thought but from thought to life. But anyone who takes abstract thought as his starting-point will never make it to life, for there is no road leading from metaphysics to life. An abyss separates them. No one has yet succeeded, nor will anyone ever succeed, in jumping across it, in making a *salto mortale*, or what Hegel himself called a *qualitative leap* (*qualitativer Sprung*), from the world of logic to the world of nature, of living reality. Anyone who relies on abstraction will die in it.

The living, concretely rational method of science is to proceed from the real fact to the idea that encompasses it, expresses it, and thereby explains it. In the practical world it is the movement from social life to the most rational possible organization of it, in accordance with the specifications, conditions, needs, and more or less passionate demands of social life itself.

That is the broad popular method, the method of real and total liberation, accessible to anyone and therefore truly popular. It is the method of the *anarchist* social revolution, which arises spontaneously within the people and destroys everything that opposes the broad flow of popular life so as to create new forms of free social organization out of the very depths of the people's existence.

The metaphysicians' method is entirely different. By "metaphysicians" we mean not just the followers of Hegel's doctrines, few of whom are left in the world, but also positivists and in general all the present-day worshippers of the goddess science; all those who by one means or another (if only by a very diligent but necessarily always imperfect study of the past and present) have created for themselves an ideal social organization into which, like new Procrustes, they want to force the life of future generations whatever the cost; in short, all those who, instead of regarding thought or science as one of the necessary manifestations of natural and social life, take such a narrow view of that poor life that they see in it only the practical manifestation of their own thought and their own always imperfect science.

Metaphysicians or positivists, all these knights of science and thought, in the name of which they consider themselves ordained to prescribe the laws of life, are reactionaries, conscious or unconscious. This is very easy to prove.

We are not speaking of metaphysics in general, with which only a few individuals occupied themselves even in those periods when it flourished most brilliantly. Even today, science in the broad sense of the term, serious science that is at all worthy of the name, is accessible only to a very insignificant minority. For example, out of 80 million inhabitants of Russia, how many serious scholars do we have? People who talk about science may number in the thousands, but there are barely a few hundred who are truly knowledgeable about it. If science is to prescribe the laws of life, however, then the great majority of mankind, millions of people, must be governed by one or two hundred scholars. In fact, the number is much smaller, for it is not just any science that renders an individual capable of governing society but the science of sciences, the crown of all the sciences – sociology, which presumes in the fortunate scholar a prior sound knowledge of all other sciences. Are there many such scholars even in the whole of Europe, let alone in Russia? Perhaps twenty or thirty! And those twenty or thirty scholars are to govern the entire world! Can you imagine a despotism more preposterous or abominable than that?

In the first place, those thirty scholars will most likely quarrel among themselves, and if they do unite it will be to the detriment of all mankind. By his very nature a scholar is disposed to intellectual and moral depravity of every kind, but his principal vice is to exalt his own knowledge and intellect and scorn all the ignorant. Let him govern, and he will become the most unbearable tyrant, for scholarly pride is repulsive, offensive, and more oppressive than any other. To be the slaves of pedants – what a fate for mankind! Give them free rein, and they will start performing the same experiments on human society that for the sake of science they now perform on rabbits, cats, and dogs.

We will esteem scholars according to their merits, but for the salvation of their intellect and morality they must not be given any social privileges or accorded any other right than the common one of freedom to propagate their convictions, ideas, and knowledge. Power should no more be given to them than to anyone else, for anyone who is invested with power by an invariable social*a* law will inevitably become the oppressor and exploiter of society.

It will be said that science will not always be the property of only a few people; the time will come when it will be accessible to each and every individual. Well, that time is still far off, and a great many social upheavals will have to be carried out before it begins. Until it does, who will consent to put his fate in the hands of scholars, in the hands

The text reads "socialist," but "social" appears to be called for.

of priests of science? Why bother, then, to wrest it from the hands of Christian priests?

It seems to us that anyone who imagines that after the social revolution all will be equally learned is profoundly mistaken. Science as such, then as now, will remain one of the numerous social specializations, the sole difference being that once classes have been abolished this specialization, which is accessible today only to members of the privileged classes, will become accessible to any individual with the vocation and desire to devote himself to it, though not at the expense of general manual labor, which will be obligatory for everyone.

Only general scientific education will become common property, particularly a familiarity with scientific method as a way of thinking, that is, of generalizing facts and drawing more or less correct conclusions from them. But there will always be very few encyclopedic minds, and, therefore, learned sociologists. Woe to mankind if thought ever became the source and sole guide of life, if science and learning began to govern society. Life would dry up, and human society would be turned into a dumb and servile herd. The government of life by science could have no other result than to turn all mankind into fools.

We revolutionary anarchists are proponents of universal popular education, liberation, and the broad development of social life, and hence are enemies of the state and of any form of statehood. By contrast to all metaphysicians, positivists, and scholarly or unscholarly worshippers of the goddess science, we maintain that natural and social life always precedes thought (which is merely one of its functions) but is never its result. Life develops out of its own inexhaustible depths by means of a succession of diverse facts, not a succession of abstract reflections; the latter, always produced by life but never producing it, like milestones merely indicate its direction and the different phases of its spontaneous and self-generated development.

In keeping with this conviction, we have neither the intention nor the least desire to impose on our own people or on any other an ideal social organization that we have drawn from books or thought up on our own. In the belief that the masses bear all the elements of their future organizational norms in their own more or less historically evolved instincts, in their everyday needs and their conscious and unconscious desires, we seek that ideal within the people themselves.

135

Since every state power, every government, by its nature and by its position stands outside the people and above them, and must invariably try to subject them to rules and objectives which are alien to them, we declare ourselves the enemies of every government and every state power, the enemies of state organization of any kind. We believe that the people can be happy and free only when they create their own life, organizing themselves from below upward by means of independent and completely free associations, subject to no official tutelage but open to the free and diverse influences of individuals and parties.

Those are the convictions of social revolutionaries, and for them we are called anarchists. We do not object to this term because we are in fact the enemies of all power, knowing that power corrupts those invested with it just as much as those compelled to submit to it. Under its pernicious influence the former become ambitious and avaricious despots, exploiters of society for their own personal or class advantage, and the latter become slaves.

Idealists of every stripe, metaphysicians, positivists, defenders of the predominance of science over life, and doctrinaire revolutionaries – all of them with identical ardor though different arguments uphold the idea of the state and of state power. *With perfect logic* (in their own terms), they regard it as the sole salvation of society. I say *with perfect logic* because once they have adopted the position – utterly false, in our view – that thought precedes life, that abstract theory precedes social practice, and that sociology must therefore be the point of departure for social upheavals and reconstructions, they necessarily conclude that since thought, theory, and science, at least for the present, are the property of a very few individuals, those few must be the directors of social life. They must be not only the instigators but the managers of all popular movements, and on the morrow of the revolution a new social organization must be created not by the free union of popular associations, communes, districts, and provinces from below upward, in conformity with popular needs and instincts, but solely by means of the dictatorial power of this learned minority, which *supposedly* expresses the will of all the people.

Both the theory of the state and the theory of so-called revolutionary dictatorship are based on this fiction of pseudo-popular representation – which in actual fact means the government of the masses by an insignificant handful of privileged individuals, elected (or even not elected) by mobs of people rounded up for voting and never knowing what or whom they are voting for – on this imaginary and abstract expression of the imaginary thought and will of all the people, of which the real, living people do not have the faintest idea.

The only difference between revolutionary dictatorship and the state is in external appearances. Essentially, they both represent the same government of the majority by a minority in the name of the presumed stupidity of the one and the presumed intelligence of the other. Therefore they are equally reactionary, both having the direct and inevitable result of consolidating the political and economic privileges of the governing minority and the political and economic slavery of the masses.

Now it is clear why the *doctrinaire revolutionaries*, whose objective is to overthrow existing governments and regimes so as to create their own dictatorship on their ruins, have never been and will never be enemies of the state. On the contrary, they have always been and will always be its most ardent defenders. They are enemies only of existing governments, because they want to take their place. They are enemies of existing political institutions because these preclude the possibility of their own dictatorship. At the same time, however, they are the most impassioned friends of state power, for were it not retained the revolution, having liberated the masses in earnest, would eliminate this pseudo-revolutionary minority's hope of putting a new harness on them and conferring upon them the blessings of their own governmental measures.

This is so true that even now we see the doctrinaire revolutionaries under Marx's leadership everywhere taking the side of the state and its supporters against popular revolution – at a time when reaction is triumphing throughout Europe; when all states, seized by the most malicious spirit of self-preservation and popular oppression, have clad themselves from head to toe in a threefold military, police, and financial armor, and under Bismarck's supreme leadership are preparing for a desperate struggle against social revolution; and when it would seem that all sincere revolutionaries ought to unite in order to repulse the desperate attack of international reaction.

In France, starting in 1870, they defended the statist republican-reactionary Gambetta against the revolutionary League of the South (*La Ligue du Midi*),[93] which alone could have saved France from German enslavement and from the still more dangerous and now victorious coalition of clericalists, legitimists, Orleanists, and Bonapartists. In Italy they are flirting with Garibaldi and the remnants of Mazzini's party. In Spain they openly took the side of Castelar, Pi y Margall, and the Madrid constituent Cortes.[94] Finally, in and around Germany, in Austria, Switzerland, Holland, and Denmark, they serve Prince Bismarck, whom they regard, by their own admission, as a highly useful revolutionary, and they are assisting him in the task of pan-Germanizing all those countries.

Now it is clear why the doctors of philosophy of the school of Hegel, despite their fiery revolutionism in the world of abstract ideas, in actuality turned out to be not revolutionaries in 1848 and 1849 but for the most part reactionaries, and why the majority of them today have become avowed supporters of Bismarck.

VI

In the 1830s[a] and 1840s, however, their pseudo-revolutionism, as yet untested in any way, found widespread credence. They believed in it themselves, though they manifested it for the most part in writings of a highly abstract character, so that the Prussian government paid no attention to it. Perhaps the government understood even then that they were working in its behalf.

On the other hand, the government was striving resolutely toward its principal objective – first the establishment of Prussian hegemony in Germany, then the outright subjection of all Germany to Prussia's undivided sway – through the use of a method which it felt to be incomparably more advantageous and appropriate than liberal reforms or even the encouragement of German science. This was the economic method, which would win it the heartfelt sympathy of the rich commercial and industrial bourgeoisie and the Jewish financial world of Germany, since both required extensive state centralization in order to flourish. We see a new example of this today in German Switzerland, where the big merchants, industrialists, and bankers are already beginning to voice open support for a very close political union with the vast German market – meaning the pan-German empire, which exerts the magnetic attraction (or suffocating pressure) of a boa constrictor on all the small countries around it.

[a] The text reads "1820s."

138

The idea of a *Customs Union*[95] came initially not from Prussia but from Bavaria and Württemberg, which formed such a union in 1828. But Prussia quickly seized upon the idea and its implementation.

Previously, Germany had as many custom-houses and as many different kinds of duty regulations as it had states. It was a truly intolerable situation and brought about the stagnation of German trade and industry. By lending its powerful hand to customs unification, therefore, Prussia did Germany a real service. By 1836, under the supreme administration of the Prussian monarchy, both Hesses, Bavaria, Württemberg, Saxony, Thuringia, Baden, Nassau, and the free city of Frankfurt belonged to the Customs Union – in all, a population of more than 27 million. Only Hanover, the Duchies of Mecklenburg and Oldenburg, the free cities of Hamburg, Lübeck, and Bremen, and, lastly, the entire Austrian Empire, remained outside the union.

Prussia's vital interest, however, lay precisely in the Austrian Empire's exclusion from the German Customs Union, for this exclusion, economic to begin with, would eventually lead to political exclusion as well.

In 1840 the *third period* of German liberalism began. It is very difficult to characterize. It was extraordinarily rich in its many-sided development of diverse orientations, schools, interests, and ideas, but equally poor in events. It was dominated by the unbalanced personality and chaotic writings of King Frederick William IV, who came to his father's throne in that year, 1840.[96]

With him came a complete change in Prussia's attitude toward Russia. In contrast to his father and to his brother, the current emperor of Germany, the new king detested Emperor Nicholas. Later on, he paid dearly for that and repented of it bitterly and loudly – but at the beginning of his reign he did not even fear the devil. Semi-educated and a semi-poet, physically frail and a drunkard to boot, patron and friend of wandering romantics and pan-German patriots, in the last years of his father's life he had been the hope of German patriotism. Everyone was hoping that he would grant a constitution.

His first act was a total amnesty. Nicholas knit his brows, but all of Germany applauded and the liberals' hopes intensified. He did not grant a constitution, however, but instead uttered so much nonsense, political, romantic, and ancient Teutonic, that even the Germans could not understand a word of it.

It was actually a very simple matter. Vain, glory-loving, restless, agitated, but at the same time incapable either of perseverance or of action, Frederick William IV was simply an epicurean, a hard drinker, a romantic and a petty tyrant on the throne. As a man incapable of actually doing anything, he doubted nothing. It seemed to him that royal power, in the mystical, divine mission of which he sincerely believed, gave him the right and the strength to do absolutely anything he took it into his head to do: to accomplish the impossible, to unite the categorically incompatible, in defiance of logic and all the laws of nature and society.

Thus he wanted total freedom to exist in Prussia while the king's power remained absolute and his arbitrariness unlimited. In this spirit he began to decree constitutions, first provincial ones, then, in 1847, something akin to a general constitution. But there was nothing serious in any of this. He accomplished only one thing: by his constant efforts, which kept supplementing and contradicting each other, he turned the whole of the old order upside down and thoroughly shook up his subjects from top to bottom. Everyone began to anticipate something.

That "something" was the revolution of 1848. Everyone sensed its approach, not only in France and Italy but even in Germany – yes, Germany, which in the course of this third period, from 1840 to 1848, had picked up the French spirit of sedition. This French cast of mind was in no way impeded by Hegelianism, which, on the contrary, loved to express its abstract revolutionary conclusions in French – though, of course, with appropriate ponderousness and a German accent. Germany had never read so many French books as it did now. It seemed to have forgotten its own literature. Instead, French literature, especially of a revolutionary variety, penetrated everywhere. Lamartine's history of the Girondists, and the works of Louis Blanc and Michelet,[97] were translated into German along with the latest novels. The Germans began to fantasize about the heroes of the Great Revolution and to assign themselves roles for the future: one would fancy himself Danton or the amiable Camille Desmoulins (*der liebenswürdige* Camille Desmoulins!), another Robespierre or Saint-Just, a third Marat. Hardly anyone was himself, because for that one has to be endowed with real character. The Germans have everything – profound thought, elevated sentiments – but not character, and if they do have any it is servile.

Many German men of letters settled in Paris, following the example of Heine and the already deceased Börne. Notable among them were Dr. Arnold Ruge, the poet Herwegh, and Karl Marx. Their original intention was to publish a journal together, but they quarreled.[98] The latter two were already socialists.

Germany began to familiarize itself with socialist doctrines only in the 1840s. The Viennese professor Stein was virtually the first to write a book in German about them.[99] The first practical German socialist, or, rather, communist, was undoubtedly the tailor Weitling, who at the beginning of 1843 came to Switzerland from Paris, where he had been a member of a secret society of French communists.[100] He created a number of communist societies among the German artisans of Switzerland, but at the end of 1843 he was handed over to Prussia by Bluntschli, the ruler of the canton of Zurich at the time and now an eminent jurist and law professor in Germany.[101]

The chief propagandist of socialism in Germany, however, first clandestinely but soon publicly, was Karl Marx.

Marx has played too important a role in the socialist movement of the German proletariat for us to pass over this remarkable personality without attempting to depict it in some of its true characteristics.

By origin Marx is a Jew. One might say that he combines all of the positive qualities and all of the shortcomings of that capable race. A nervous man, some say to the point of cowardice, he is extremely ambitious and vain, quarrelsome, intolerant, and absolute, like Jehovah, the Lord God of his ancestors, and, like him, vengeful to the point of madness. There is no lie or calumny that he would not invent and disseminate against anyone who had the misfortune to arouse his jealousy – or his hatred, which amounts to the same thing. And there is no intrigue so sordid that he would hesitate to engage in it if in his opinion (which is for the most part mistaken) it might serve to strengthen his position and his influence or extend his power. In this respect he is a thoroughly political man.

Those are his negative features, but he also has a great many positive ones. He is highly intelligent and a man of many-sided learning. A doctor of philosophy, while he was still in Cologne, around 1840, he was the soul and center of the notable circle of progressive Hegelians with whom he began to publish an opposition journal, soon closed down by government order. This circle also included the brothers Bruno and Edgar Bauer, Max Stirner, and later, in Berlin, the first circle of German nihilists, who far surpassed the most frenzied Russian nihilists with their cynical logic.[102]

In 1843 or 1844 Marx settled in Paris. Here for the first time he came into contact with a society of French and German communists[103] and with his compatriot, the German Jew Moses Hess, who was a learned economist and a socialist before Marx and at this time had a considerable influence on Marx's scholarly development.[104]

Rarely can a man be found who knows so much and reads so much, and reads so intelligently, as Marx. At this time economics had already become the exclusive subject of his studies. With particular zeal he studied the English economists, who surpassed all others in the scientific character of their knowledge, their practical cast of mind, nurtured on English economic facts, their rigorous criticism, and the scrupulous boldness of their conclusions. Marx added two new elements: the highly abstract and fantastically subtle dialectic which he acquired from the school of Hegel and which he often reduces to a perverted game, and communism as a point of departure.

It goes without saying that Marx read all the French socialists, from Saint-Simon to Proudhon,[105] and it is well known that he hates the latter. Undoubtedly there is a good deal of truth in the merciless critique he directed against Proudhon. For all his efforts to ground himself in reality, Proudhon remained an idealist and a metaphysician. His starting-point is the abstract idea of right. From right he proceeds to economic fact, while Marx, by contrast, advanced and proved the incontrovertible truth, confirmed by the entire past and present history of human society, nations, and states, that economic fact has always preceded legal and political right. The exposition and demonstration of that truth constitutes one of Marx's principal contributions to science.

What is most remarkable, however, and what Marx, of course, has never admitted, is that in respect to politics he is a direct disciple of Louis Blanc. Marx is incomparably more intelligent and incomparably more learned than that unsuccessful little revolutionary and statesman. But as a German, despite his estimable stature, he fell in with the diminutive Frenchman's doctrines.[106]

This strange fact has a simple explanation, however: the French rhetorician, as a bourgeois politician and avowed admirer of Robespierre, and the German scholar, in his threefold capacity as an Hegelian, a Jew, and a German, are both hopeless statists, and both advocate state communism. The only difference between them is that one contents himself with rhetorical declamations instead of arguments, while the other, as befits a learned and ponderous German, decorates this principle, which is equally dear to both of them, with all the contrivances of the Hegelian dialectic and all the riches of his many-sided knowledge.

By about 1845 Marx had become the leader of the German communists. Together with Engels, his devoted friend (who is just as intelligent though less learned, but to make up for it is more practical and no less adept at political slander, lies, and intrigue), he founded a secret society of German communists, or state socialists. Their central committee, which Marx and Engels headed, of course, was transferred to Brussels when they were expelled from Paris in 1846, and remained there until 1848.[107] Until that year, however, their propaganda, though it was disseminated to some extent throughout Germany, remained clandestine and was not carried on openly.

The "poison" of socialism certainly penetrated into Germany by the most diverse channels. It even found expression in religious movements. Who has not heard of the ephemeral religious doctrine called New Catholicism, which arose in 1844 and sank in 1848? (A new heresy against the Roman Church has now appeared in Germany under the name Old Catholicism.)[108]

New Catholicism emerged in the following manner. In Germany in 1844, as in France today, the Catholic clergy took it into its head to arouse the fanaticism of the Catholic population with a great procession in honor of the seamless cloak of Christ which was supposedly preserved in Trier. Around a *million* pilgrims gathered for this festival from all corners of Europe. They solemnly carried the holy garment and sang "holy cloak, pray to God for us!" It created an enormous scandal in Germany and provided the German radicals with an opportunity to denounce this travesty. In 1848 we happened to see the beer-hall in Breslau where, soon after the procession, some Silesian radicals gathered, among others the celebrated Count Reichenbach and his university friends, the gymnasium teacher Stein and the former Catholic priest Johannes Ronge. At their dictation Ronge wrote an open letter, an eloquent protest, to the bishop of Trier, whom he called the Tetzel of the nineteenth century. That is how the New Catholic heresy began.[109]

It spread rapidly throughout Germany, even to the Duchy of

Poznan, and under the pretext of a return to the ancient Christian practice of the love feast, communism began to be propagated openly. The government was in a quandary and did not know what to do. These doctrines did bear a religious character, after all, and within the Protestant population, too, *free congregations* were being formed which also manifested a political and social orientation, albeit more modestly.[110]

In 1847 an industrial crisis, which condemned tens of thousands of weavers to starvation, aroused an even stronger interest in social issues throughout Germany. The chameleon poet Heine on this occasion wrote a magnificent poem, "The Weaver," which predicted an imminent and merciless social revolution.

Indeed, everyone in Germany was expecting if not a social, then at least a political, revolution, from which the resurrection and renewal of the great German fatherland were anticipated. The principal note in this universal expectation, this chorus of hopes and desires, was patriotic and statist. The Germans were offended at the ironic amazement with which the English and French, while referring to them as a learned and sagacious people, denied them any practical aptitude or sense of reality. Therefore all their desires and demands were directed toward a single objective: *the formation of a unified and powerful pan-German state.* It did not matter what form it took, republic or monarchy, as long as it was strong enough to arouse the astonishment and fear of all its neighbors.

In 1848, with the general European revolution, the fourth period of German liberalism began, its final crisis, a crisis which ended in its complete bankruptcy.

In 1525 the combined forces of feudalism, which was manifestly nearing its end, and of the modern states which had just begun to take shape in Germany, achieved a lamentable victory over the great peasant rebellion. Not since that victory, which decisively condemned all of Germany to prolonged slavery under the yoke of the bureaucratic state, had the country amassed so much combustible material, so many revolutionary elements, as on the eve of 1848. Except within the upper bureaucracy and the nobility, discontent and the expectation of and desire for a revolution were universal. What had not happened in Germany after the fall of Napoleon, in the 1820s, or in the 1830s, now occurred: among the bourgeoisie itself there were not just dozens but many hundreds of people who called themselves revolutionaries and had every right to do so. Not satisfied with literary prattle and rhetorical hot air, they were truly prepared to lay down their lives for their convictions.

We knew many such individuals. They did not belong to the world of the rich or to the learned and literary bourgeoisie, of course. There were very few lawyers among them, slightly more doctors, and, remarkably, scarcely a single student, except for those at the University of Vienna. In 1848 and 1849 the University of Vienna displayed quite serious revolutionary tendencies, probably because in respect to science it was vastly inferior to the other German universities. (We are not referring to the University of Prague, which is a Slavic university.)

The great majority of the students in Germany by that time had already taken the side of reaction – not feudal reaction, of course, but conservative-liberal reaction: they were upholders of the state order at all costs. One can imagine what these young people have become today.

The radical party was divided into two categories. Both had formed under the direct influence of French revolutionary ideas. There was a great difference between them, however. The first category consisted of the flower of the educated younger generation of Germany: doctors of various faculties, physicians, lawyers, not a few officials, writers, journalists, and orators. All of them, of course, were shrewd politicians, impatiently awaiting a revolution that would open up broad careers to their talents. Scarcely had the revolution begun than these people assumed the leadership of the entire radical party and after many learned evolutions, which exhausted it uselessly and paralyzed its last vestiges of energy, reduced it to utter insignificance.

There was another category of people, however, composed of petty bourgeois, less brilliant and ambitious but more sincere and therefore incomparably more serious. It included a number of schoolteachers and poor clerks in commercial and industrial establishments. Of course, it also included lawyers, physicians, professors, journalists, book-sellers, and even officials, though in insignificant numbers. These were truly saintly people and very serious revolutionaries, in the sense of boundless dedication and readiness to sacrifice themselves to the utmost, and without phrase-making, to the revolutionary cause. There is no doubt that if they had had different leaders, and if German society as a whole had been disposed to a popular revolution, and capable of one, they would have been of inestimable service.

But these people were revolutionaries, and prepared to serve the revolution honestly, without giving themselves any clear account of what a revolution is and what should be demanded of it. They did not have, and could not have, any collective instinct, will, or principle. They were individual revolutionaries, without any ground beneath their feet, and since they had no guiding principle of their own they had to entrust themselves blindly to the prodigal leadership of their learned elder brothers, in whose hands they became tools for the conscious or unconscious deception of the masses. Their personal instincts impelled them toward universal liberation, equality, and prosperity for all, but they were forced to work for the triumph of a pan-German state.

Then, as now, a more serious revolutionary element existed in Germany: the urban proletariat. In Berlin, Vienna, and Frankfurt in 1848, and in Dresden, Hanover, and Baden in 1849, it showed that it was capable of and ready for a serious uprising if only it found some intelligent and honest leadership. In Berlin there was even an element of which only Paris had been able to boast hitherto: the street urchin, the gamin, a revolutionary and hero.

At that time Marx's propaganda and his communist party organization had almost no influence over the urban proletariat of Germany, or at least the great majority of it. Marx's organization had spread mainly to the industrial towns of the Prussian Rhineland, especially Cologne. It had branches also in Berlin, Breslau, and Vienna, but they were very weak. Of course, the German proletariat, like the proletariat of other countries, harbored in embryonic form, as an instinctive demand, all the socialist aspirations which the masses had put forth more or less resolutely in all the revolutions of the past, religious as well as political. There is a great difference, however, between an instinctive expression and a conscious, clearly defined demand for a social revolution or social reforms. No such demand was made in Germany in 1848 or 1849, even though the famous manifesto of the German communists, composed by Marx and Engels, had been published in March of 1848. It passed by the German people almost without a trace. In all the towns of Germany the revolutionary proletariat was directly subordinate to the political radicals, or the party of *extreme democracy*, which gave the latter enormous strength. But bourgeois democracy, itself confused by the bourgeois-patriotic program and by the complete bankruptcy of its leaders, deceived the people.

Finally, there was yet another element in Germany, which no longer exists: a revolutionary peasantry, or, at least, a peasantry capable of becoming revolutionary. At that time, in the greater part of Germany, vestiges of serfdom still existed, as they do today in the two Duchies of Mecklenburg. In Austria, serfdom predominated. There was no doubt that the German peasantry was capable of an insurrection and was ready for one. As in the Bavarian Palatinate in 1830, in almost the whole of Germany in 1848, no sooner had the proclamation of the French republic become known than the entire peasantry began to stir and to take an enthusiastic, lively, and active part in the first elections of deputies to the numerous revolutionary parliaments. The German peasants still believed that parliaments could and would do something for them, and they sent as their representatives the most desperate, "reddest" individuals – as desperate and red as a German politician can be, of course. Soon, upon realizing that they could expect no benefit from the parliaments, the peasants cooled to them; initially, however, they were ready for anything, even a general uprising.

In 1848, as in 1830, the German liberals and radicals feared this kind of uprising most of all. Even socialists of the school of Marx have no love for it. Everyone knows that Ferdinand Lassalle was, by his own admission, a direct disciple of that supreme leader of the German communist party (which did not prevent his teacher, upon Lassalle's death, from venting his jealousy and envy of his brilliant pupil, who far outstripped him in practical matters). And everyone knows that Lassalle several times expressed the thought that the defeat of the peasant rebellion of the sixteenth century and the consequent strengthening and flourishing of the bureaucratic state in Germany that followed it were true victories for the revolution.

For the German communists or social democrats the peasantry, any peasantry, stands for reaction, while the state, any state, even the Bismarckian state, stands for revolution. Let them not think that we are slandering them. As proof that this is what they actually believe, we can point to their speeches, pamphlets, journal articles, and letters; it will all be presented to the Russian public in due course. Moreover, Marxists cannot believe otherwise. As statists come what may, they are obliged to curse any popular revolution, especially a peasant revolution, which is by nature anarchistic and leads directly to the abolition of the state. As all-devouring pan-Germanists, they are

147

obliged to reject a peasant revolution for the very fact alone that it is a specifically Slavic revolution.

In their hatred for peasant uprisings they are in most affectionate and touching agreement with all parties and strata of bourgeois German society. We have already seen that in 1830 it was enough for the peasants of the Bavarian Palatinate to rise up with their scythes and pitchforks against the lords' castles for the revolutionary fever which had gripped the south German *Burschen* suddenly to cool down. In 1848 the same thing was repeated, and the decided rebuff which the German radicals gave to attempts at a peasant insurrection at the very beginning of the revolution was virtually the main reason for the revolution's dismal outcome.

It began with an unprecedented series of popular victories. Within about a month of the February days in Paris, all state institutions and government forces were swept from German soil almost without effort on the part of the people. Scarcely had popular revolution triumphed in Paris than German rulers and governments, panic-stricken and filled with self-contempt, began to topple one after the other. There was something akin to military resistance in Berlin and Vienna, to be sure, but it was so insignificant as to be scarcely worth mention.

Thus, the revolution was victorious in Germany almost without bloodshed. All chains were broken, all barriers had fallen of their own accord. The German revolutionaries could have done anything. And what did they do?

It will be said that the revolution proved bankrupt not just in Germany but throughout Europe. In every other country, however, the revolution was defeated by foreign forces after prolonged and serious struggle: in Italy by Austrian troops, in Hungary by a joint Russian and Austrian army. In Germany, however, it was crushed by the bankruptcy of the revolutionaries themselves.

Perhaps it will be said that the same thing happened in France. No, in France it was an entirely different matter. There, a terrible revolutionary question arose that suddenly thrust all the bourgeois politicians, even the red revolutionaries, into reaction. In France, during the memorable June Days, the bourgeoisie and the proletariat confronted each other for a second time as enemies between whom no reconciliation was possible. (Their first such encounter had been in Lyons in 1834.)[111]

In Germany, as we have already noted, the social question had scarcely begun to penetrate the consciousness of the proletariat through underground channels, and although mention was being made of it, it was in theoretical terms, as a French question more than a German one. Therefore it was not yet able to separate the German proletariat from the democrats, whom the workers were prepared to follow without argument if only the democrats had wanted to lead them into battle.

But street battles were precisely what the leaders and politicians of the democratic party in Germany did not want. They preferred safe and bloodless battles in the parliaments, which Count Jelačić,[112] the Ban of Croatia and one of the tools of Habsburg reaction, graphically termed "institutions for rhetorical exercises."

At the time there were countless parliaments and constituent assemblies in Germany. The National Assembly in Frankfurt, which was supposed to draw up a common constitution for the whole of Germany, was considered paramount among them. It consisted of approximately 600 deputies, representatives of all the German lands elected directly by the people. There were also deputies from the strictly German provinces of the Austrian Empire. The Bohemian and Moravian Slavs, however, refused to send deputies, to the great indignation of the German patriots, who were unable and, above all, unwilling to understand that Bohemia and Moravia, at least to the extent that they are populated by Slavs, are not German lands at all. Thus from all corners of Germany the flower of German patriotism and liberalism, of the German intellect and German learning, gathered in Frankfurt. All the patriots and revolutionaries of the 1820s and 1830s who had had the luck to survive, and all the liberal luminaries of the 1840s, met in this supreme all-German parliament. And suddenly, to everyone's amazement, from the very first days it turned out that at least three-quarters of the deputies, who had been directly elected by universal suffrage, were reactionaries! And not just reactionaries but political schoolboys, very learned but extremely naive.

They seriously imagined that all they had to do was extract a constitution for the whole of Germany from their wise brains and proclaim it in the name of the people, and all the German governments would immediately submit to it. They believed the promises and vows of the German princes, as though for more than thirty years, from 1815 to 1848, they and their colleagues had not experienced the brazen and systematic perfidy of those princes. The astute historians and jurists among them did not understand the simple truth, which they could have found explained and confirmed on every page of history, that the only way to render any political power harmless, to pacify it and subdue it, is to destroy it. The philosophers did not understand that there can be no guarantee against political power except its complete abolition. Words, promises, and vows mean nothing in politics, as an arena of mutually contending forces and facts, for the simple reason that any political power, as long as it remains a real power, by its very nature and under the threat of self-destruction must inexorably and at all costs strive for the realization of its objectives, regardless of or even against the will of the authorities and princes wielding it.

The governments of Germany in March 1848 were demoralized and frightened but by no means destroyed. The old state, bureaucratic, legal, financial, political, and military organizations remained intact. Yielding to the pressure of the time they had loosened the bit somewhat, but the reins remained firmly in the hands of the princes. The overwhelming majority of officials, accustomed to carrying out orders mechanically, the police, and the army, were all as devoted to them as before – even more than before, because amidst the popular storm that threatened their entire existence, they could expect salvation only from the princes. Finally, despite the triumph of revolution everywhere, taxes continued to be paid and collected punctiliously.

True, at the beginning of the revolution a few isolated voices did demand that tax payments and all dues in money and kind be suspended throughout Germany until a new constitution was introduced. Against this proposal, however, which encountered many doubts among the people themselves, especially the peasants, a thunderous and unanimous chorus of reproofs arose from the entire bourgeois world, not just the liberals but the reddest revolutionaries and radicals, too. Indeed, such measures led directly to state bankruptcy and the abolition of all state institutions – and this at the very moment when everyone was clamoring for the creation of a new, stronger, one and indivisible pan-German state! Mercy me! Abolition of the state! For the stupid crowd of laboring people that might have meant liberation and been cause for them to celebrate, but for respectable people, for the entire bourgeoisie, which exists solely by the power of the state, it would have been a catastrophe. On the one hand, it could not even enter the minds of the Frankfurt National Assembly, or of any of the German radicals, to abolish the state power which the German princes wielded. On the other, they did not know how to organize a popular force incompatible with state power, and in fact did not want to. Therefore, nothing remained for them but to console themselves with trust in the sanctity of the promises and vows of those very princes.

People who talk about the special mission of science and scholars to organize societies and govern states would do well to recall a bit more often the tragicomic fate of the hapless Frankfurt parliament. If any political assembly deserved to be called learned, it was this pan-German parliament, wherein sat the most illustrious professors from all the German universities and faculties, especially jurists, political economists, and historians.

In the first place, as we have already mentioned, the majority of the assembly turned out to be terribly reactionary. For example, Radowitz,[113] the friend, constant correspondent, and faithful servant of King Frederick William IV, had formerly been a Prussian envoy to the German Confederation and in May of 1848 became a deputy to the National Assembly. And when he proposed to the assembly that it solemnly declare its sympathy for the Austrian army – that *German* army (composed largely of Magyars and Croats) which had been sent by the Viennese cabinet against the rebellious Italians – the great majority of the deputies, enraptured by the German patriotism of his speech, stood and applauded the Austrians. Thereby they solemnly declared, in the name of Germany as a whole, that the principal objective – and, it can be said, the only serious one – of the German revolution was not to achieve liberty for the German people but to erect a vast new patriotic prison for them in the name of a unified and indivisible *pan-German empire*.

The assembly treated the Poles of the Duchy of Poznan and all the Slavs in general with the same crude injustice. All those peoples, who hated the Germans, would have to be swallowed up by the pan-German state. The future might and grandeur of the German father-land demanded it.

The first domestic issue presented to the wise and patriotic assembly for decision was whether the all-German state should be a republic or a monarchy. It goes without saying that the issue was decided in favor of a monarchy. The professorial deputies and legislators should not be blamed for this, however. Of course, as good Germans, and learned ones to boot, that is, as consciously convinced dolts, they wanted with all their hearts to preserve their precious princes. But even if they had not had such a desire, they would have had to decide in favor of a monarchy anyway, for with the exception of the few hundred sincere revolutionaries whom we mentioned above, that was what the entire German bourgeoisie wanted.

As proof, let us cite the words of the venerable patriarch of the democratic party, now a social democrat, the aforementioned Königsberg patriot Dr. Johann Jacoby. In a speech to the electors of Königsberg in 1858, this is what he said: "Now, gentlemen, and I am most deeply convinced of this, in our entire country and in the entire democratic party there is not a single individual who, I will not say would desire a form of state other than a monarchy, but would even dream of it." Further on, he adds: "If any moment showed us what deep roots the monarchical element has put down in the hearts of the people, it was 1848."

The second issue was the form the German Empire should take, centralized or federal. The former would have been logical and much more consistent with the objective of forming a unified, indivisible, and mighty German state. Its realization, however, required that all the sovereigns except one be deprived of their power and thrones and expelled from Germany – that is, it required that a number of local insurrections be initiated and carried out. That was too repugnant to the loyalty and fidelity of German subjects, so the issue was decided in favor of a federal monarchy in conformity with the old ideal: a multitude of petty and middling princes and as many parliaments, headed by a single all-German emperor and all-German parliament.

But who would be emperor? That was the main question. It was clear that only the Austrian emperor or the Prussian king could be appointed to this position. Neither Austria nor Prussia would have tolerated anyone else.

The sympathies of the majority of the assembly were in favor of the Austrian emperor. There were a number of reasons: first, all the non-Prussian Germans hated Prussia (and still do), just as Piedmont is hated in Italy. Then, Frederick William IV, by his eccentric and willful behavior both before and after the revolution, had forfeited all the sympathy that had greeted him upon his accession to the throne. Moreover, all of south Germany, owing to the character of its population, which is mostly Catholic, and its historical traditions and customs, was decidedly inclined toward Austria.

Nevertheless, the selection of the Austrian emperor was impossible, for the Austrian Empire, shaken by revolutionary movements in Italy, Hungary, Bohemia, and, finally, in Vienna itself, was on the verge of ruin, while Prussia was armed and ready, despite disturbances in the streets of Berlin, Königsberg, Poznan, Breslau, and Cologne.

The Germans wanted a unified and powerful empire far more than they wanted liberty. It was clear to everyone that Prussia alone could give Germany a serious emperor. Therefore, if the professors who constituted a virtual majority of the Frankfurt parliament had had even a particle of common sense, a particle of energy, they would immediately have offered the imperial crown to the Prussian king, grudgingly but without pondering it and without postponing it.

At the beginning of the revolution Frederick William IV would certainly have accepted it. The Berlin uprising, the victory of the people over the army, struck him to the quick. He felt humiliated and sought some way of saving and restoring his royal honor. For lack of any other means, he had reached for the imperial crown on his own initiative. On March 21, three days after his defeat in Berlin, he issued a manifesto to the German nation in which he declared that for the sake of Germany's salvation he would head a common German fatherland. Having written the manifesto with his own hand, he mounted his horse and, surrounded by a military retinue, solemnly rode through the streets of Berlin carrying a tricolor pan-German flag.

The Frankfurt parliament, however, did not understand, or did not want to understand, this unsubtle hint. As short-sighted and indecisive people will do, instead of simply proclaiming Frederick William the emperor immediately, they resorted to a half measure which resolved nothing but was a direct affront to the king. The professors believed[a] that before they chose a German emperor they had to concoct an all-German constitution, and before they did that they had to formulate "*the fundamental rights of the German people.*"

[a] The text reads "did not understand," which seems to be an error.

The learned legislators spent half a year on the legal definition of those rights. They handed over practical affairs to the provisional government they had set up, consisting of a non-responsible ruler of the state and a responsible ministry. As ruler, however, they chose not the king of Prussia but, to spite him, the Archduke of Austria.[114]

Having chosen him, the Frankfurt assembly demanded that all the armies of the German Confederation swear allegiance to him. Only the insignificant armies of the small states obeyed, while those of Prussia, Hanover, and even Austria bluntly refused. Thus it became clear to everyone that the power, influence, and significance of the Frankfurt assembly were nil, and that Germany's fate was being decided not in Frankfurt but in Berlin and Vienna – especially the former, since the latter was too preoccupied with its own exclusively Austrian affairs to have time to concern itself with German matters.

What was the radical, or so-called revolutionary, party doing all this time? The majority of its non-Prussian members were in the Frankfurt parliament, where they constituted a minority. The rest were in local parliaments and were likewise paralyzed, first because these parliaments were insignificant and therefore their influence on the general course of events in Germany was necessarily insignificant, too, and secondly because even in Berlin, Vienna, and Frankfurt parliamentary activity was ridiculous and amounted to idle chatter.

The Prussian constituent assembly, which opened in Berlin on May 22, 1848 and included virtually the entire flower of radicalism, gave clear proof of this. The speeches delivered in the assembly were extremely fiery and eloquent, even revolutionary, but it accomplished nothing. In its first sessions it rejected the draft constitution presented by the government, and like the Frankfurt assembly spent several months discussing its own draft, while the radicals outdid one another in declaring their revolutionism, to the astonishment of the entire nation.

The incapacity for revolution on the part of the German democrats and revolutionaries, not to say their utter stupidity, revealed itself clearly. The Prussian radicals were totally immersed in parliamentary games and lost sight of everything else. They seriously believed in the power of parliamentary resolutions, and the most intelligent among them thought that the victories they were scoring in parliamentary debates were deciding the fate of Prussia and Germany.

They had assigned themselves an impossible task: to reconcile democratic self-government and equality of rights with monarchical institutions. As proof, let us cite the speech one of the principal leaders of this party, Dr. Jacoby, gave to his electors in Berlin, a speech that clearly reflects the entire democratic program: "The idea of a republic is the highest and purest expression of civic self-government and equality of rights. But whether the realization of a republican form of government is possible given the reality of existing conditions at a particular time and in a particular country is another question. Only the general, unanimous will of the citizens can decide it. Any individual who dared take upon himself the responsibility for such a decision would be acting senselessly. A party that took it into its head to *impose* this form of government upon the people would be senseless and even criminal. Not just today but in March, at the pre-parliament in Frankfurt, I said the same thing to the deputies from Baden and tried to dissuade them – though, alas, in vain – from a republican uprising. Throughout Germany – with the sole exception of Baden – the revolution has stopped respectfully before the tottering thrones and has thereby demonstrated that although it may place limits on the arbitrary power of its princes it has no intention of driving them out. We must submit to the public will, and therefore a *constitutional monarchy* is the sole foundation on which we should erect a new political edifice."

So, building a new monarchical structure on democratic foundations was the difficult, downright impossible task which the astute but highly unrevolutionary radicals and red democrats of the Prussian constituent assembly set for themselves. The more absorbed in it they got, devising new constitutional chains with which to fetter not just the popular will but the monarchical arbitrariness of their adored, half-mad sovereign, the farther they strayed from their real task.

However great their practical short-sightedness, it could not prevent them from seeing that the monarchy, defeated in the March Days but not destroyed, was blatantly gathering around it and conspiring with the forces of the old reactionary-aristocratic, military, police, and bureaucratic world, waiting for a suitable occasion to disperse the democrats and restore its unlimited power. Jacoby's speech shows that the Prussian radicals saw this clearly. "Let us not deceive ourselves," he said. "Absolutism and the Junker party* have

* In Prussia that is the term for the aristocratic orientation and the military-aristocratic party. The word Junker is used in the sense of a nobleman.

by no means disappeared or changed their opinions. They scarcely consider it necessary to take the trouble to play dead. One would have to be blind not to see the aspirations of the reaction . . ."

Thus the Prussian radicals saw quite clearly the danger that threatened them. What did they do to forestall it? Monarchical-feudal reaction was not a theory but a force, an awesome force. It had behind it the entire army, burning with impatience to purge the shame of the March defeat in the people's blood and restore the besmirched and insulted authority of the king; it had the entire bureaucracy, the state organism with its enormous financial resources. Did the radicals really think they could bind this menacing force with new laws and a constitution, with nothing but paper?

Yes, they were sufficiently wise and practical to have nurtured such hopes. What else can explain the fact that instead of taking a series of practical and effective measures against the threat hanging over them, they spent whole months discussing the new constitution and the new laws which were supposed to subordinate all state power and authority to parliament? They had such faith in the efficacy of their parliamentary debates and legislative proposals that they neglected the sole means of opposing the reactionary forces of the state – organizing the revolutionary force of the people.

The unprecedented ease with which popular uprisings triumphed over the army in almost all the capitals of Europe at the beginning of the revolution of 1848 was detrimental to the revolutionaries, not only in Germany but in all the other countries. It made them foolishly confident that the slightest popular demonstration would be enough to shatter any military resistance. As a result, the Prussian and all the other German democrats and revolutionaries, believing that it would always lie in their power to intimidate the government with a popular movement if need be, did not deem it necessary either to organize the revolutionary passions and forces of the people or to give them any direction, much less to increase them.

On the contrary, as was befitting of good bourgeois, even the most revolutionary among them feared those passions and those forces, were always ready to take the side of the state and the bourgeois social order against them, and in general believed that the less frequently they resorted to the dangerous expedient of a popular uprising, the better.

Thus the official revolutionaries of Germany and Prussia disdained the one instrument they had for winning a real and decisive victory over the resurgent forces of reaction. They not only had no thought of organizing a popular revolution, but they tried everywhere to pacify and subdue it, thereby demolishing the only serious weapon they possessed.

The June Days, the victory of the military dictator and republican general Cavaignac[115] over the proletariat of Paris, should have opened the eyes of the German democrats. The June catastrophe was not only a misfortune for the Parisian workers, it was the first and, it can be said, decisive defeat of the revolution in Europe. The reactionaries everywhere understood the tragic – and, for them, advantageous – significance of the June Days better and more quickly than the revolutionaries did, especially in Germany.

One had to have seen the ecstasy which the first news of the June Days aroused in all the reactionary circles; it was received as tidings of salvation. Guided by a sure instinct, they saw in Cavaignac's victory not only the triumph of French reaction over French revolution, but the victory of international reaction over international revolution. In every country the military men, the general staff, hailed it as the international redemption of military honor. It is well known that army officers in Prussia, Austria, Saxony, Hanover, Bavaria, and other German states immediately sent General Cavaignac, the provisional ruler of the French republic, a congratulatory address – with the permission of their commanders and the approval of their princes, of course.

Cavaignac's victory was in fact of enormous historic significance. It initiated a new era in the international struggle of reaction and revolution. The insurrection of the Parisian workers, which lasted four days, from June 23 to June 26, in its savage energy and bitterness surpassed any popular uprising Paris had ever witnessed. It marked the beginning of the social revolution: it was the first act, while the recent, even more desperate resistance of the Paris Commune was the second.

In the June insurrection two forces for the first time confronted each other unmasked, face to face: the savage force of the people, no longer struggling in behalf of others but for themselves, with no one leading them, rising up on their own initiative to defend their most sacred interests; and a savage military force, unrestrained by any considerations of respect for the demands of civilization or humanity, of social custom or civil law, and in the intoxication of battle mercilessly burning, slashing, and destroying everything in its path.

In all previous revolutions, when the army, in its struggle against the people, found itself opposed not only by the masses but by the respectable citizens who were leading them, by university and polytechnic students, and, finally, by the National Guard, the majority of which consisted of bourgeois, it rapidly became demoralized, and before actually being defeated it yielded and retreated, or fraternized with the people. Even in the heat of battle, a compact of sorts had existed and been observed between the contending sides which did not allow even the most furious passions to transgress certain boundaries, as though both sides by mutual agreement were fighting with blunted weapons. It never occurred either to the people or to the army that houses and streets could be destroyed or tens of thousands of unarmed people cut down with impunity. There was a common saying which the conservative party constantly repeated whenever it was trying to justify some reactionary measure and wanted to lull the suspicions of the opposing party: "Any government that would take it into its head to bombard Paris for the sake of victory over the people would immediately become impossible."*

This limitation on the use of military force was highly advantageous for revolution, and it explains why previously the people had for the most part emerged the victors. General Cavaignac now decided to put an end to these easy victories by the people over the army.

When asked why he had ordered a massive attack, so that a large number of insurgents were certain to be killed, he replied: "I did not want the military standard to be dishonored for a second time by a popular victory." Guided by this purely military but thoroughly anti-popular notion, he was the first to have the audacity to use cannon to destroy houses and entire streets occupied by the insurgents. Finally, on the second, third, and fourth days after his victory, despite all his touching proclamations to his errant brothers, to whom he offered his fraternal embrace, he allowed the army and the infuriated National Guard for three days in succession to cut down and shoot without trial some 10,000 insurgents, among whom, of course, were many innocent individuals.

---

* These words were spoken in the Chamber of Deputies by Thiers in 1840, when, as Louis-Philippe's minister, he introduced a plan for the fortification of Paris. Thirty-one years later, Thiers, as president of the French republic, bombarded Paris to suppress the Commune.

All this was done for a twofold purpose: to purge *military honor*(!) in the blood of the insurgents, and at the same time to eliminate the proletariat's penchant for revolutionary movements by instilling it with proper respect for the superiority of military force and fear of its mercilessness.

Cavaignac did not achieve the latter goal. We have seen that the lesson of June did not prevent the proletariat of the Paris Commune from rising up in its turn, and we hope that even the new and incomparably more brutal lesson of the Commune will not stop or even delay the social revolution but, on the contrary, will multiply the energy and passion of its adherents tenfold and thereby bring closer the day of its victory.

If Cavaignac did not succeed in killing the social revolution, he did achieve his other objective: he finally killed liberalism and bourgeois revolutionism. He killed the republic and on its ruins established a military dictatorship.

Having freed military force from the fetters bourgeois civilization had placed upon it, having restored in full its natural savagery and its right to give free rein to it inhumanly and mercilessly, he made any bourgeois resistance henceforth impossible. Once mercilessness and annihilation became the watchwords of military action, the old, classical, innocent bourgeois revolution by means of street barricades became child's play. To contend successfully with a military force which now respects nothing, is armed with the most terrible weapons of destruction, and is always ready to use them to wipe out not just houses and streets but entire cities with all their inhabitants – to contend with such a wild beast one needs another beast, no less wild but more just: an organized uprising of all the people, a social revolution which, like military reaction, spares nothing and stops at nothing.

Cavaignac, though he rendered such an invaluable service to French and international reaction, was nonetheless a very sincere republican. Is it not remarkable that a republican was fated to lay the initial foundations for military dictatorship in Europe, to be the direct precursor of Napoleon III and the German emperor? In just the same way, another republican, his illustrious predecessor Robespierre, was fated to prepare the way for the state despotism personified by Napoleon I. Does this not prove that military discipline, which devours and crushes everything – the ideal of the pan-German empire – is in essence the last word of bourgeois state centralization, of the bourgeois republic, and of bourgeois civilization itself?

Be that as it may, German officers, nobles, bureaucrats, rulers, and princes became fiercely enamored of Cavaignac and, inspired by his success, were visibly heartened and began to prepare for a new battle.

And what did the German democrats do? Did they understand the danger that threatened them, and that they had only two means of averting it: to kindle revolutionary passions in the people, and to organize a popular force? No, they did not. On the contrary, they seemed deliberately to absorb themselves all the more in parliamentary debates, and, turning their backs on the people, abandoned them to the influence of all sorts of agents of reaction.

It is no wonder that the people grew completely cold toward them and lost all confidence in them and in their cause. In November, the Prussian king brought his Guard back to Berlin, appointed General Brandenburg[116] prime minister with the obvious intention of full-scale reaction, decreed the dissolution of the constituent assembly, and granted Prussia his own constitution (a thoroughly reactionary one, it goes without saying). Now the same Berlin workers who in March had risen up in such unanimity and fought so bravely that they had forced the Guard to withdraw from Berlin, did not make a move, did not even utter a word, but looked on with indifference as "the soldiers chased out the democrats."

This in effect brought to an end the tragicomedy of the German revolution. Earlier, in October, Prince Windischgrätz had restored order in Vienna, albeit not without considerable bloodshed – on the whole the Austrian revolutionaries proved more revolutionary than those of Prussia.

What was the National Assembly in Frankfurt doing at this time? At the end of 1848 it finally voted the *fundamental rights* and a new all-German constitution and offered the imperial crown to the Prussian king. But the governments of Austria, Prussia, Bavaria, Hanover, and Saxony rejected the fundamental rights and the newly fledged constitution, while the Prussian king refused to accept the imperial crown and then recalled his deputies from the assembly.

Reaction triumphed throughout Germany. The revolutionary party, having come to its senses late in the day, decided to organize a general insurrection in the spring of 1849. In May the dying revolution hurled its last flames into Saxony, the Bavarian Palatinate, and Baden. They were extinguished everywhere by Prussian soldiers, who, after a brief but bloody enough struggle, restored the old order throughout Germany. Meanwhile, the Prince of Prussia (the present emperor and king William I), who commanded the Prussian forces in Baden, did not let slip the opportunity to hang a few insurgents.

That was the sad end of the only and, for a long time, the last, German revolution. Now it may be asked, what was the main reason for its failure?

Aside from the political inexperience and practical ineptitude often characteristic of scholars; aside from a decided absence of revolutionary boldness and the Germans' ingrained aversion to revolutionary measures and actions and their passionate love for subordinating themselves to authority; finally, aside from their conspicuous lack of any sense of liberty, any instinct or passion for it, the main reason for the failure was the common desire of all the German patriots for the formation of a pan-German state.

This desire, emanating from the depths of the German character, renders the Germans totally incapable of revolution. A society that wishes to create a strong state necessarily wants to submit to authority; a revolutionary society, on the contrary, wants to cast off authority. How are these two contradictory and mutually exclusive demands to be reconciled? They must inevitably paralyze each other, as happened with the Germans, who in 1848 achieved neither liberty nor a strong state, but instead suffered a terrible defeat.

The two desires are so contradictory that they cannot in fact be found in the same nation at the same time. One of them must necessarily be an illusory desire which conceals the real one, as was the case in 1848. The imaginary desire for freedom was a self-delusion, a deception, while the desire for a pan-German state was the serious one. That is undeniable, at least in regard to the whole of educated bourgeois society in Germany, including the great majority of the reddest democrats and radicals. It might be thought, suspected, and hoped that an anti-social instinct exists within the German proletariat that would render it capable of winning liberty, because it bears the same economic yoke, and hates it just as much, as the proletariat of other countries, and because neither the German proletariat nor any other can liberate itself from economic bondage without destroying the centuries-old prison called the state. That can only be assumed and hoped, for there is no factual proof of it. On the contrary, we have seen that not only in 1848 but today as well the German workers blindly obey their leaders, and those leaders, the organizers of the *German Social-Democratic Workers' Party*, are leading them not to liberty and international brotherhood but directly under the yoke of the pan-German state.

In 1848 the German radicals, as noted above, found themselves in the unfortunate, tragicomic position of having to rebel against state power in order to force it to become stronger and more extensive. Hence not only did they not want to destroy it, but, on the contrary, they evinced the most tender concern for its preservation even while struggling against it. Consequently all their actions were thwarted and paralyzed from the start. The actions of the authorities reflected no such contradiction. Without a moment's hesitation they set out to suppress at whatever cost their strange, unsolicited, and unruly friends, the democrats. One fact will suffice to indicate that the radicals were thinking not about liberty but about the creation of an empire.

The Frankfurt assembly, in which the democrats had already triumphed, offered the imperial crown to Frederick William IV on March 28, 1849 – that is, when Frederick had completely destroyed all the so-called revolutionary gains or popular rights, had dispersed the constituent assembly elected directly by the people, had granted the most reactionary, most contemptible constitution, and, filled with anger at the insults he and the crown had suffered, was hunting down the hated democrats with police and soldiers.

They could not have been so blind as to demand liberty from such a prince! What was it they were hoping for and expecting? *A pan-German state*!

The king was not in a position to give them even that. The feudal party, which had triumphed along with him and had once again seized state power, was extremely hostile to the idea of German unity. It hated German patriotism, regarding it as seditious, and knew only its own Prussian patriotism. The entire army, all the officers and all the cadets in the military schools, at that time would sing with frenzy the well-known Prussian patriotic song: "I am a Prussian, do you know my flag?"[117]

Frederick wanted to be emperor, but he was afraid of his own men, he was afraid of Austria and France, and above all he was afraid of Emperor Nicholas. In reply to a Polish deputation that came to demand liberty for the Duchy of Poznan in March 1848, he said: "I cannot consent to your request, because it would be contrary to the wishes of my brother-in-law, Emperor Nicholas, who is truly a great man! When he says yes, it means yes, when he says no, it means no."

The king knew that Nicholas would never agree to the imperial crown. Therefore, and therefore especially, he refused point-blank to accept it from the Frankfurt deputation.

He had to do something for German unity and Prussian hegemony, however, if only to redeem his honor, which had been compromised by his March manifesto. Taking advantage of the laurels the Prussian troops had won in suppressing the German democrats, and of the domestic difficulties of Austria, which was displeased with his successes in Germany, he made an attempt in May 1849 to create a league of Prussia, Saxony, and Hanover. It would have had the effect of concentrating all their diplomatic and military affairs in the hands of Prussia, but it did not last long. As soon as Austria had suppressed Hungary with the help of the Russian army in September of 1849, Schwarzenberg threateningly demanded of Prussia that everything in Germany revert to the old pre-March order, meaning that the German Confederation, which had been so conducive to Austria's hegemony, be restored. Saxony and Hanover immediately broke with Prussia and joined Austria, Bavaria followed their example, and the bellicose king of Württemberg declared loudly and clearly that wherever the Austrian emperor ordered him to go with his army, thither he would go.

Unhappy Prussia thus found itself completely isolated. What was it to do? To agree to Austria's demand seemed impossible to the vain but weak king, so he appointed his friend, General Radowitz, prime minister and ordered his troops to begin moving. The situation nearly came to blows. But Emperor Nicholas cried "halt!" to the Germans, galloped to Olmütz (November 1850) for a conference, and pronounced sentence. The humiliated king submitted, Austria triumphed, and in the old palace of the Confederation in Frankfurt, in May 1851, after a three-year eclipse, the German Confederation shone once again.

It was as though there had been no revolution. Its sole trace was ferocious reaction, which should have served the Germans as a salutary lesson: anyone who wants not liberty but a state should not play at revolution.

The history of German liberalism strictly speaking comes to an end with the crisis of 1848 and 1849. It showed the Germans that they were not only incapable of attaining liberty but did not even want it. It showed them also that without the initiative of the Prussian monarchy they were incapable even of achieving their real and serious objective: they were not strong enough to create a unified and powerful state. The ensuing reaction differed from that of 1812 and 1813 in that during the latter, for all its bitterness and oppressiveness, the Germans had been able to preserve the illusion that they loved liberty, and that if the power of the allied governments, which far exceeded their own seditious strength, had not prevented them, they could have created a free and unified Germany. Now this comforting self-deception was impossible. During the first months of the revolution there was absolutely no governmental force in Germany capable of resisting them had they wanted to do anything; and subsequently they, more than anyone else, aided the reestablishment of such a force. Hence the lack of any results from the revolution stemmed not from external obstacles but solely from the German liberals' and patriots' own bankruptcy.

Recognition of this bankruptcy seemed to become the basis of political life and the guiding sentiment of the new public opinion in Germany. The Germans evidently had changed and become practical people. Renouncing the broad abstract ideas that constituted the universal significance of their classical literature from Lessing to Goethe and from Kant to Hegel, and renouncing French liberalism, democracy, and republicanism, they now began to seek the fulfillment of German destiny in the aggressive policy of Prussia.

To their honor, it should be added, this turnabout was not accomplished overnight. The last twenty-four years, from 1849 to the present, which for the sake of brevity we have included in a single fifth period, should actually be divided into four periods:

5.   The period of hopeless subjugation, from 1849 to 1858, that is, to the beginning of the regency in Prussia.

6.   The period from 1858 to 1866, the final, death-bed struggle of expiring liberalism against Prussian absolutism.

7.   The period from 1866 to 1870, the capitulation of defeated liberalism.

8.   The period from 1870 to the present, the triumph of victorious
     bondage.

In the fifth period Germany's internal and external humiliation
reached its extremity. Internally, there was the silence of slaves: in
south Germany the Austrian minister, Metternich's successor, commanded unconditionally; in the north Manteuffel,[118] who had humiliated the Prussian monarchy beyond measure at Olmütz in 1850 to the
delight of Austria and the immense satisfaction of the Prussian court,
noble, and military-bureaucratic party, hounded the surviving
democrats. It added up to zero as far as liberty was concerned, and to
less than zero as far as the external dignity, weight, and significance of
Germany as a state were concerned. The Schleswig-Holstein question, on which Germans of every land and every party (except that of
the court, military, bureaucracy, and nobility) had been expressing the
most vehement passions since 1847, thanks to Prussian meddling was
finally resolved in favor of Denmark. In all other questions the voice
of united Germany – or, rather, Germany disunited by the German
Confederation – was not even taken into consideration by the other
powers. Prussia more than ever became the slave of Russia. The
hapless Frederick, who formerly had detested Nicholas, now swore by
him. His devotion to the interests of the Petersburg court went so far
that the Prussian war minister and the Prussian ambassador to the
English court, a friend of the king's, were both replaced for expressing sympathy for the Western powers.

The story of the "ingratitude" of Prince Schwarzenberg and
Austria, which so deeply pained and offended Nicholas, is well
known. Austria, the natural enemy of Russia on account of its interests in the East, openly took the side of England and France against it,
while Prussia, to the great indignation of the whole of Germany,
remained faithful to the end.

The sixth period begins with the regency of the present king-
emperor William I. Frederick finally went mad, and his brother,
William, hated throughout Germany as Prince of Prussia, became
regent in 1858 and king in January 1861, upon the death of his elder
brother. It is notable that this royal drill-sergeant and notorious hangman of democrats also had a honeymoon of liberalism to ingratiate
himself with the people. Upon acceding to the regency, he gave an
address in which he expressed his firm intention of elevating Prussia,

and through it all of Germany, to its proper eminence, while respecting the limits placed upon royal power* by the constitution and relying always on the wishes of the people as expressed by parliament.

In accordance with this promise, the first act of his rule was to dismiss Manteuffel's ministry, which was one of the most reactionary ever to govern Prussia and seemed to personify its political defeat and annihilation.

Manteuffel had become prime minister in November 1850, as though for the purpose of signing the conditions of the Olmütz Conference, which were extremely humiliating for Prussia, and of completely subjecting Prussia and the whole of Germany to Austrian hegemony. That was Nicholas's wish, it was the arrogant and passionate desire of Prince Schwarzenberg, and it was also the aspiration of the great majority of the Prussian Junkers, or nobles. They did not want to hear of Prussia merging with Germany and were almost more devoted to the Austrian and Russian emperors than to their own king, whom they obeyed out of duty, not out of love. For eight years Manteuffel governed Prussia in this spirit, humbling it before Austria on every suitable occasion and mercilessly and relentlessly persecuting anything in Prussia and throughout Germany that smacked of liberalism or a popular movement and popular rights.

This hated ministry was replaced by the liberal ministry of Prince Hohenzollern-Sigmaringen,[119] who immediately declared the regent's intention of restoring Prussia's honor and independence vis-à-vis Vienna, as well as its lost influence on Germany.

A few words and steps in this direction were sufficient to send all the Germans into ecstasy. All the recent insults, cruelties, and atrocities were forgotten; the hangman of democrats, the regent and then king, William I, who yesterday had been hated and cursed, suddenly became a favorite, a hero, the sole hope. In corroboration, let us cite the words of the famous Jacoby to the electors of Königsberg on November 11, 1858: "The address of the Prince upon his assumption of the regency, truly manly and in conformity with the constitution,

---

* This respect, it appears, should have come the more easily to him in that the constitution, which had been granted by favor of the king, in no way limited royal power, except on one point: the right to conclude new loans or decree new taxes without the approval of the Chamber of Deputies. To levy taxes that had already received parliamentary approval once, however, did not require a new vote, for parliament did not have the right to rescind them. This innovation turned German constitutionalism and parliamentarism into a completely meaningless game. In other countries, England,

filled the hearts of all Prussians and all Germans with new confidence and new hopes. With unusual eagerness all are hastening to the electoral urns."

In 1861 the same Jacoby wrote the following: "When the Prince-Regent by his own decision took the government of the country into his own hands, everyone expected that *Prussia would advance unimpeded toward its intended goal*. Everyone expected that the men to whom the regent entrusted the administration of the country would first of all eliminate all the evils committed by the government in the last ten years, would put an end to bureaucratic arbitrariness in order to arouse and revive a common patriotic spirit, the free self-esteem of the citizenry . . .

"Have those hopes been fulfilled? Loud and clear, a unanimous voice replies: *In these two years Prussia has not advanced one step forward and is as far from fulfilling its historic destiny as it was before.*"

The venerable Dr. Jacoby, the last believer and last representative of German political democracy, will doubtless die faithful to his program, which has been broadened in recent years to reach the not very wide boundaries of the German social democrats' program. His ideal, the formation of a pan-German state of means of nation-wide liberty, is a utopia, an absurdity. We have already spoken of this. The great majority of German patriots after 1848 and 1849 came to believe that the creation of pan-German power was possible only by means of cannon and bayonets, and therefore Germany awaited its salvation from warlike and monarchical Prussia.

In 1858 the entire National-Liberal Party, taking advantage of the first signs of a change in the government's policy, went over to its side. The old democratic party split: the majority formed a new party, the Progressive Party, while the remainder continued to call itself democratic. The former from the start burned with a desire for unity with the government, but, wishing to preserve its honor, begged it to provide a decorous pretext for coming over and demanded at least outward respect for the constitution. It flirted with the government and crossed swords with it until 1866, and then, won over by the brilliance of the victories against Denmark and Austria, unconditionally surrendered to it. The democratic party, as we shall see, did the same in 1870.

France, Belgium, Italy, Spain, Portugal, Sweden, Denmark, Holland, and so forth, parliaments retain their one real and essential right of refusing taxes to the government

Jacoby did not follow, and never will follow, the general example. Democratic principles constitute his life. He hates violence and does not believe that a powerful German state can be created by means of it. Therefore he has remained an enemy – a solitary and powerless one, to be sure – of current Prussian policy. His powerlessness stems mainly from the fact that as a statist from head to toe he sincerely dreams of freedom while at the same time wanting a unified pan-German state.

The present German emperor, William I, does not suffer from contradictions, and like the unforgettable Nicholas I is fashioned as though from a single piece of metal; in a word, he is an integrated personality, albeit a limited one. He and the Count of Chambord[120] are virtually alone in believing in their divine anointment, their divine mission, and divine right. William, like Nicholas a pious soldier-king, places the principle of legitimacy, meaning the hereditary right to rule, above all other principles. It presented a serious difficulty to his mind and conscience when it came to the unification of Germany, for a number of legitimate princes had to be pushed off their thrones. In the moral code of the state, however, there is another principle, *the sacred right of conquest*, and that resolved the question. A prince who is true to his monarchical obligations will not agree for anything in the world to occupy a throne offered to him by a rebellious nation which has liberated it from a legitimate ruler. But he will consider himself entitled to *conquer* that nation and throne as long as God blesses his arms and he has a suitable pretext for declaring war. Princes have always recognized that principle and the right based on it, and they recognize it to this day.

Therefore, William I needed a minister who was able to create *legitimate* pretexts and methods for expanding the state by means of war. Such a man was Bismarck, whom William fully appreciated and appointed his minister in October 1862.

VII

Prince Bismarck is the most powerful man in Europe today. He is a Pomeranian nobleman of the purest sort, with a quixotic devotion to

and can, if they wish, make any government impossible. As a result, they carry considerable weight in governmental affairs. The Prussian constitution, which removed this right from the Prussian parliament, granted it only the right to refuse the imposition of new taxes and the conclusion of new loans. We will soon see William I, however, three years the royal house, a typical cold and military bearing, and an arrogant, dryly polite, for the most part scornful and sarcastic manner in dealing with bourgeois-liberal politicians. He does not get angry at being called a "Junker," that is, an aristocrat, usually replying to his opponents: "be assured, we will know how to uphold the honor of the Junkers." An extraordinarily intelligent man, he is completely free of Junker prejudices or of any other kind.

We have called Bismarck the direct political disciple of Frederick II. Like the latter, he believes first of all in power and then in intelligence, which wields power and frequently increases it tenfold. A statesman through and through, like Frederick the Great he does not believe in God or the devil, in humanity or even the nobility – they are all merely tools as far as he is concerned. In pursuit of his statist objectives he will not hesitate before divine or human laws. He does not recognize morality in politics: base deeds and crimes are immoral only when they are not crowned with success. Colder and more impassive than Frederick, he is just as unceremonious and arrogant. A nobleman who owes his rise to the noble party, he is systematically suppressing it for the benefit of the state and curses it just as he previously cursed liberals, progressives, and democrats. In essence, he curses everything and everyone, except for the emperor, without whose favor he could undertake nothing and do nothing – though perhaps in secret, with his friends (if he has any), he curses him, too.

In order to appreciate fully everything that Bismarck has done, we must keep in mind who surrounds him.* The king, a dull-witted man with the education of a theologian and a drill-sergeant, is surrounded by the aristocratic-clerical party, which is openly hostile to Bismarck,

after promising to observe the rights of parliament religiously, finding himself forced to violate them.

* Here is an anecdote, drawn from a direct and reliable source, that characterizes Bismarck. Everyone has heard of Schurz, one of the reddest German revolutionaries of 1848, who liberated the pseudo-revolutionary Kinkel from a fortress-prison.[121] Schurz took him for a serious revolutionary, though politically he was basically not worth a cent, and, placing his own freedom in jeopardy, boldly and ingeniously overcame enormous obstacles to liberate him. He himself then fled to America. An intelligent, capable, and energetic man, qualities esteemed in America, he soon became the leader of the multi-million-member German party. During the recent war he attained the rank of general in the northern army (earlier he had been elected a senator). After the war the United States sent him as ambassador extraordinary to Spain. He took advantage of this appointment to visit south Germany, but not Prussia, where a death sentence hung over him for having freed the pseud.-rev. Kinkel. When Bismarck learned of his presence in Germany, he wanted to win over a man of such influence among the Germans in

so that he has to do battle for each new measure, each new step. This domestic struggle takes up at least half of his time, intellect, and energy, and of course it very much retards, hinders, and paralyzes his activity. To a certain degree that is good for him, because it keeps him from overreaching himself in his enterprises, like the celebrated tyrant Napoleon I, who was no stupider than Bismarck.

Bismarck's public activity began in 1847: he became the head of the most extreme noble party in the United Diet of Prussia. In 1848 he was an avowed enemy of the Frankfurt parliament and of an all-German constitution, and a passionate ally of Russia and Austria, that is, of internal and external reaction. In this spirit he took a very active part in the ultra-reactionary newspaper *Kreuzzeitung*,[122] which was founded in that year and is still in existence. It goes without saying that he was an ardent defender of the ministries of Brandenburg and Manteuffel, and therefore of the resolutions of the Olmütz Conference. In 1851 he became envoy to the German Confederation in Frankfurt. At this time he radically changed his attitude toward Austria. "It was as though the scales fell from my eyes when I examined its policies closely," he said to his friends. Only now did he understand how hostile Austria was to Prussia, and from its ardent defender he became its implacable enemy. From that moment he became preoccupied with the idea of excluding Austria from Germany and eliminating its influence over it.

Under these circumstances he made the acquaintance of William, the Prince of Prussia, who, after the Olmütz Conference, hated Austria as much as he hated revolution. As soon as William became regent, he turned his attention to Bismarck, appointing him ambassador first to Russia and then to France, and finally prime minister.

While serving as ambassador, Bismarck brought his program to maturity. In Paris he took some valuable lessons in state swindling from Napoleon III. The latter, finding him an eager and able listener, opened his heart and made some transparent allusions to the *necessity* of redrawing the map of Europe, demanding the Rhine frontier and

America. He invited him to Berlin, ordering that he be told: "laws are not made for men like Schurz." Upon Schurz's arrival in Berlin, Bismarck gave a dinner for him to which he invited all of his fellow ministers. After dinner, when everyone had left and Schurz remained alone with Bismarck for a private conversation, the latter said to him: "You have seen and heard my colleagues; with such donkeys I am condemned to create and govern Germany."

Belgium for himself and leaving the rest of Germany to Prussia. The results of these conversations are well known: the pupil outwitted the teacher.

Upon becoming prime minister, Bismarck gave a speech in which he set forth his program: "Prussia's frontiers are confining and unsuitable for a first-class state. To achieve new frontiers we must expand and perfect our military organization. We must prepare ourselves for the forthcoming struggle, and in anticipation of it we must assemble and increase our forces. The error of 1848 was the desire to unify Germany into a single state by means of popular institutions. Great issues of state are decided not by right but by force – force always precedes right."

For this last expression Bismarck really caught it from the German liberals between 1862 and 1866. After 1866, that is, after the victory over Austria, and especially after 1870 and the defeat of France, all those reproaches turned into ecstatic dithyrambs.

With his usual audacity, characteristic cynicism, and scornful bluntness, Bismarck expressed in these words the very essence of the political history of nations, the whole secret of statecraft. The constant predominance and triumph of force – that is its real essence, while everything that political language calls right is merely the consecration of a fact created by force. Clearly, the masses thirsting for liberation cannot expect it from the theoretical triumph of abstract right; they must conquer freedom by force, and to do so they must organize their own spontaneous forces outside of the state and against it.

The Germans, as we have said, wanted not freedom but a strong state. Bismarck understood that, and with the bureaucracy and military force of Prussia he felt capable of achieving it. Therefore he proceeded boldly and firmly toward his objective, paying no heed either to rights or to the fierce polemics and attacks on him by the liberals and democrats. Contrary to preceding rulers, he believed that both liberals and democrats would become his impassioned allies once he had achieved his objective.

The drill-sergeant king and the politician Bismarck wanted to strengthen the army, for which new taxes and credits were necessary. The Chamber of Deputies, on which the approval of new taxes and loans depended, repeatedly refused to give it, and as a result it was dissolved several times. In another country such a conflict might have called forth a political revolution, but not in Prussia, and Bismarck understood this. Despite the refusals, therefore, he took the funds he needed anywhere he could, by means of loans and taxes. With its refusals the chamber became the laughing-stock, if not of Germany then of Europe.

Bismarck was not mistaken. Once he had achieved his objectives, he became the idol of both the liberals and the democrats.

Perhaps in no other country has there been such a rapid and complete turnaround of opinion as occurred in Germany between 1864, 1866, and 1870. Until the Austro-Prussian War against Denmark, Bismarck was the most unpopular man in Germany. During that war, and especially after it, he displayed the most profound contempt for all the rights of nations and states. It is well known how unceremoniously Prussia and stupid Austria, which Prussia had enticed, drove out of Schleswig and Holstein the Saxon-Hanoverian corps which had occupied those provinces by order of the German Confederation; how arrogantly Bismarck divided the conquered provinces with deceived Austria; and how he ended by declaring them exclusively the spoils of Prussia.

One might have supposed that such behavior would arouse the strong indignation of all *honest, freedom-loving, and just* Germans. To the contrary, it was from this very moment that Bismarck's popularity began to grow – the Germans felt themselves dominated by patriotic reason of state and a strong governmental authority. The war of 1866 only enhanced his significance. The rapid campaign in Bohemia, which recalled the campaigns of Napoleon I, the succession of brilliant victories which brought Austria down, the triumphal procession through Germany, the pillaging of enemy territory, the declaration of Hanover, Hesse-Cassel, and Frankfurt as military spoils, the formation of a North German Confederation under the protection of the future emperor – these events enraptured the Germans. The leaders of the Prussian opposition, Virchow, Schulze-Delitzsch,[123] and the rest, suddenly fell silent, declaring themselves morally vanquished. A very small group headed by the noble old Jacoby remained in opposition and joined the German People's Party, which was formed in the south of Germany after 1866.

Upon conclusion of the treaty between victorious Prussia and shattered Austria, the old German Confederation was abolished and in its place a *North German Confederation* was created under Prussia's leadership. Austria, Bavaria, Württemberg, and Baden were granted the right to form a southern confederation.

Baron Beust, the Austrian minister appointed after the war, understood the great significance of such a confederation and directed all his efforts to creating it. He was prevented from doing so by unresolved domestic problems and by the great obstacles placed in his way by those very states for which a confederation was important. Bismarck duped them all: Russia, France, and the German princes, for whom it was a matter of importance to form a confederation that would not have allowed Prussia to achieve its current position.

The People's Party, which was formed at this time by the south German bourgeoisie with the exclusive objective of opposing Bismarck, had a program essentially identical to Beust's: to create a south German confederation closely tied to Austria and based on the most broadly popular institutions.

The center of the People's Party was Stuttgart. Besides confederation with Austria, it had a number of other inclinations. In Bavaria it flirted with the ultra-Catholics, meaning the Jesuits; it wanted confederation with France, confederation with Switzerland. The group that wanted confederation with republican Switzerland was the main founder of the League of Peace and Freedom.[124]

On the whole the party's program was naive and filled with contradictions: democratic popular institutions were combined in a fantastic manner with a monarchical form of government, the sovereignty of princes was combined with pan-German unity, and the latter with a European-wide republican federation. In short, almost everything was to remain as before and everything was to be filled with a new spirit, primarily philanthropic in nature. Freedom and equality were to flower under conditions that destroy them. Such a program could have been drawn up only by the sentimental burghers of south Germany, who were distinguished first by their systematic disregard of contemporary socialist aspirations and then by their passionate denial of them, as the Congress of the League in 1868 showed.

Clearly, the People's Party was obliged to adopt a hostile attitude toward the *General German Workers' Association*,[a] which Ferdinand Lassalle founded in the 1860s.

---

[a] The text reads "the Workers' Party of the Social Democrats," but since Bakunin now proceeds to discuss Lassalle he evidently meant the party Lassalle created in 1863, and not the Social-Democratic Party, which was founded in 1869, after Lassalle's death.

In the second part of this book[125] we will relate in detail the development of worker associations in Germany and in Europe as a whole. For now let us note that at the end of the last decade, in 1868 to be precise, the workers of Germany were divided into three categories. The first and most numerous remained outside of any organization. The second, also quite numerous, consisted of the so-called "societies for worker education."[126] The third and least numerous, but most energetic and sensible, formed the phalanx of Lassallean workers under the name of the General German Workers' Association.

Nothing need be said of the first category. The second represented a kind of federation of small associations of workers under the direct leadership of Schulze-Delitzsch and bourgeois socialists of his ilk. "Self-help" (*Selbsthülfe*) was its slogan, in the sense that laboring people were persistently advised not to anticipate either deliverance or help from the state and the government, but only from their own efforts. This advice would have been excellent had it not been accompanied by the false assurance that liberation of the laboring people is possible under *current conditions of social organization*, given the existence of *economic monopolies*, which oppress the workers, and the *political state*, which protects those monopolies against a popular uprising. Under this delusion (and as far as the bourgeois socialists and the leaders of this party were concerned, it was a fully conscious deception), the workers subject to their influence were supposed to disengage themselves systematically from all political and social concerns and questions about the state, property, and so forth. Taking as their point of departure the rationality and legitimacy of the existing social order, they were to seek improvement and relief through the organization of cooperative consumers', producers', and credit associations. For their political education, Schulze-Delitzsch recommended to the workers the full program of the Progressive Party, to which he and his colleagues belonged.

In its economic aspect, as everyone can now see, Schulze-Delitzsch's system led directly to the protection of the bourgeois world from any social threat, while in its political aspect it completely subordinated the proletariat to the bourgeoisie which exploits it and for which it was to remain an obedient and mindless tool.

Ferdinand Lassalle took up arms against this crude twofold deception. It was easy for him to demolish Schulze-Delitzsch's economic system and to show the utter worthlessness of his political system. No one but Lassalle could have explained and proved so convincingly to the German workers that under existing economic conditions the proletariat's position not only cannot be reversed, but, on the contrary, by virtue of an incontrovertible economic law, must worsen with each passing year, regardless of all cooperative endeavors, which are capable only of bringing temporary, ephemeral benefits to a trivial number of workers.

In demolishing Schulze-Delitzsch's political program, he showed that its pseudo-popular policies would lead merely to the strengthening of bourgeois economic privileges.

Up to this point we are in agreement with Lassalle. But then we part company with him and with all the German social democrats or communists in general. In opposition to Schulze-Delitzsch, who recommended to the workers that they seek salvation only in their own efforts and neither demand nor expect anything from the state, Lassalle showed them, in the first place, that under existing economic conditions not merely their liberation but even the slightest improvement in their lot is impossible and its deterioration unavoidable; and, in the second place, that as long as the bourgeois state exists, bourgeois economic privileges will remain unassailable. But then he came to the following conclusion: in order to obtain real liberty, liberty based on economic equality, *the proletariat must seize the state* and turn the state's power against the bourgeoisie for the benefit of the workers, in just the same way that it is now turned against the proletariat for the exclusive benefit of the exploiting class.

And how are they to seize the state? There are only two methods: a political revolution, or legal popular agitation for peaceful reform. Lassalle, as a German, a Jew, a scholar, and a rich man, advised them to choose the second path.

With this objective in mind, he founded a sizable and primarily political party of German workers, organized it hierarchically, and subjected it to strict discipline and to his own dictatorship – in short, he did what Marx in the last three years wanted to do in the International. Marx's endeavor proved a failure, but Lassalle's was a complete success. The direct and immediate goal he set for the party was peaceful nation-wide agitation for the election of state representatives and authorities by universal suffrage.

Once they had achieved this objective by means of legal reform, the people would send only their own representatives to a people's parliament, which by a series of decrees and laws would transform the bourgeois state into a people's state. The first task of the people's state would be to make unlimited credit available to the producers' and consumers' associations of the workers, which only then would be in a position to contend with bourgeois capital and in a short time would defeat it and swallow it up. When the swallowing-up process was completed, a period of radical transformation of society would begin.

That was Lassalle's program, and it is also the program of the Social-Democratic Party. Strictly speaking, it belongs not to Lassalle but to Marx, who expressed it fully in the famous *Manifesto of the Communist Party*, which he and Engels published in 1848. A clear allusion to it can also be found in the *Inaugural Address of the International Working Men's Association*, which Marx wrote in 1864, in the words: "the first duty of the working class consists of winning political power for itself," or, as the *Communist Manifesto* says, "the first step toward revolution by the workers must consist of raising the proletariat to the level of a ruling class. The proletariat must concentrate all the means of production in the hands of the state, that is, of the proletariat raised to the level of a ruling class."[127]

Is it not clear that Lassalle's program in no way differs from that of Marx, whom he acknowledged as his teacher? In his pamphlet against Schulze-Delitzsch, Lassalle, with the truly inspired clarity characteristic of his writings, after setting forth his basic ideas on the social and political evolution of modern society, explicitly states that these ideas and even the terminology belong not to him but to Marx, who first expressed and developed them in a remarkable, as yet unpublished work.[128]

Marx's protest, then, printed *after Lassalle's death* in the preface to *Capital*,[129] seems all the more strange. Marx complains bitterly that Lassalle robbed him, that he appropriated his ideas. It is a particularly odd protest coming from a communist, who advocates collective property but does not understand that once an idea has been expressed it ceases to be the property of an individual. It would be a different story if Lassalle had copied a page, or several pages – that would be plagiarism, and proof of the intellectual bankruptcy of a writer incapable of digesting borrowed ideas and reproducing them in independent form through his own intellectual labor. Only vain and dishonest individuals who are devoid of intellectual ability – crows in peacock feathers – do that.

Lassalle was too intelligent and independent to have to resort to such pitiful methods of gaining the public's attention. He was vain, very vain, as befits a Jew, but at the same time he was brilliant enough to be able to satisfy the demands of the most exquisite vanity without difficulty. He was clever, learned, rich, adroit, and extremely bold; he was endowed to the highest degree with dialectical reasoning, the gift of speech, and clarity of understanding and expression. In contrast to his teacher Marx, who is strong on theory, on behind-the-scenes or underground intrigue, but loses all significance and force in the public arena, Lassalle seemed to have been expressly created for open struggle in the practical realm. Dialectical dexterity and force of logic, aroused by a self-esteem inflamed by struggle, substituted within him for the force of passionate convictions. He had a very strong impact on the proletariat, but he was by no means a man of the people.

By his whole way of life, by his circumstances, habits, and tastes, he belonged to the upper bourgeoisie, the so-called gilded or dandified youth. Of course, he raised himself head and shoulders above it and gained ascendancy by means of his intellect, thanks to which he became the leader of the German proletariat. Within a few years he achieved enormous popularity. The entire liberal and democratic bourgeoisie profoundly detested him. His like-minded comrades, the socialists, Marxists, and his teacher, Marx himself, concentrated against him the full force of their malicious envy. Indeed, they hated him as deeply as the bourgeoisie did; as long as he was alive, however, they could not give voice to their hatred because he was too strong for them.

We have already expressed several times our profound aversion to the theory of Lassalle and Marx, which recommends to the workers, if not as their ultimate ideal, then at least as their immediate and principal objective, *the creation of a people's state*. As they explain it, this will be nothing other than "the proletariat raised to the level of a ruling class."

If the proletariat is to be the ruling class, it may be asked, then whom will it rule? There must be yet another proletariat which will be subject to this new rule, this new state. It might be the peasant rabble, for example, which, as we know, does not enjoy the favor of the Marxists, and which, finding itself on a lower cultural level, will probably be governed by the urban and factory proletariat. Or, if we look at this question from the national point of view, then, presumably, as far as the Germans are concerned it is the Slavs who, for the same reason, will occupy in regard to the victorious German proletariat the same position of servile subordination that the latter now occupies in relation to its own bourgeoisie.

If there is a state, then necessarily there is domination and consequently slavery. A state without slavery, open or camouflaged, is inconceivable – that is why we are enemies of the state.

What does it mean, "the proletariat raised to a governing class?" Will the entire proletariat head the government? The Germans number about 40 million. Will all 40 million be members of the government? The entire nation will rule, but no one will be ruled. Then there will be no government, there will be no state; but if there is a state, there will also be those who are ruled, there will be slaves.

In the Marxists' theory this dilemma is resolved in a simple fashion. By popular government they mean government of the people by a small number of representatives elected by the people. So-called popular representatives and rulers of the state elected by the entire nation on the basis of universal suffrage – the last word of the Marxists, as well as of the democratic school – is a lie behind which the despotism of a ruling minority is concealed, a lie all the more dangerous in that it represents itself as the expression of a sham popular will.

So, from whatever point of view we look at this question, it always comes down to the same dismal result: government of the vast majority of the people by a privileged minority. But this minority, the Marxists say, will consist of workers. Yes, perhaps of *former* workers, who, as soon as they become rulers or representatives of the people will cease to be workers and will begin to look upon the whole workers' world from the heights of the state. They will no longer represent the people but themselves and their own pretensions to govern the people. Anyone who doubts this is not at all familiar with human nature.

But those elected will be passionately committed as well as learned socialists. The words "learned socialist" and "scientific socialism," which recur constantly in the writings and speeches of the Lassalleans and Marxists, are proof in themselves that the pseudo-popular state will be nothing but the highly despotic government of the masses by a new and very small aristocracy of real or pretended scholars. The people are not learned, so they will be liberated in entirety from the cares of government and included in entirety in the governed herd. A fine liberation!

The Marxists sense this contradiction, and, recognizing that a government of scholars, the most oppressive, offensive, and contemptuous kind in the world, will be a real dictatorship for all its democratic forms, offer the consoling thought that this dictatorship will be temporary and brief. They say that its sole concern and objective will be to educate the people and raise them both economically and politically to such a level that government of any kind will soon become unnecessary and the state, having lost its political, that is, ruling, character, will transform itself into a totally free organization of economic interests and communities.

There is a flagrant contradiction here. If their state is to be truly a people's state, then why abolish it? But if its abolition is essential for the real liberation of the people, then how do they dare call it a people's state? Our polemics against them have forced them to recognize that freedom, or anarchy – that is, the voluntary organization of the workers from below upward – is the ultimate goal of social development, and that any state, including their people's state, is a yoke which gives rise to despotism on the one hand and slavery on the other.

They say that this state yoke, this dictatorship, is a necessary transitional device for achieving the total liberation of the people: anarchy, or freedom, is the goal, and the state, or dictatorship, the means. Thus, for the masses to be liberated they must first be enslaved.

For the moment we have concentrated our polemic on this contradiction. They claim that only a dictatorship (theirs, of course) can create popular freedom. We reply that no dictatorship can have any other objective than to perpetuate itself, and that it can engender and nurture only slavery in the people who endure it. Liberty can be created only by liberty, by an insurrection of all the people and the voluntary organization of the workers from below upward.

In the second part of this book, we will examine this question more closely and in greater detail, for the fate of contemporary history turns on it. Now, however, let us direct the attention of our readers to the following very significant and continually repeated fact.

The political and social theory of the anti-state socialists, or anarchists, leads them directly and inexorably to a complete break with all governments and all forms of bourgeois politics, leaving no alternative but social revolution. Meanwhile, the opposing theory, the theory of the state communists and scientific authority, inexorably enmeshes and entangles its adherents, under the pretext of political tactics, in endless accommodations with governments and the various bourgeois political parties – that is, it thrusts them directly into reaction.

The best proof of this is Lassalle. Who is unaware of his relations and negotiations with Bismarck? The liberals and democrats, against whom he waged relentless and very successful war, took advantage of it to accuse him of venality. Marx's personal adherents in Germany whispered the same thing among themselves, though not so openly. But they all lied. Lassalle was rich and had no reason to sell himself. He was too intelligent and too proud not to prefer the role of independent agitator to the unseemly position of an agent of the government, or of anyone else.

We said that Lassalle was not a man of the people because he was too much of a dandy to mingle with the proletariat outside of meetings, where he usually mesmerized his audience with his clever and brilliant speeches; he was too spoilt by wealth and its attendant habits of elegance and refinement to find satisfaction in the popular milieu; he was too much of a Jew to feel comfortable among the people; and he was too aware of his intellectual superiority not to feel a certain disdain for the uneducated crowd, to which he related more as doctor to patient than as brother to brother. Within these limits he was sincerely devoted to the people's cause, the way an honest doctor is devoted to curing his patient, in whom, nevertheless, he sees not so much a man as a case. We are profoundly convinced that he was so honorable and proud that nothing in the world would have made him betray the people's cause.

There is no need to resort to base suppositions in order to explain Lassalle's relations and transactions with the Prussian minister. Lassalle, as we said, was openly at war with liberals and democrats of all shades and very much scorned these naive rhetoricians, whose helplessness and bankruptcy he perceived clearly. Bismarck, though for different reasons, was also hostile to them, and that served as the initial ground for their rapprochement. The principal basis for it, however, was Lassalle's political and social program, the communist theory created by Marx.

The fundamental point of this program is the liberation (imaginary) of the proletariat *solely by means of the state*. But that requires that the state agree to liberate the proletariat from the yoke of bourgeois capital. How is the state to be imbued with such a desire? There are only two possible methods. The proletariat must carry out a revolution to seize the state – that is the heroic method. In our opinion, once it has seized the state it must immediately destroy it as the eternal prison of the masses. According to Marx's theory, however, the people not only must not destroy it, they must fortify it and strengthen it, and in this form place it at the complete disposal of their benefactors, guardians, and teachers – the leaders of the communist party, in a word, Marx and his friends, who will begin to liberate them in their own way. They will concentrate the reins of government in a strong hand, because the ignorant people require strong supervision. They will create a single state bank, concentrating in their own hands all commercial, industrial, agricultural, and even scientific production, and will divide the people into two armies, one industrial and one agrarian, under the direct command of state engineers, who will form a new privileged scientific and political class.[130]

You see what a splendid goal the school of German communists sets for the people! But to attain all these benefits one innocent little step must first be taken – a revolution! Well, just wait for the Germans to make a revolution! They will discuss it endlessly, but as for actually doing it . . .

The Germans themselves do not believe in a German revolution. Some other nation must initiate it, or some external force must draw or push them into it. By themselves they will never go beyond philosophizing. Consequently another method of seizing the state must be sought. The sympathies of the people who head the state, or who might head it, must be won over.

In Lassalle's time Bismarck headed the state, just as he does today. And who could have replaced him? The liberal and democratic-progressive parties had been defeated; only the purely democratic party remained, which subsequently adopted the name People's Party. In the north, however, it was insignificant, while in the south it the Austrian Empire. Recent events showed that this exclusively bourgeois party had no intrinsic independence or strength. In 1870 it finally disintegrated.

Lassalle was particularly endowed with a practical instinct and practical sense, which neither Marx nor his followers possess. Like all theorists, Marx is an inveterate and incorrigible dreamer when it comes to practical activity. He proved it in his hapless campaign to establish his dictatorship in the International, and through the International over the entire revolutionary movement of the proletariat of Europe and America. One would have to be either a madman or a very abstract scholar to set oneself such a goal. This year Marx suffered a total and well-deserved defeat, but it is not likely to rid him of his ambitious dreams.[131]

Because of these dreams, and also because of his desire to gain admirers and adherents within the bourgeoisie, Marx has continually pushed the proletariat into accommodations with bourgeois radicals. By education and by nature he is a Jacobin, and his favorite dream is of a political dictatorship. Gambetta and Castelar are his true ideals. His heart and all his thoughts are with them, and if he has recently been obliged to renounce them, it is only because they did not know how to pretend to be socialists.

A twofold dream lies within this desire to compromise with the radical bourgeoisie, which Marx has manifested more strongly in recent years: first, that the radical bourgeoisie, if it succeeds in seizing state power, will want, will be capable of wanting, to use it for the benefit of the proletariat; and secondly, that the radical party, having seized the state, will be in a position to resist reaction, the roots of which lie hidden within itself.

The bourgeois-radical party is separated from the mass of laborers by the fact that it is profoundly, one might say organically, tied to the exploiting class by its economic and political interests and by all its habits of life, its ambition, its vanity, and its prejudices. How, then, can it have any desire to use the power it has won for the benefit of the people (even if it has won it with the people's help)? That would mean the suicide of the entire class, and class suicide is inconceivable. The reddest, most fervent democrats were, are, and will remain so bourgeois that any serious declaration of socialist demands and instincts by the people that goes beyond mere lip service will always be enough to make them hurl themselves immediately into the most vehement and insane reaction.

This is logically necessary, and in addition to logic, the whole of recent history proves it to be necessary. It is enough to remember the

utter betrayal by the red republican party in the June Days of 1848 –
though that example and the harsh lesson Napoleon III gave in the
following twenty years do not seem to have prevented the same thing
from repeating itself in France in 1870–71. Gambetta and his party
turned out to be the fiercest enemies of revolutionary socialism. They
handed France over, bound hand and foot, to the outrageous reaction
we see today. Another example is Spain. The most radical political
party, the Intransigent Party, turned out to be the fiercest enemy of
international socialism.[132]

Now for the other question: is the radical bourgeoisie in a position
to carry out a victorious revolution without a popular insurrection?
Merely posing this question is enough to answer it in the negative: of
course not. It is not the people who need the bourgeoisie, but the
bourgeoisie who need the people to carry out a revolution. This has
become clear everywhere, but clearer in Russia than anywhere else.
Take all our gentry and bourgeois youth who dream and philosophize
about revolution. First, how are they to be formed into a single living
body, with one thought and one purpose? They can be united only by
submerging themselves in the people. Outside of the people they will
always remain a senseless crowd of empty windbags, devoid of will
and completely powerless.

The best people of the bourgeois world, bourgeois by origin but not
by convictions or aspirations, can be useful only on the condition that
they immerse themselves in the people, solely in the people's cause. If
they continue to exist outside of the people, they will not only be
useless to them but positively harmful.

The radical party, however, constitutes a separate party, living and
acting outside of the people. What does its desire for an alliance with
the laboring people indicate? Nothing more and nothing less than
recognition of its own impotence, recognition that it needs the
people's help to seize state power (not, of course, for the people's
benefit but for its own). And as soon as it seizes power, it will inevitably become the people's enemy. Having become their enemy, it will
lose its former point of support in the people, and in order to maintain
power even temporarily it will be forced to seek new sources of
support against the people, in alliances and compromises with the
defeated reactionary parties. Proceeding thus from concession to concession, from betrayal to betrayal, it will hand over both itself and the
people to reaction. Listen to what Castelar, that fierce republican,

says now that he has become a dictator: "Politics is a matter of concessions and compromises. Therefore I intend to place generals from the moderate monarchist party at the head of the republican army." What the end result of that will be, of course, is clear to everyone.

Lassalle, as a practical man, understood this perfectly. Besides, he had profound contempt for the whole German bourgeoisie, so he could not advise the workers to link themselves to any bourgeois party.

Revolution was one alternative. But Lassalle knew his compatriots too well to expect any revolutionary initiative from them. What was left? Only one thing – to get together with Bismarck.

Marx's theory provided a meeting point: a vast, unified, strongly centralized state. This was what Lassalle wanted, and Bismarck was already doing it. Why should they not join forces?

From the moment he entered the government, or even from the time of the Prussian Diet in 1848, Bismarck showed that he was the enemy, a contemptuous enemy, of the bourgeoisie. His actual behavior, however, indicates that he is no fanatic and no slave of the noble-feudal party, to which he belongs by origin and education. With the help of the defeated, subjugated, and slavishly obedient party of bourgeois liberals, democrats, republicans, and even social-ists, he is taking the noble-feudal party down a few pegs and seeks ultimately to reduce it to a common denominator in relation to the state.

His principal objective, like that of Lassalle and Marx, is the state. Therefore Lassalle was incomparably more logical and practical than Marx, who regards Bismarck as a revolutionary (in his own way, of course) but dreams of overthrowing him, probably because Bismarck occupies the paramount position in the state, which, in Marx's opinion, ought to belong to him.

Lassalle evidently did not have such a high opinion of himself and therefore had no aversion to entering into relations with Bismarck. Conforming strictly to the political program Marx and Engels had set forth in the *Communist Manifesto*, Lassalle demanded only one thing of Bismarck: that state credit be made available to the workers' producer associations. But at the same time (and this shows how much he trusted Bismarck), again in conformity with the *Communist Manifesto*'s pro-gram, he conducted a peaceful and legal campaign among the workers for the achievement of voting rights – another dream about which we have already expressed our opinion.

Lassalle's unexpected and premature death did not allow him to complete his plans or even to develop them to any degree.

After the death of Lassalle, under the direct influence of the friends and followers of Marx, a third party began to form in Germany between the free federation of the *Association of German Workers' Societies* and Lassalle's *General German Workers' Association*. This was the *German Social-Democratic Workers' Party*. It was headed by two very talented men, one a semi-worker, the other a writer and direct disciple and agent of Marx: Bebel and Liebknecht.

We have already recounted the lamentable consequences of Liebknecht's expedition to Vienna in 1868. It resulted in the Nuremberg Congress of August 1868, at which the *Social-Democratic Party* was finally organized.[133]

It was intended by its founders, who were acting under the direct guidance of Marx, to become the pan-German section of the International Working Men's Association. But German, and especially Prussian, law prohibited such an affiliation. Therefore it was proclaimed only in an oblique fashion, specifically in the following words: "The German Social-Democratic Workers' Party is associated with the International to the extent permitted by German law."

Unquestionably, this new party was founded with the secret hope and intention of using it to introduce Marx's entire program into the International, which had rejected it at its first Congress at Geneva in 1866.

Marx's program became the program of the Social-Democratic Party. It begins by repeating several of the main articles of the International's program as adopted by the Geneva Congress. Then, suddenly, there is an abrupt transition to "the conquest of political power," which is recommended to the German workers as "the immediate and direct objective" of the new party, with the addition of the following significant sentence: "The conquest of political rights (universal suffrage, freedom of the press, freedom of association and public assembly, and so forth), is the necessary *preliminary* condition for the economic emancipation of the workers."

This is what the sentence means: before they undertake a social revolution, the workers must carry out a political revolution, or (to accord better with the character of the Germans) must win, or, more simply, obtain political rights by means of peaceful agitation. Since a political movement prior to, or (what amounts to the same thing) *apart from* a social one can be nothing other than a bourgeois movement, it follows that this program recommends to the German workers that they first adopt bourgeois interests and objectives and carry out a political movement for the benefit of the radical bourgeoisie – which then, in gratitude, will not liberate the people but will subject them to a new government, a new exploitation.

On the basis of this program the touching reconciliation of the German and Austrian workers with the bourgeois radicals of the People's Party was effected. When the Nuremberg Congress ended, delegates elected for this purpose by the congress set out for Stuttgart, where a formal defensive and offensive alliance was concluded between these representatives of the deceived workers and the leaders of the bourgeois-radical party.

As a result of this alliance, the two groups showed up together, as brethren, at the second Congress of the League of Peace and Freedom, which opened in September in Berne. Quite a remarkable event took place there. Many if not all of our readers have heard of the schism which first manifested itself at this congress between the bourgeois socialists and democrats and the revolutionary socialists who belonged to the so-called Alliance or joined it afterwards.*[134]

The question that served as the ostensible reason for the split (it had already become inevitable much earlier) was posed by the Alliancists in very clear and definite terms. They wanted to expose the bourgeois democrats and socialists, to make them declare out loud not only their indifference but their active hostility to the only question that can be called a popular one – the social question.

To this end they proposed that the League of Peace and Freedom recognize as the principal objective of all its efforts "the equalization of individuals" (not merely in the political or legal sense but above all in the economic sense) "and of classes" (in the sense of their total abolition). In other words, they invited the League to adopt a social-revolutionary program.

They deliberately gave their proposal a very moderate form, so that their opponents, the majority of the League, would have no oppor-

---

* Those who do not know of it can gather the essential information from the second volume of our publications: *The Historical Development of the International*, Part I, pp. 301–65, 1873.[135]

tunity to mask their refusal with objections to an excessively strident formulation of the question. They told them clearly: "For now we are not touching on the question of the means of achieving this objective. We are asking you, do you want the objective itself? Do you acknowledge it as a legitimate objective, and as the principal, not to say the only, objective at the present moment? Do you want to attain complete equality – not physiological, not ethnographic, but social and economic equality – of all individuals, whatever part of the earth they belong to, whatever their nation or gender? We are convinced, and the whole of modern history serves to confirm it, that as long as mankind is divided into a minority of exploiters and a majority that is exploited, liberty is inconceivable and becomes a lie. If you want liberty for all, then you must want universal equality, as we do. Do you want it, yes or no?"

Had the bourgeois democrats and socialists been smarter, they would have answered "yes" in order to preserve their honor but as *practical* people would have postponed the realization of the objective to the distant future. The Alliancists, fearing such a reply, had arranged beforehand in such case to raise the question of the ways and means of achieving the objective. Then they would have brought forward the question of individual and collective property, and the question of abolishing legal rights and the state.

The majority of the congress would have found this second question much more suitable as a field of battle. The clarity of the first question was such as to allow of no evasions. The second question, however, is much more complex and is open to a countless number of interpretations, so that with a certain amount of agility one can speak and vote against popular socialism and still seem to be a socialist and a friend of the people. The school of Marx has given us many examples in this regard, and the German dictator is so hospitable (on the indispensable condition that everyone bow down to him) that he now takes under his standard a vast number of thoroughly bourgeois socialists and democrats – even the League of Peace and Freedom could have found refuge there, if only it had agreed to acknowledge his primacy.

Had the bourgeois congress acted thus, the position of the Alliancists would have become incomparably more difficult. The same struggle would have taken place between them and the League that now exists between them and Marx. But the League proved more stupid, and at the same time more honest, than the Marxists: it accepted battle on the first field offered to it, and to the question "do you want economic equality, yes or no?," the great majority answered "no." Thereby it cut itself off completely from the proletariat and condemned itself to imminent death. And it did die, leaving behind only two wandering and bitterly complaining ghosts: Amand Gögg and the Saint-Simonian millionaire Lemonnier.[136]

Now let us return to a strange episode that occurred at this congress. The delegates from Nuremberg and Stuttgart – that is, the workers dispatched by the Nuremberg Congress of the new Social-Democratic Party and the bourgeois Schwabians of the People's Party – voted unanimously along with the majority of the League against equality. That the bourgeoisie voted this way is no cause for astonishment; they are not bourgeois for nothing. No bourgeois, even the reddest revolutionary, can want economic equality, because such equality is death to him.

But how could workers, members of the Social-Democratic Party, have voted against equality? Does it not prove that the program to which they are now subject is leading them directly toward a goal completely contrary to the one prescribed by their social position and social instinct, and that their alliance with the bourgeois radicals, concluded for political purposes, is based not on the swallowing up of the bourgeoisie by the proletariat but, to the contrary, on the subjugation of the proletariat by the bourgeoisie?

There was another remarkable event: the Brussels Congress of the International, which ended its sessions a few days before the Berne Congress of the League, rejected any solidarity with the latter, and all the Marxists who participated in the Brussels Congress spoke and voted to this effect. How, then, could other Marxists, acting like these under the direct influence of Marx, achieve such touching unanimity with the majority of the Berne Congress?

It has remained an unsolved riddle to this day. The same contradiction appeared throughout 1868 and even after 1869 in the *Volksstaat*, the main, one may say the official, newspaper of the Social-Democratic Party, edited by Bebel and Liebknecht. Sometimes it would print quite strong articles against the bourgeois League, but they would be followed by unmistakable declarations of affection, or sometimes friendly reproaches. A newspaper that is supposed to represent purely popular interests seemed to be begging the League to tone down its excessively vehement expressions of its bourgeois instincts, which were compromising the defenders of the League in the eyes of the workers.

This sort of vacillation within Marx's party continued until September 1869, that is, until the Basle Congress. That congress marks a watershed in the development of the International.

Hitherto, the Germans had taken very little part in the congresses of the International. The workers of France, Belgium, Switzerland, and to some degree England had played the major role. But now the Germans, having organized a party on the basis of a program more political and bourgeois than social and popular, appeared at the Basle Congress like a well-drilled regiment and voted as one man, under the strict supervision of one of their leaders, Liebknecht.

Their first concern, of course, was to introduce their program, with a proposal that the political question be considered ahead of all others. A heated battle occurred, in which the Germans suffered a decisive defeat. The Basle Congress preserved the integrity of the International's program and did not allow the Germans to distort it by introducing bourgeois politics into it.

Thus began the schism in the International, the cause of which was and remains the Germans. They had the gall to propose to a preeminently international association – they tried to impose upon it almost by force – their narrowly bourgeois, exclusively German or pan-German program of national politics.

They were thoroughly routed, and the members of the Alliance of Social Revolutionaries, the Alliancists, made no small contribution to their defeat. Hence the Germans' fierce hatred for the Alliance. The end of 1869 and the first half of 1870 were filled with malicious abuse and even more malicious (and sometimes sordid) intrigues by the Marxists against its members.

But all this soon came to a halt in the face of the military and political thunderstorm which gathered over Germany and broke out over France. The outcome of the war is well known: France fell, and Germany, transformed into an empire, took its place.

We just said that Germany took France's place. No, it took a place that no state had occupied before in modern history, not even Charles V's Spain. Perhaps only the empire of Napoleon I can compare with it in power and influence.

We do not know what would have happened if Napoleon III had

won. Without doubt, things would have been bad, perhaps very bad; but nothing could have been more unfortunate for the entire world and for the liberty of nations than the situation that exists today. For other countries the effects of a victory by Napoleon III would have been like an acute disease, painful but not prolonged, because no stratum of the French nation has a sufficient measure of that organic statist element which is essential for the consolidation and perpetuation of victory. The French themselves would have destroyed their temporary predominance, which might have flattered their vanity but which their temperament cannot abide.

The German is something else again. He is created simultaneously for slavery and for domination. The Frenchman is a soldier by temperament and boastfulness, but he cannot tolerate discipline. The German submits willingly to the most unbearable, humiliating, and onerous discipline. He is even prepared to love it, as long as it places him, or, rather, his German state, above all other states and nations.

How else can one explain the insane rapture that seized the entire German nation – all, absolutely all strata of German society – when news came of the series of brilliant victories won by the German army, and, finally, of the taking of Paris? Everyone in Germany knew very well that the direct result of those victories would be the decisive predominance of the military element, which was already notable for its inordinate arrogance, and that the triumph of the crudest reaction would ensue in domestic life. And what happened? Not a single German, or scarcely a single one, grew alarmed. On the contrary, they all joined in the unanimous rapture. The entire Schwabian opposition melted away like snow beneath the radiance of the new imperial sun. The People's Party disappeared, and burghers, nobles, peasants, professors, artists, writers, and students began to sing in unison of pan-German triumph. All the German associations and circles abroad held celebrations and cried "long live the emperor!" (that same individual who had hanged democrats in 1849*[a]*). All the liberals, democrats, and republicans became Bismarckians. Even in the United States, where one might have thought they had learned something about freedom and grown accustomed to it, millions of ecstatic German immigrants celebrated the victory of pan-German despotism.

Such a universal fact cannot be a passing phenomenon. It reveals the deep passion dwelling in the soul of every German, a passion

[a] The text reads 1848.

which comprises the seemingly inseparable elements of command and obedience, domination and slavery.

And the German workers? They did nothing. They did not issue a single energetic declaration of sympathy for the workers of France. There were a few meetings where a few phrases were spoken in which jubilant national pride seemed to fall silent before the expression of international solidarity. But no one went beyond phrase-making, even though that might have been the time to start something and do something in Germany, which had been emptied of troops. It is true that a number of workers had been drafted into the army, where they fulfilled their obligations as soldiers splendidly, meaning that they beat, choked, slashed, and shot everyone as ordered by their commanders, and pillaged as well. Some of them, even as they carried out their military obligations in this fashion, wrote doleful letters to the *Volksstaat* describing in vivid colors the acts of barbarism perpetrated by the German army in France.

There were, however, some examples of more steadfast opposition, such as the protests of the valiant old Jacoby, for which he was imprisoned in a fortress, and the protests of Liebknecht and Bebel, who are still in prison today. But these were isolated and very rare examples. We cannot forget the article that appeared in September 1870 in the *Volksstaat* blatantly displaying pan-German exultation. It began with the following words: "Thanks to the victories won by the German army, the historical initiative has finally passed from France to Germany; we Germans . . ."

In short, it can be said that without exception *an enthusiastic sentiment of military, political, and national triumph* prevailed among the Germans and continues to prevail today. That is what the power of the pan-German empire and of its great chancellor, Prince Bismarck, relies on in the main.

The rich provinces that have been annexed, the countless masses of captured weapons, and the 5 billion franc indemnity which allows Germany to maintain a huge, extremely well-armed and perfected army; the creation of the empire and its organic subordination to the Prussian autocracy; the building of new fortresses and the creation of a navy – all these factors, of course, are significant contributions to the expansion of pan-German power. Nevertheless, its main support lies in the profound and undeniable sympathy of the people.

As one of our Swiss friends put it: "Now every German tailor living in Japan, China, or Moscow feels that he has the German navy and all of Germany's power behind him. This proud consciousness sends him into an insane rapture: the German has finally lived to see the day when he can say with pride, relying on his own state, like an Englishman or an American, 'I am a German.' True, when the Englishman or American says 'I am an Englishman,' or 'I am an American,' he is saying 'I am a free man.' The German, however, is saying 'I am a slave, but my emperor is stronger than all other princes, and the German soldier who is strangling me will strangle all of you.' "

Will the German people content themselves with this feeling of pride for long? Who can say? They have thirsted so long for the grace of a unified state, a single cudgel, that has now descended upon them that one must assume they will want to enjoy it for quite some time yet. Every nation has its own tastes, and the German nation has a particular taste for a strong cudgel in the form of the state.

No one can doubt that with state centralization Germany will develop – indeed, has already begun to develop – all the evils, all the depravity, all the causes of internal disintegration that vast centralized states inevitably entail. It is even less possible to doubt that the process of moral and intellectual decay is already taking place before everyone's eyes. One only has to read the German journals, the most conservative or the most moderate, to encounter horrifying descriptions everywhere of the corruption that has seized the German public, which has the reputation of being the most honest in the world.

It is the inevitable result of capitalist monopoly, which always and everywhere accompanies the strengthening and expansion of state centralization. It can be said that privileged capital, concentrated in a few hands, has today become the soul of every state. The state is financed by it, and by it alone, and in return guarantees it the unlimited right to exploit the people's labor. Financial monopoly is inseparable from stock-market speculation, which squeezes the last kopeck out of the masses (and the increasingly impoverished petty and middle bourgeoisie as well) by means of joint-stock industrial and commercial companies.

With stock speculation the old bourgeois virtues based on thrift, moderation, and work begin to decline. A common desire to get rich quick arises, and since that is impossible without fraud or so-called legal (as well as illegal) but cunning theft, the old philistine honesty and scrupulousness must necessarily disappear.

It is remarkable how rapidly the celebrated German honesty is vanishing before our eyes. The honest German philistine was indescribably narrow and stupid, but the corrupt German is such a repulsive creature that words fail in trying to characterize him. A Frenchman's corruption is concealed by elegance, by a quick and attractive wit. The German's corruption knows no measure, and nothing conceals it. It stands exposed in all its repugnant, crude, and stupid nakedness.

The excellence of German thought, German art, and German science is also manifestly disappearing with this new economic orientation which has seized the whole of German society. The professors have become lackeys more than ever, and the students are drinking even more beer to the health and honor of their emperor.

And the peasants? They remain bewildered. Shunted aside and for several centuries driven systematically into the camp of reaction by the liberal bourgeoisie itself, for the most part they are now the staunchest support of reaction, especially in Austria, central Germany, and Bavaria. Much time must pass yet before they see and understand that the unified pan-German state and the emperor with his innumerable military, civil, and police minions are choking and plundering them.

Finally, we come to the workers. They are confused by their leaders – politicians, *literati*, and Jews. Their position, it is true, is becoming more intolerable year by year, as demonstrated by the serious troubles occurring among them in all the major industrial centers of Germany. Scarcely a month or a week goes by without a street disturbance or sometimes even a clash with the police in some German city. But it should not be concluded that a popular revolution is imminent, first of all because the leaders themselves hate and fear revolution no less than any bourgeois, even though they constantly pay lip service to it!

Because of this hatred and fear, they have directed the entire worker population into so-called legal and peaceful agitation, which usually has as its result the election to the German parliament of one or two workers (or even bourgeois scribblers) from the Social-Democratic Party. Not only is this not dangerous, it is highly useful to the German state as a lightning-rod, or a safety-valve.

In the last analysis, a German revolution cannot be expected because there are very few revolutionary elements in the mind, character, and temperament of the German. The German will argue against any authority and even against the emperor as much as you might wish. There will be no end to his philosophizing – but this very tendency to philosophize, by dissipating his intellectual and moral forces, so to speak, and preventing them from building up, delivers him from the danger of a revolutionary explosion.

Indeed, how could a revolutionary disposition be combined in the German people with the innate habit of obedience and the desire for domination which, as we have already reiterated several times, constitute the fundamental traits of their character? And what is the desire that prevails today in the consciousness or instinct of every German? *The desire to expand far and wide the boundaries of the German Empire.*

Take a German of any social stratum, and you will be lucky to find one in a thousand, or even ten thousand, who will not reply to you in the words of Arndt's famous song: "No, no, no, the German's fatherland must be broader."

Every German believes that the task of forming a great German Empire has only begun, and that its completion requires the annexation of all of Austria (except Hungary), Sweden, Denmark, Holland, a portion of Belgium, another portion of France, and all of Switzerland up to the Alps. That is his passion, and at the present time it overwhelms everything else within him. It also determines all the actions of the Social-Democratic Party today.

Do not think that Bismarck is as ferocious an enemy of this party as he pretends. He is too clever not to see that it serves him as a pioneer, disseminating the German concept of the state in Austria, Sweden, Denmark, Belgium, Holland, and Switzerland. The propagation of this Germanic idea is now the chief aspiration of Marx, who, as we have already noted, tried to resume within the International, to his own advantage, the exploits and victories of Prince Bismarck.

Bismarck holds all the parties in his hands, and he is not about to turn them over to Marx. Much more than the pope or clerical France, he is now the leader of European reaction, one can even say of world reaction.

French reaction is ugly, ridiculous, and highly deplorable, but it is not dangerous. It is too mindless, it too stupidly contradicts all the aspirations of contemporary society (not just of the proletariat, but of the bourgeoisie itself), all the conditions for the existence of the state, for it to become a real force. It is nothing but a sickly, desperate convulsion of the dying French state.

Pan-German reaction is something else entirely. It does not boast of its crude and stupid opposition to the contemporary demands of bourgeois civilization. On the contrary, it takes every possible care to act in complete accord with it on all issues. In the art of concealing its despotic actions and deeds behind the most liberal and even democratic forms, it surpasses its teacher, Napoleon III.

Look at the religious question, for example. Who boldly seized the initiative in resolutely opposing the medieval pretensions of the papal throne?[137] It was Germany, it was Bismarck. He did not fear the intrigues of the Jesuits, who scheme against him everywhere – among the people, whom they incite, and particularly at the imperial court, which still has a great penchant for hypocrisy of every kind. He did not even fear their daggers or poison, with which, as is well known, they have long been in the habit of ridding themselves of dangerous opponents. So strongly did Bismarck attack the Roman Catholic Church that the old and good-hearted Garibaldi – a hero on the field of battle, though a very poor philosopher and politician, who hates priests so much that it is enough to declare oneself their enemy to win his praise as the most progressive and liberal individual – even Garibaldi not long ago published an ecstatic dithyramb to the great German chancellor and proclaimed him the liberator of Europe and the world. The poor general did not understand that today state reaction is incomparably worse and more dangerous than church reaction, which is evil but impotent because it is categorically impossible. State reaction is more dangerous because it is now the last and only possible form of reaction. Many so-called liberals and democrats still do not understand this, and therefore many of them, like Garibaldi, view Bismarck as the champion of popular liberty.

Bismarck is dealing with the social question in exactly the same way. Just a few months ago he convened a veritable social congress of learned German jurists and political economists for a rigorous and profound discussion of all issues of concern to the workers today. To be sure, these gentlemen did not decide anything, nor could they have decided anything, because only one question was put to them: how to improve the situation of the workers without in any way altering the existing relations between capital and labor – or, what amounts to the same thing, how to make the impossible possible. Clearly, they had to disperse without having reached any decisions, but still, it redounded to Bismarck's glory that unlike the other statesmen of Europe he understands the full importance of the social question and is examining it carefully.

Finally, he has completely satisfied the political vanity of the patriotic German bourgeoisie. Not only did he create a powerful, unified pan-German empire, he even endowed it with the most liberal and democratic forms of government. He gave it a parliament based on universal suffrage and with the unlimited right to discuss every conceivable issue, reserving for himself only the right to do and to put into practice whatever he and his sovereign please. Thus he opened to the Germans a new field for unlimited chatter while leaving himself only three things: *finances, the police, and the army* – the very essence of the contemporary state, the very power of reaction.

Thanks to these three trifles, he now holds absolute sway over Germany, and through Germany over the entire continent of Europe. We have provided evidence, and, it seems to us, have proved, that all the other continental states are either so weak that they are not worth talking about; have not yet established themselves – and, indeed, never will – as serious states, like Italy; or are in the process of disintegrating, like Austria, Turkey, Russia, Spain, and France. Amid half-built structures, on the one side, and ruins, on the other, in all its beauty and strength rises the majestic edifice of the pan-German state – the last refuge of all privileges and monopolies (that is, of bourgeois civilization), the last and mighty bulwark of statism (that is, of reaction). Indeed, only one real state exists on the European continent, the pan-German state; all the rest are mere vice-royalties of the great German Empire.

Through the lips of its great chancellor, this empire has declared life-and-death war on the social revolution. Bismarck pronounced its death sentence in the name of the 40 million Germans who stand behind him and serve as his support. Meanwhile, Marx, his envious rival, and following him all the leaders of the German Social-Democratic Party, as though in endorsement of Bismarck, for their part have also declared desperate war on the social revolution. We will set all of this forth in detail in the next part of this work.

We will see that at the present moment on one side stands full-scale reaction, embodied in the German Empire and in the German people, who are gripped solely by a passion for conquest and domination – that is, for the rule of the state. On the other side, as the sole champion of the liberation of nations, of the millions of laborers of all countries, social revolution raises its head. For the present it has consolidated its forces only in the south of Europe, in Italy, Spain, and France. But soon, we hope, under its banner will stand the nations of northwestern Europe as well: Belgium, Holland, particularly England – and, finally, all the Slavic nations, too.

On the pan-German banner is written: *Maintain and strengthen the state at all costs.* On the social-revolutionary banner, our banner, in letters of fire and blood, is inscribed: *Abolish all states, destroy bourgeois civilization, organize freely from below upward, by means of free associations – organize the unshackled laboring hordes, the whole of liberated humanity, create a new world for all mankind.*

In the next part we will show how these two opposing principles have emerged and developed in the consciousness of the European proletariat.

Appendix A

To avoid misunderstanding, we feel it necessary to remark that what we call the people's *ideal* has nothing to do with those political and social constructs, formulas, and theories which bourgeois scholars or semi-scholars devise at their leisure, in isolation from popular life, and graciously offer to the *ignorant crowd* as the necessary form of their future organization. We have no faith whatsoever in those theories, and even the best of them seem to us Procrustean beds, too narrow to encompass the broad and powerful sweep of popular life.

Even the most rational and profound science cannot divine the form social life will take in the future. It can determine only the *negative* conditions, which follow logically from a rigorous critique of existing society. Thus, by means of such a critique, social and economic science rejected hereditary individual property and, consequently, took the abstract and, so to speak, *negative* position of collective property as a necessary condition of the future social order. In the same way, it rejected the very idea of the state or of statism, meaning the government of society from above downward in the name of some imaginary right – theological or metaphysical, divine or intellectual and scientific. Therefore it took the opposite, or negative, position: anarchy, meaning the free and independent organization of all the units and parts of the community and their voluntary federation from below upward, not by the orders of any authority, even an elected one, and not by the dictates of any scientific theory, but as a result of the natural development of all the varied demands put forth by life itself.

Therefore no scholar can teach the people or even define for himself how they will and must live on the morrow of the social revolution. That will be determined first by the situation of each people, and secondly by the desires that manifest themselves and operate most strongly within them – not by guidance and explanations from above and not by any theories invented on the eve of the revolution.

We know that a distinct current advocating the formation of so-called teachers of the people has now developed in Russia.[138] It maintains that the people must first be educated, and only when they are educated and understand their rights and obligations can they be incited to revolt. The question immediately arises: what are you going to teach the people? Is it not what you yourselves do not know and cannot know, and must first learn from the people?

Within this current or party (which, however, is not at all new), two categories of people must be distinguished.

The more numerous one is the category of doctrinaires, charlatans, who for the most part deceive themselves as well. Without renouncing any of the satisfactions and advantages that existing society affords the rich and privileged minority, they want to acquire or preserve the reputation of people truly dedicated to the cause of popular liberation, or even of revolutionaries – as long as it does not entail excessive inconvenience. All too many such gentlemen have appeared in Russia. They establish people's banks, consumer cooperatives, and producer associations, they study the question of women, of course, and they loudly term themselves proponents of science, positivists, and now Marxists. The common trait that distinguishes them is that they make no sacrifices. They look out for and take care of their own dear persons above all, while at the same time wanting to pass for progressive individuals in every respect.

Discussion is useless with these people, however numerous they may be. Until the revolution, they can only be exposed and shamed; when the revolution comes . . . well, we hope they will disappear of their own accord.

There is another category, however, consisting of honest and truly dedicated young people who have lately fallen in with this party as though out of desperation, only because it seems to them that under current conditions there is no other cause and no other alternative. We will not describe them more precisely lest they attract the attention of the police, but those among them who read these lines will understand that our words are addressed directly to them.

We would like to ask them what they intend to teach the people. Do they want to teach them rational science? As far as we know, that is not their objective. They know that the government would immediately stop anyone who tried to introduce science into the popular schools, and they also know that our people are too poverty-stricken to have any interest in science. For theory to be made accessible to them their practical circumstances must be changed, and first of all their economic conditions must be radically transformed and they must be wrested from their general, almost universal hunger and poverty.

But how can honest individuals change the people's economic life? They have no power, and even the power of the state itself, as we will try to demonstrate below, is incapable of improving the people's economic situation. The only thing it can do for them is to abolish itself, to disappear, for its existence is incompatible with the good of the people, which can be created only by the people themselves.

What can the friends of the people do, then? Incite them to independent initiative and action, and first of all – as even the conscientious proponents of the party we have just been speaking of maintain – show them the ways and the means of their liberation.

Those ways and means can be of two kinds: purely revolutionary ones, leading directly to the organization of a universal uprising; and other, more peaceful ones, which begin the liberation of the people with a slow and systematic but at the same time radical transformation of their economic life. This second method, if it is to be followed sincerely, of course excludes the trite sermons about savings that are so beloved by bourgeois economists, for the simple reason that laboring people in general, and ours in particular, have absolutely nothing to save.

But what can honest individuals do in order to draw our people onto the path of a slow but radical economic transformation? Are they to establish chairs of sociology in the villages? In the first place, our paternally vigilant government again would not allow it; in the second place, the peasants would understand nothing and would laugh at the professors; and finally, sociology itself is a science of the future. At present it is incomparably richer in unresolved questions than in positive answers, and even aside from the fact that our poor peasants have no time to study it, one can have an impact on them only by means of practical activity, not theory.

What can this practical activity consist of? Should it set as its main objective, if not its only one, to draw the whole enormous mass of our peasantry onto the path of independent economic change in the spirit of contemporary sociology? That can consist of nothing but the formation of workers' *artels*[a] and credit, consumers', and producers' cooperatives – especially the last, as they lead more directly than the others to the goal of emancipating labor from the sway of bourgeois capital.

But is that emancipation possible under the economic conditions prevailing in contemporary society? Science, on the basis of facts, and specifically a whole series of experiments made in the last twenty years in various countries, tells us categorically: no. Lassalle (of whom, however, we are by no means followers) in the most brilliant and popularized fashion proved in his pamphlets that it is impossible, and all the latest economists agree with him, even bourgeois (but serious) economists, however reluctant they are to reveal the impotence of the cooperative system, which they quite rightly regard as a lightning-rod protecting against the thunderbolts of social revolution.

The International, for its part, raised the question of cooperative associations frequently over the course of several years. On the basis of a number of arguments, it came to the following conclusion, set forth at the Lausanne Congress of 1867 and confirmed at the Brussels Congress of 1868.

Cooperation in all its forms is undeniably a rational and just mode of future production. But for it to achieve its objective – liberation of all the workers and their full compensation and satisfaction – all forms of land and capital must become collective property. Until that occurs, cooperation in the majority of cases will be crushed by the almighty competition of big capital and big landholding. In the rare cases when some producers' association, invariably more or less isolated, does succeed in withstanding and surviving this struggle, the result of its success will merely be the rise of a new privileged class of fortunate collectivists within the destitute mass of the proletariat. Thus, under the existing conditions of social economy, cooperation cannot liberate the worker masses. Nevertheless, it does offer the benefit, even now,

[a] An *artel* was a traditional Russian kind of cooperative association of artisans or laborers.

of accustoming the workers to unite, organize, and independently manage their own affairs.

Despite recognition of its undeniable usefulness, however, the cooperative movement, which at first advanced rapidly, has of late weakened considerably in Europe. The reason is very simple: having lost the conviction that they can achieve their liberation by this method, the worker masses have not deemed it necessary to resort to it to complete their practical education. Once they lost confidence that they could attain their objective, they scorned the path leading to it also – or, rather, the path not leading to it. They have no time to engage in gymnastic exercises, even though they may be useful.

What is true in the West cannot be false in the East, and we do not believe that the cooperative movement can attain very sizable dimensions in Russia. Cooperation is even less of a possibility in Russia today than in the West. One of the chief conditions for its success wherever it has succeeded is individual initiative, persistence, and prowess, but individuality is much more developed in the West than in Russia, where the herd instinct still prevails. In addition, external circumstances, both political and social, as well as the educational level in the West are incomparably more favorable for the formation and development of cooperative societies – and even so, the cooperative movement has begun to decline there. How, then, can it thrive in Russia?

It will be said that the herd-like character of the Russian people's instincts may be favorable to cooperation. The elements of progress, the uninterrupted improvement of the organization of work, of production and its products, without which the struggle against the competition of capital, so unequal to begin with, will become completely impossible, are incompatible with herd-like activity, which invariably leads to routinization. Cooperation, therefore, can flourish in Russia only on the most insignificant, not to say minute, scale, and only as long as it remains unnoticed and unfelt by the all-oppressive forces of capital and the even more oppressive forces of the government.

We find it understandable, however, why young people, seeing no other alternative, throw themselves into the so-called cooperative movement. On the one hand, they are too honest and serious to amuse themselves with liberal phrase-making and to camouflage their selfishness with the doctrinaire, soulless, meaningless scholarly twaddle of a Mirtov or Kedrov,[139] and, on the other hand, too alive and passionate to remain with their arms folded in shameful inactivity. This at least gives them the opportunity to come in contact with workers, to join their ranks, to get to know them, and, insofar as possible, to unite them for the purpose of attaining some objective. That is far more consoling and useful than doing nothing at all.

From that point of view we have nothing against cooperative endeavors. At the same time, however, we believe that the young people who undertake them should not deceive themselves as to the results they can obtain. In the large towns and manufacturing settlements, among the factory workers, those results may be quite considerable. They will be highly insignificant among the rural population, however, where they will be lost like grains of sand in the steppe, like drops in the sea . . .

But is it true that in Russia today there is no other alternative, no other cause, than cooperative enterprises? We believe it is decidedly untrue.

The two primary elements we would point to as the necessary preconditions for social revolution exist on the broadest scale among the Russian people. They can boast of inordinate poverty and of exemplary servitude. Their sufferings are without number, and they bear them not with patience but with profound and passionate desperation which has already found expression twice in history, in two terrible outbursts – the Stenka Razin and Pugachev uprisings – and to this day has not ceased to manifest itself in an uninterrupted series of local peasant insurrections.

What prevents them from carrying out a fully victorious revolution? Do they lack a common ideal capable of giving meaning to a popular revolution, of giving it a well-defined objective, and without which, as we said above, a simultaneous and universal uprising of the entire people, and, consequently, the success of the revolution itself, is impossible? But it would scarcely be correct to say that the Russian people have not yet developed such an ideal.

If such an ideal did not exist in the people's consciousness, at least in its main outlines, one would have to give up all hope of a Russian revolution, because such an ideal arises from the very depths of popular life. It is the product of the people's historical experiences, of their strivings, sufferings, protests, and struggle, and at the same time it is a graphic expression, as it were, always simple and comprehensible to all, of their real demands and hopes.

If the people do not develop this ideal themselves, of course, no one can give it to them. In general, it must be noted that nobody – neither an individual, a society, nor a people – can be given what does not already exist within him, not just in embryonic form but at a certain level of development. Take the individual. If an idea does not already exist within him as a vital instinct, and as a more or less clear concept which serves, as it were, as the first reflection of that instinct, you will never explain it to him or get him to understand it. Look at a bourgeois who is satisfied with his fate. Can you ever hope to explain to him the proletarian's right to full human development and equal participation in all the enjoyments, satisfactions, and blessings of social life, or prove to him the legitimacy and salutary necessity of social revolution? No, unless you have taken leave of your senses you will not even attempt it. And why not? Because you will be convinced that even if this bourgeois were by nature good, intelligent, noble, magnanimous, and disposed to justice – you see what concessions I am making, but in fact there are not many such bourgeois on earth – even if he were educated, even learned, he still would not understand you and would not become a social revolutionary. And why not? For the simple reason that his life has not generated within him instinctive strivings that would correspond to your social-revolutionary idea. On the other hand, if those strivings did exist within him, even in embryonic form or as the most absurd sorts of concepts, then however much his social position might please his sensibilities and satisfy his vanity, he could not rest content with himself.

On the other hand, take the least educated and most ridiculous fellow: if you can only find within him instincts and honest, though vague, aspirations that correspond to the social-revolutionary idea, however primitive his actual conceptions may be, do not shy away, but occupy yourself with him seriously, with love, and you will see how broadly and passionately he will embrace and assimilate your idea – or, rather, his own idea, for it is nothing other than the clear, full, and logical expression of his own instinct. In essence, you have not given him anything, you have not brought him anything new, but merely clarified for him what existed in him long before he encountered you. That is why I say that no one can give anyone anything.

But if this is true in regard to the individual, it is all the more true in regard to an entire people. One would have to be a complete idiot or an incurable doctrinaire to imagine that one can give anything to the people, that one can bestow upon them any kind of material blessing or a new intellectual or moral outlook, a new truth, and arbitrarily give their lives a new direction, or, as the late Chaadaev put it thirty-six years ago, speaking specifically of the Russian people, write on them what you will, as though they were a blank sheet of paper.[140]

Among the greatest geniuses to date, few have actually done anything for the people. A nation's geniuses are highly aristocratic, and everything they have done up to now has served only to educate, strengthen, and enrich the exploiting minority. The poor masses, forsaken and abused by everyone, have had to break their own martyr's path to freedom and light by means of an infinite number of obscure and fruitless efforts. The greatest geniuses did not and could not bring society a new content. Created by society themselves, they continued and developed the work of many centuries, bringing only new forms to a content which is continually born anew and broadened by the movement of social life itself.

But, I repeat, the most renowned geniuses have done nothing, or very little, specifically for the people, for the many millions of laboring proletarians. Popular life, popular development, popular progress belong exclusively to the people themselves. That progress is achieved, of course, not by book learning but by the natural accumulation of experience and thought, transmitted from generation to generation and necessarily broadening and deepening its content and perfecting itself and assuming its forms very slowly. An infinite number of severe and bitter historical experiences have finally brought the masses in all countries, or at least in all the European countries, to the realization that they can expect nothing from the privileged classes and contemporary states or from political revolutions in general, and that they can liberate themselves only by their own efforts, by means of social revolution. That is what defines the universal ideal that lives within them and acts upon them today.

Does such an ideal exist in the minds of the Russian people? There is no doubt that it does, nor is it even necessary to delve very deeply into the historical consciousness of our people to define the main features of that ideal.

Its first and principal feature is their universal conviction that the land, all the land, belongs to the people, who have watered it with their sweat and fertilized it with the labor of their own hands. Its second major feature is the belief that the right to use the land belongs not to the individual but to the whole commune, to the *mir*,^a which temporarily distributes it to individuals. The third feature, equal in importance to the preceding two, is the quasi-absolute auton-omy and self-government of the commune, and hence its categorical hostility to the state.

Those are the three main features that lie at the basis of the Russian people's ideal. In essence, they correspond fully to the ideal that has developed in recent years in the consciousness of the pro-letariat of the Latin countries, which today are incomparably closer to social revolution than the Germanic countries. Three other features, however, cloud the Russian people's ideal, distorting its character and very much impeding and retarding its realization. We must therefore struggle against them with all our might – a struggle rendered more possible by the fact that it already exists among the people themselves.

The three dark features are: (1) patriarchalism; (2) the swallowing up of the individual by the *mir*; and (3) faith in the tsar.

One might add as a fourth feature the Christian religion, in the form of official Orthodoxy or of sectarianism. In our opinion, however, this issue does not have nearly the importance in Russia that it has in Western Europe, not only in the Catholic countries but even in the Protestant ones. Social revolutionaries, of course, do not ignore it, and they take every opportunity to speak the murderous truth, in the presence of the people, to the Lord of Hosts and his theological, metaphysical, political, legal, police, and bourgeois-economist representatives on earth. But they do not place the religious issue in the forefront, for they believe that the people's superstition, while a natural accompaniment of their ignorance, is rooted not so much in their ignorance as in their poverty, in their material sufferings and the unheard-of oppressions of every sort which they endure each day. Their religious conceptions and fables, their fantastic predilection for the absurd, are phenomena more practical than theoretical, and not so much a mental delusion as a protest of life, will, and passion against

---

^a The term *mir*, generally used interchangeably with "commune," refers more specifi-cally to the peasant commune as a self-governing community rather than an economic or geographical unit. Communal decisions were made by an assembly, consisting of heads of households, which elected officers and representatives of the *mir* and apportioned tax burdens and other joint obligations to the *mir*'s households. In some parts of Russia, though not all, the *mir* periodically redistributed the commune's arable landholdings to its various households in order to maintain a rough economic equality. The land was then cultivated by and for the benefit of the individual household. It was the practice of

the unbearable burden of their existence. For the people, the church is a kind of celestial tavern, just as the tavern is a sort of celestial church on earth. In church and tavern alike they forget, at least momentarily, their hunger, their oppression, and their humiliation, and they try to dull the memory of their daily afflictions, in the one with mindless faith and in the other with wine. One form of intoxication is as good as the other.

Social revolutionaries know these things and therefore are convinced that the people's religiosity can be eliminated only by a social revolution, and not by the abstract, doctrinaire propaganda of the so-called free-thinkers. Those gentlemen are bourgeois from head to toe, incorrigible metaphysicians in their methods, habits, and way of life, even when they call themselves positivists and fancy themselves materialists. It always seems to them that life follows from thought, that it is in some way the realization of a preconceived idea, and hence they believe that thought (their impoverished thought, of course) should direct life. They do not understand that thought, to the contrary, follows from life, and that in order to alter thought one must first of all change life. Give the people a broad human existence, and they will amaze you with the profound rationality of their ideas.

The inveterate doctrinaires who call themselves free-thinkers have yet another reason for making theoretical, anti-religious propaganda a prerequisite for practical activity. For the most part they are bad revolutionaries, simply vainglorious egotists and cowards. Moreover, by their social position they belong to the educated classes, and they very much cherish the comfort and refined elegance, and the gratification of intellectual vanity, with which the life of those classes is filled. They understand that a popular revolution, by its nature and objective, is crude and unceremonious, that it will not hesitate to destroy the bourgeois world in which they live so well. Therefore, aside from the fact that they have no intention whatsoever of inflicting upon themselves the great inconveniences that accompany honest service to the revolutionary cause, and have no desire to provoke the indignation of their less liberal and audacious but still valued patrons, admirers, friends, and colleagues, with whom they share education, worldly ties, refinement, and material comfort, they simply fear and do not want such a revolution, which would pull them down from

communal land redistribution that persuaded Populist intellectuals that the peasant commune could be a steppingstone to Russian socialism.

their pedestal and suddenly deprive them of all the advantages of their present position.

But they do not want to own up to this, and they feel compelled to shock the bourgeois world with their radicalism and to draw the revolutionary youth, and if possible the people themselves, behind them. How is this to be done? They must shock the bourgeois world but not anger it, and they must attract the revolutionary youth but avoid the revolutionary abyss! There is only one way: to direct all of their pseudo-revolutionary fury against the Lord God. They are so sure of his non-existence that they do not fear his wrath. The authorities are another matter – authorities of any kind, from the tsar to the last policeman! The rich and powerful are another matter, too, from the banker and the Yid tax farmer to the last *kulak*[a] merchant and landowner! Their wrath might make itself felt all too painfully.

On the strength of such reasoning, they declare relentless war on God, in the most radical fashion rejecting religion in all its forms and manifestations and fulminating against theology, metaphysical fantasies, and all popular superstitions in the name of science – which, of course, they carry in their pockets and sprinkle into all their verbose screeds. At the same time, however, they treat with extraordinary delicacy all the political and social powers of this world, and if, compelled by logic and public opinion, they do allow themselves to reject them, they do it so courteously and mildly that one would have to have a very stern temper to get angry at them, and they invariably leave loopholes and express the hope that those powers can be reformed. Their capacity for hoping and believing in them is so great that they even suppose it possible that our Governing Senate will sooner or later become the organ of popular liberation. (See the third and latest program of the non-periodical *Forward!*, which is expected to appear soon in Zurich.)[141]

But let us leave these charlatans and return to our subject.

The people should never be deceived, under any pretext or for any purpose. It would not only be criminal but detrimental to the revolutionary cause, for deception of any kind, by its very nature, is short-sighted, petty, narrow, always sewn with rotten threads, so that it inevitably tears and is exposed. For the revolutionary youth it is a false, arbitrary, and tyrannical course that is repugnant to the people. A person is strong only when he stands upon his own truth, when he

[a] A pejorative term for a well-to-do peasant.

speaks and acts in accordance with his deepest convictions. Then, whatever situation he may be in, he always knows what he must say and do. He may fall, but he cannot bring shame upon himself or his cause. If we seek the liberation of the people by means of a lie, we will surely grow confused, go astray, and lose sight of our objective, and if we have any influence at all on the people we will lead them astray as well – in other words, we will be acting in the spirit of reaction and to its benefit.

Therefore, since we ourselves are deeply convinced atheists, enemies of any religious creed, and materialists, whenever we have occasion to speak with the people about religion we are obliged to give full expression to our lack of belief – I will go further and say our hostile attitude to religion. We should reply honestly to all their questions on this subject, and, when necessary, that is, when there is a prospect of success, we must even try to explain and prove to them the correctness of our views. But we should not ourselves seek opportunities for such discussions. We should not place the religious question in the forefront of our propaganda among the people. It is our profound conviction that to do so is synonymous with betrayal of the people's cause.

The people are neither doctrinaires nor philosophers. They are not in the habit of concerning themselves with a number of questions simultaneously, nor do they have the leisure to do so. When absorbed in one question, they forget all others. Therefore, it is our direct obligation to place before them the principal question on the resolution of which their liberation most depends. But that question is indicated by their very situation, by their whole existence – it is the economic and political question, economic in the sense of social revolution and political in the sense of destruction of the state. To occupy them with the religious question is to distract them from their real cause and thus to betray it.

The people's cause consists solely of the realization of their ideal, perhaps correcting it in accordance with the people's own desires and directing it along the straightest and quickest path to its objective. We have pointed out the three unfortunate traits that particularly cloud the Russian people's ideal. Now let us note that the latter two, the swallowing up of the individual by the *mir* and worship of the tsar, strictly speaking follow from the first, patriarchalism, as its natural consequences. Patriarchalism is therefore the main historical evil –

but unfortunately a thoroughly popular one – against which we are obliged to struggle with all our might.

That evil has distorted the whole of Russian life and given it the characteristics that make it unendurable: obtuse immobility, hopeless filth, ingrained falsehood, greedy hypocrisy, and, finally, servile bondage. The despotism of the husband, the father, and the elder brother turned the family – already immoral in its legal and economic foundations – into a school of triumphant force and tyranny, of daily domestic baseness and depravity. A "whited sepulcher" is the perfect expression to describe the Russian family. The good Russian family man, if he is in fact a good man but lacking in character – meaning a good-natured swine, innocent and irresponsible – is a being who has no clear consciousness of anything, has no definite desires, and does good and evil indifferently and, as it were, unwittingly, almost at one and the same time. His actions are determined much less by goals than by circumstances, by his mood at the moment, and especially by his environment. Habituated to obedience within the family, he continues to obey and to bend with the wind in society as well. He is created to be and to remain a slave, but he will not be a despot. He does not have the strength for that. Therefore, he will not flog anyone himself, but he will without fail hold down the unfortunate individual, guilty or innocent, whom the authorities want to flog. Those authorities appear before him in three principal and sacred forms: as father, as *mir*, and as tsar.

If he is a man of mettle and fire, however, he will be a slave and at the same time a despot who tyrannizes over anyone who stands beneath him and is dependent on his good will. His masters, though, are the *mir* and the tsar. If he is the head of a family, he will be an unlimited despot at home but a servant of the *mir* and a slave of the tsar.

The commune is his world. It is nothing but a natural extension of his family, his clan. Therefore the same patriarchal principle, the same vile despotism, and the same base obedience prevail within it, and therefore the same innate injustice and radical denial of any personal rights, as in the family itself. The decisions of the *mir*, whatever they may be, are law. "Who dares to go against the *mir*!" the Russian peasant exclaims with astonishment. We will see that besides the tsar, his officials, and the nobles, who stand outside the *mir*, or, rather, above it, among the Russian people themselves there is an individual who dares to go against the *mir*: the bandit. That is why banditry is an important historical phenomenon in Russia – the first rebels, the first revolutionaries in Russia, Pugachev and Stenka Razin, were bandits.

In the *mir*, only the elders, the heads of families, have the right to vote. An unmarried young man, or even a married one who has not established his own household, must obey and carry out orders. Over the commune, however, over all the communes, stands the tsar, the common patriarch and progenitor, the father of all Russia. Therefore his power is unlimited.

Each commune forms a self-contained whole, as a result of which – and this is one of Russia's principal misfortunes – no commune has, or even feels the need to have, any independent organic bond with other communes. All that links them together is the supreme, paternal power of the "tsar and little father."

We say that this is a great misfortune. It is clear that the lack of cohesion weakens the people and dooms all their uprisings, which are almost always local and unconnected, to inevitable defeat, thereby consolidating the victory of despotic power. Hence, one of the chief obligations of the revolutionary youth must be to establish by all possible means and at whatever cost a vital bond of rebellion among the separate communes. It is a difficult but not impossible task, for history shows us that in troubled times, such as the False Dmitry's civil strife, the Stenka Razin and Pugachev revolutions, and the Novgorod uprising at the beginning of the reign of Tsar Alexis,[a] the communes themselves, on their own initiative, strove to establish this salutary bond.[142]

The number of communes is incalculable, and their common "tsar and little father" stands too high above them – just a little lower than God – to rule them all personally. If God himself needs the services of countless heavenly hosts and ranks to rule the world – seraphim, cherubim, archangels, six-winged angels and ordinary-winged angels – then the tsar can hardly do without officials. He needs an entire military, civil, judicial, and police administration. Thus, between the tsar and the people, between the tsar and the commune, stands the military, police, bureaucratic, and, inevitably, strictly centralized state.

The imaginary tsar-father, the guardian and benefactor of the

[a] The text reads Emperor Nicholas.

people, is located high, high up, all but in heaven, while the real tsar, the tsar-knout, tsar-thief, and tsar-destroyer – the state – takes his place. From this naturally follows the strange fact that our people simultaneously deify the imaginary, fabled tsar and hate the real tsar manifested in the state.

Our people deeply and passionately hate the state and all its representatives, whatever form they may take. Not long ago, that hatred was still divided between nobles and officials, and sometimes it even seemed that the people hated the former more than the latter, though in essence they hated them both equally. From the time serfdom was abolished, however, and the nobility visibly began to go to ruin, to disappear, and to revert to what it was originally, exclusively a state service class, the people began to include it in their general hatred for officialdom as a whole. It hardly needs to be shown how legitimate their hatred is!

The state once and for all crushed and corrupted the Russian commune, which was already corrupted in any case by its patriarchal principle. Under the state's oppression, communal elections became a fraud, and the individuals temporarily elected by the people them-selves – the village headmen, elders, and policemen – became, on the one hand, tools of the government, and, on the other, paid servants of the rich peasants, the *kulaks*. Under such conditions the last vestiges of justice, truth, and simple humanity necessarily disappeared from the communes, which were, moreover, ruined by state taxes and dues and squeezed to the limit by the arbitrariness of the authorities. More than ever, the sole recourse for the individual remained banditry, and for the people as a whole a universal uprising, a revolution.

In such a situation, what can our intellectual proletariat do, our honest, sincere, utterly dedicated social-revolutionary Russian youth? Without question they must go to the people, because today – and this is true everywhere, but especially in Russia – outside of the people, outside of the multi-million-strong laboring masses, there is neither life, nor cause, nor future. But how and why are they to go to the people?

At the present time, after the unfortunate outcome of the Nechaev enterprise, opinions on this score seem very much divided.[143] From the general confusion of ideas, however, two main, and opposing, parties are now beginning to emerge. One is more peace-loving and preparatory in character, the other is insurrectionary and strives directly for the organization of popular defense.

The proponents of the first orientation do not believe in the possibility of a revolution at present. But since they cannot and will not remain passive spectators of the people's misfortunes, they are resolved to go to the people in order to share those misfortunes fraternally with them, while at the same time instructing them and preparing them, not theoretically but in practice, by their own living example. Some will go among the factory workers, and, working with them as equals, will try to spread the spirit of communalism among them . . .

Others will try to establish rural colonies. There, besides common use of the land, which is so well known to our peasants, they will introduce and apply a principle which is still completely unfamiliar to them but economically necessary: the principle of collective cultivation of the common land and equal division of its products, or the value of its products, on the basis of the strictest justice – not legal but human justice, demanding more work from the strong and able, less from the weak and unable, and distributing earnings not according to the work but according to the needs of each.

They hope to succeed in attracting the peasants by their example, and particularly by the benefits they hope to gain from the organization of collective labor. That was the hope Cabet nurtured when he set out after the unsuccessful revolution of 1848 with his Icarians for America, where he founded his New Icaria.[144] It had a very brief existence, and it should be noted that American soil was more favorable for the success of such an experiment than Russian soil. In America total freedom reigns, while in our blessed Russia . . . the tsar reigns.

But the hopes of those who intend to prepare and peacefully reason with the people go further. By organizing their own domestic life on the basis of complete freedom of the individual, they want to counteract the vile patriarchalism that underlies the whole of our Russian slavery. They want to strike at the root of our principal social evil and thereby contribute directly to the correction of the people's ideal and to the dissemination among them of practical concepts of justice, freedom, and the methods of liberation.

That is all fine, very magnanimous and noble, but scarcely realizable. And even if it does succeed somewhere, it will be a drop in the sea, and a drop is far from sufficient to prepare, arouse, and liberate our people. It will take many resources and a great deal of vital strength, and the results will be exceedingly paltry.

Those who draw up such plans and sincerely intend to realize them undoubtedly do so with their eyes closed, so as not to see our Russian reality in all its ugliness. One can predict in advance all the severe, terrible disappointments that will befall them right at the start of their efforts to carry out their plans, and except perhaps in a few – a very few – fortunate cases the majority of them will get no farther and will not have the strength to go on.

Let them try, if they see no alternative, but also let them know that it will do little, too little, for the liberation and deliverance of our poor martyred people.

The other course is the militant, insurrectionary one. This is the one we believe in, and it is the only one from which we expect deliverance.

Our people obviously need help. They are in such desperate straits that any village can be stirred up without effort. Although an uprising, however unsuccessful it may be, is always useful, individual outbursts are insufficient. All the villages must rise up at once. The vast popular movements under the leadership of Stenka Razin and Pugachev show us that this is possible. Those movements show us that an ideal truly lives in the consciousness of our people and that they are striving for its realization; from the failure of those movements we conclude that this ideal contains fundamental defects which have prevented it from being realized.

We have identified those defects and expressed our conviction that it is the direct obligation of our revolutionary youth to counteract them and to bend all their efforts to combating them in the people's consciousness. To indicate the possibility of such a struggle, we have shown that it long since began among the people themselves.

The war against patriarchalism is now being waged in virtually every village and every family. The commune and the *mir* have now become tools of the hated state power and bureaucratic arbitrariness to such a degree that a revolt against the latter simultaneously becomes a revolt against the despotism of the commune and the *mir*.

Worship of the tsar remains. We believe that it has very much palled on the people and grown weaker in their consciousness in the last ten or twelve years, thanks to the wise and philanthropic policies of Emperor Alexander the Benevolent. The landed noble serfowner is no more, and he was a lightning-rod who for the most part attracted the thunderbolts of the people's hatred. The noble or merchant landowner has remained, the rich *kulak*, and particularly the official, the tsar's angel or archangel. But the official carries out the will of the tsar. However beclouded our peasant may be by his senseless historical faith in the tsar, he is finally beginning to understand that himself. And how could he help but understand it! For ten years now, from all corners of Russia he has been sending his deputies to petition the tsar, and they have all heard but one answer from the tsar's own lips: *"You will have no other freedom!"*[145]

No, say what you will, the Russian peasant may be ignorant, but he is no fool. And with so many facts thrown in his teeth and so many tortures inflicted on his own skin, he would have to be a perfect fool not to begin to understand at last that he has no worse enemy than the tsar. To explain this to him and to employ every possible means of making him feel it; to make use of all the lamentable and tragic instances with which the daily life of the people is filled to show him that all the brutalities, thefts, and robberies by the officials, landowners, priests, and *kulaks* who make life impossible for him come directly from the tsar's power, rely on it, and are possible only because of it; to show him, in short, that the state which he hates so much is the tsar himself, and nothing but the tsar – that is now the direct and principal obligation of revolutionary propaganda.

But it is not enough. The chief defect which to this day paralyzes and makes impossible a universal popular insurrection in Russia is the self-containment of the communes, the isolation and separateness of the local peasant worlds. At all costs we must shatter that isolation and introduce the vital current of revolutionary thought, will, and deed to those separate worlds. We must link together the best peasants of all the villages, districts, and, if possible, regions, the progressive individuals, the natural revolutionaries of the Russian peasant world, and, where possible, create the same vital link between the factory workers and the peasantry. These links cannot be anything but personal ones. While observing, of course, the most studious discretion, the best or most progressive peasants of each village, each district, and each region must get to know their counterparts in all the other villages, districts, and regions.

We must first convince these progressive individuals – and through them, if not all the people then at least a sizable segment of them, the most energetic segment – that the people as a whole, all the villages, districts, and regions throughout Russia, and even outside of Russia, share one common misfortune and therefore one common cause. We must convince them that an invincible force lives in the people, which nothing and no one can withstand, and that if it has not yet liberated the people it is because it is powerful only when it is concentrated and acts simultaneously, everywhere, jointly, in concert, and until now it has not done so. In order to concentrate that force, the villages, districts, and regions must be linked and organized according to a common plan and with the single objective of universal liberation of the people. To create in our people a feeling and consciousness of real unity, some sort of popular newspaper must be established – printed, lithographed, handwritten, or even oral – which would immediately spread information to every corner of Russia, to every region, district, and village, about any peasant or factory uprising that breaks out in one locality or another, and also about the significant revolutionary movements produced by the proletariat of Western Europe. Then our peasant and our factory worker will not feel isolated, but on the contrary will know that behind them, under the same yoke but with the same passion and will to liberate themselves, stands a vast, countless world of laborers preparing for a universal outburst.

That is the task and, we will say bluntly, the sole objective of revolutionary propaganda. It is inappropriate to specify in print how our young people are to carry out this objective.

We will say only one thing: the Russian people will acknowledge our educated youth as their own only when they encounter them in their own lives, in their own misfortunes, in their own cause, in their own desperate rebellion. The youth must be present from now on not as witnesses but as active participants, in the forefront of all popular disturbances and uprisings, great and small, always and everywhere – participants who have doomed themselves to destruction. Acting in accordance with a rigorously conceived and fixed plan, and subjecting all their activity to the strictest discipline in order to create that unanimity without which there can be no victory, they must ready both themselves and the people not just for desperate resistance but also for a bold attack.

Let us add one more word in conclusion. The class which we call our intellectual proletariat, and which is already in a social-revolutionary situation (meaning simply a desperate and impossible one), must be imbued with a conscious passion for the cause of social revolution if it does not want to perish shamefully and in vain. This class is now called upon to prepare, that is, to organize, a popular revolution. It has no other alternative. Thanks to the education it has received, it might, of course, seek to obtain some more or less profitable position in the already overcrowded and very inhospitable ranks of the robbers, exploiters, and oppressors of the people. In the first place, however, there are fewer and fewer such positions, so that they are accessible only to a very small number of people. The majority will be left only with the shame of betrayal and will perish in poverty, insignificance, and baseness. But we are addressing ourselves only to those for whom betrayal is unthinkable and impossible.

Irrevocably cutting all their ties with the world of the exploiters, destroyers, and enemies of the Russian people, they should regard themselves as precious capital belonging exclusively to the cause of the people's liberation, capital that should be expended only on popular propaganda, on gradually arousing and organizing a universal popular uprising.

Appendix B
The Program of the Slavic Section of Zurich[146]

1. The Slavic Section, while fully accepting the fundamental statutes of the International Working Men's Association adopted at its first Congress (Geneva, September 1866), sets itself the special objective of propagating the principles of revolutionary socialism and the organization of popular forces in the Slavic lands.

2. It will struggle with equal energy against the aspirations and manifestations of pan-Slavism, that is, the liberation of the Slavic peoples with the aid of the Russian Empire, and pan-Germanism, that is, their liberation with the aid of the bourgeois civilization of the Germans, who are now striving to organize themselves into a huge pseudo-popular state.

3. Adopting the anarchist revolutionary program, which alone, in our opinion, reflects all the conditions for the real and total liberation of the masses, and convinced that the existence of the state in any form whatsoever is incompatible with the liberty of the proletariat, that it does not permit the fraternal international alliance of peoples, we want to abolish all states. For the Slavic peoples in particular, that abolition is a question of life and death, and at the same time it is the sole method of reconciliation with peoples of other races, such as the Turks, Magyars, or Germans.

4. Along with the state, everything that bears the name of juridical law must inescapably perish, every structure created from above downward by means of legislation and government and never having any objective but the establishment and systematization of the exploi-

tation of the people's labor for the benefit of the ruling classes.

5. Abolition of the state and juridical law will necessarily have as its consequence the abolition of individual hereditary property and the juridical family which is based on it, since neither in any way permits human justice.

6. Abolition of the state, the right of property, and the juridical family alone will make possible the organization of popular life from below upward, on the basis of collective labor and property, which by the force of events will have become possible and obligatory for all. This will be achieved by means of the completely free federation of separate individuals into associations or autonomous communes – or, disregarding communes or any provincial or national divisions, into great homogeneous associations linked by the identity of their interests and social aspirations – and the federation of communes into nations and of nations into humanity.

7. The Slavic Section, professing materialism and atheism, will struggle against divine worship of all kinds, against all official and unofficial religious creeds. While maintaining both in word and in deed the fullest respect for the freedom of conscience of all and the sacred right of each individual to propagate his ideas, it will try to destroy the idea of divinity in all its religious, metaphysical, doctrinaire political, and legal manifestations, convinced that this harmful idea has been and remains the consecration of every kind of slavery.

8. It has the fullest respect for the positive sciences; it demands for the proletariat equal scientific education for all, irrespective of gender. But, as the enemy of all government, it rejects with indignation the government of scholars as the most arrogant and harmful.

9. The Slavic Section demands, along with liberty, the equality of rights and obligations for men and women.

10. The Slavic Section, while striving for the liberation of the Slavic peoples, in no way proposes to organize a separate Slavic world, hostile out of national sentiment to peoples of other races. On the contrary, it will strive for the Slavic peoples to enter the common family of mankind, which the International Working Men's Association has made it its mission to achieve on the basis of liberty, equality, and universal brotherhood.

11. In view of the great task – liberation of the masses from all tutelage and all government – which the International has taken upon itself, the Slavic Section does not allow of the possibility of any

supreme authority or government existing within the International. Consequently, it does not allow of any kind of organization except the free federation of autonomous sections.

12. The Slavic Section recognizes neither an official truth nor a uniform political program prescribed by the General Council or by a general congress. It recognizes only the full solidarity of individuals, sections, and federations in the economic struggle of the workers of all countries against their exploiters. It will seek particularly to draw the Slavic workers into all the practical consequences of this struggle.

13. The Slavic Section recognizes for the sections of all countries: (a) freedom of philosophical and social propaganda; (b) freedom to pursue any policy as long as it does not violate the freedom and rights of other sections and federations; freedom to organize for popular revolution; freedom to form ties with the sections and federations of other countries.

14. Since the Jura Federation has loudly proclaimed these principles, and since it sincerely puts them into practice, the Slavic Section has joined it.[147]

Biographical and other notes on the text

1. With the defeat of Emperor Napoleon III at Sedan on September 2, 1870, and his surrender to the victorious Prussians, the Legislative Body in Paris (the parliament of the Second Empire) named a provisional Government of National Defense. The central figure in the new government was the republican lawyer Léon Gambetta (1838–82), who served as minister of the interior as well as minister of war. His efforts to continue the war failed, even as the threat from without began turning into a social struggle within France. In February 1871, a newly elected National Assembly, highly conservative in composition, rejected Gambetta's policy in favor of a peace settlement. A new government, headed by Adolph Thiers (1797–1877), was installed in Versailles, outside of Paris. In March, a radical municipal government called the Commune (an echo of the Jacobin phase of the French Revolution) was elected in Paris. The Versailles government now besieged Paris and after two months brutally suppressed the Commune. Over 10,000 and possibly upwards of 20,000 communards were killed, with additional thousands wounded or deported to New Caledonia. Prussia's terms for peace, including an indemnity of 5 billion francs and German annexation of Alsace and most of Lorraine, were then accepted, and the Third Republic was organized.

   Although the International itself had virtually nothing to do with the Paris Commune, the latter was championed by both Marx and Bakunin, each one claiming it as his own. Marx devoted his *Civil War in France* to the subject, and Bakunin *The Paris Commune and the Idea of the State*.

   Jules Favre (1814–96), a lawyer, politician, and notable orator, served as foreign minister in the Government of National Defense and continued in that position in Thiers's government until August 1871.

2. On June 6, 1871, in a circular, or instruction, to French diplomatic envoys throughout Europe, Favre likened the International to "a vast Freemasonry" and proposed that all European governments join France in taking concerted measures against it.

3. In September 1868 a revolution brought to an end the tumultuous reign of Queen Isabella II of Spain. In 1870 Amadeo of Savoy, the son of King Victor Emmanuel of Italy, acceded to the Spanish throne under the arrangements of a constitution proclaimed in 1869. Práxedes Mateo Sagasta (1827–1903) served as interior minister for part of the brief reign of Amadeo I. In February 1873, after considerable political turmoil, Amadeo abdicated and was succeeded by a short-lived

republic, in the government of which Sagasta served as a cabinet minister. See n. 20.

4. A reference to Pope Pius IX's Syllabus of Errors, issued in December 1864. It condemned eighty errors of modern thought and belief, including liberalism, socialism, and communism.

5. Giuseppe Mazzini (1805–72) was an ardent Italian nationalist and advocate of the unification of Italy. Bakunin had met Mazzini in the early 1860s at the home of Alexander Herzen in London. Although he valued Mazzini's contribution to Italy's liberation from foreign rule, he repeatedly attacked his religio-mystical brand of nationalism and his democratic and republican political principles. In a series of articles just after the Paris Commune, Mazzini criticized both the Commune itself and the International, the materialist doctrines of which he held responsible for it. Bakunin's response to Mazzini was a work entitled *The Political Theology of Mazzini and the International*.

6. Bakunin's Russian readers would have caught his ironic reference to Ivan III, Grand Prince of Moscow (1462–1505), who incorporated much of northern Russia into a unified state under Muscovite rule and became known as "the gatherer of the Russian lands." In an analogous fashion, Victor Emmanuel of the Kingdom of Sardinia (comprising Piedmont on the Italian mainland and the island of Sardinia) became the first king of a unified Italy in 1861.

7. Giuseppe Garibaldi (1807–82) was an Italian nationalist and revolutionary whose invasion of Sicily and southern Italy in 1860 with a small army of followers called the Red Shirts was a key step in the unification of Italy. Bakunin heard of Garibaldi's exploits while still in Siberia, and upon his arrival in Italy in January of 1864 he hastened to meet him.

8. Alexander I was emperor of Russia from 1801 to 1825. He was succeeded by his younger brother Nicholas, who ruled from 1825 to 1855. It was Nicholas who sent Russian troops into Austria in 1849 to help quell the Hungarian revolution, as Bakunin mentions below.

9. Poland in the eighteenth century had fallen into a virtual condition of anarchy, and in the three partitions of 1772, 1793, and 1795 it was wiped off the map of Europe as an independent state by Russia, Prussia, and Austria. (Polish independence was restored only after the First World War.) Russia annexed Poland's eastern territories, inhabited largely by White Russians, Lithuanians, and Ukrainians; Prussia took the central and western portions; and Austria took the province of Galicia, inhabited not only by Poles but by Ruthenians, as the Ukrainians in the Austrian Empire were called.

    Under the terms of the Congress of Vienna of 1815, Russia received most of the territory of the Grand Duchy of Warsaw, a Polish entity which Napoleon had carved out of the Polish possessions of Prussia. It included much of the Polish heartland as well as the capital of Warsaw. It was renamed the Kingdom of Poland (also known as the Congress Kingdom) and received a constitution and autonomous status within the Russian Empire. This arrangement lasted until 1831. In 1830–31, and again in 1863, the Poles rose in rebellion against Russian rule. As a result, Russian Poland lost its autonomous status, became an integral part of the empire, and was subjected to a relentless policy of cultural and linguistic Russification.

10. Ferdinand Lassalle (1825–64), whom Bakunin discusses at length later in this work, was the founder of the General German Workers' Association, which eventually became part of the German Social-Democratic Party. A flamboyant personality, Lassalle was killed in a duel.

    Although Bakunin tries to equate Lassalle and Marx, their views on the state were fundamentally different. Unlike Marx, Lassalle believed that socialism could be realized within the existing state system. He was willing to collaborate with it, and in the 1860s he met with Bismarck on more than one occasion.

11. The Slavophiles were cultural nationalists who flourished in the 1840s and thereafter. They criticized Russia's adoption of Western values and institutions and sought a distinctively Russian path of national development based on native traditions.

    Slavophilism should not be confused with pan-Slavism. The Slavophiles glorified native Russian culture, religion, and custom. They were critical of the government for having adopted Western (especially German) practices since the time of Peter the Great, and even for its bureaucratic repression. Pan-Slavism was much more political and aggressive, anticipating the "liberation" of the other Slavic nations under the direct or indirect aegis of the Russian Empire. Pan-Slavism was never an official Russian government policy, and in fact often conflicted with Russian foreign policy. The government, however, was not above utilizing pan-Slav sentiment when it suited its purposes.

12. Johann Jacoby (1805–77), a Königsberg physician and political figure, served as a member of the Frankfurt parliament of 1848–49 and later as a member of the Prussian parliament. He was a respected democrat and constitutionalist and ultimately joined the Social-Democratic Party. Bakunin had met Jacoby in Frankfurt in 1848. The party Bakunin refers to was the German People's Party, a south German grouping of bourgeois democrats and anti-Prussian republicans.

13. Wilhelm Liebknecht (1826–1900) was one of the founders of the German Social-Democratic Workers' Party in 1869. Earlier, he had founded the Saxon People's Party, a radical-democratic and labor-oriented party. In the 1860s, Liebknecht and other socialists collaborated with middle-class liberals such as those of the German People's Party. Despite what Bakunin implies here, Marx in fact disapproved of this policy.

14. The fifth Congress of German Workers' Societies, held in Nuremberg in September 1868, declared that political democratization was an indispensable condition for the social and economic liberation of the working class. This was the position adopted by the German Social-Democratic Party at its foundation in 1869. See n. 126.

15. This monument, in the place Vendôme in Paris, was a column bearing a statue of Julius Caesar. It had been put up by Napoleon III on a site previously occupied by a statue of himself erected by Napoleon I. The column was pulled down in a public ceremony by order of the Paris Commune as a symbol of imperial pretension but was subsequently restored.

16. Désiré Barodet (1823–1906) served as mayor of the city of Lyons in 1872–73. Angered by the revolutionary attitude of the municipal authorities, the National Assembly abolished Lyons's right to be governed by a mayor, whereupon, as a protest by the left, Barodet was elected to fill a parliamentary vacancy in Paris over the official candidate of Thiers's government.

    At the time of Bakunin's attempt to raise an anarchist insurrection in Lyons in September of 1870, Barodet, a republican, had been a municipal councillor and member of the Committee of Public Safety that took over the government of the city upon the fall of Louis Napoleon.

17. The terms of the Treaty of Paris of 1856, which ended the Crimean War, neutralized the Black Sea and prohibited Russia from maintaining a navy in it. In 1870, Russia took advantage of the confused situation created by the German victory in the Franco-Prussian War to repudiate the Black Sea provisions of the Treaty of Paris.

The Khanate of Khiva was conquered by Russian troops early in 1873, one of several Central Asian territories annexed by or subordinated to the Russian Empire in the 1860s and 1870s.

18. Bakunin's Russian readers would doubtless have recognized the allusion to Alexander Pushkin's famous description of "a Russian revolt, senseless and merciless." It appears in the concluding lines of his novel about the Pugachev uprising, *The Captain's Daughter*.

19. This is a reprise of perhaps the most famous line Bakunin ever wrote, and the one most closely associated with him. In 1842, at the very start of his political career, he published in German in the *Deutsche Jahrbücher für Wissenschaft und Kunst* an article entitled "The Reaction in Germany," under the pseudonym Jules Elysard. The last sentence of the article read: "The passion for destruction is a creative passion, too."

20. As Bakunin indicates, the nineteenth century was a stormy period in Spanish history. Ferdinand VII, restored to the throne in 1814 after the Napoleonic invasion (and restored again by a French army after a revolution in 1823), was succeeded in 1833 by his daughter, Isabella II. Her accession was contested by Ferdinand's brother, Don Carlos, and his adherents, the Carlists, exponents of extreme reaction and absolutism. Even when the Carlist war ended, Isabella's reign was punctuated by numerous upheavals, and she was forced to abdicate in 1868. Baldomero Espartero, Ramón María Narváez, and Juan Prim were prominent military and political players in the events of the period. Manuel Ruiz Zorilla (or Zorrilla, 1834–95) was a rival of Sagasta and served as prime minister for part of the reign of King Amadeo. The republic of 1873–74, which followed Amadeo's abdication, was marked by another Carlist war, various regional and local separatist movements, and fundamental disagreements over the future form of the state. Shortly thereafter, the monarchy was restored in the person of Isabella's son, Alfonso XII. See n. 3.

21. In September of 1872, in Zurich, Bakunin founded his Alliance of Social Revolutionaries, essentially the successor to his Alliance of Social Democracy of 1868. It consisted of a small group of his Italian and Spanish adherents.

22. The *Consorteria* ("the Cabal") was actually a grouping of anti-Piedmontese right-wing forces in the Italian parliament.

23. The Compromise (*Ausgleich*) of 1867 transformed the Austrian Empire into the Austro-Hungarian Empire, or the Dual Monarchy. The Magyar-dominated Transleithan (east of the Leith River) segment, and the German-dominated Cisleithan (west of the Leith River) segment, each had its own constitution, parliament, and administration. They were united under a single Habsburg ruler, who reigned as Emperor of Austria and King of Hungary.

24. Prince Felix Schwarzenberg (1800–52) became prime minister of Austria in 1848 and headed the government that restored centralized absolutism in the wake of the 1848 revolution. Count Leo Thun (1811–88) served as Austrian minister of education in the post-1848 period. He was instrumental in concluding a concordat with the Holy See in 1855 which strengthened the independence of the Catholic Church in Austria and particularly its influence on education. Although Thun was a member of the German nobility of Bohemia, he supported Czech language and cultural claims.

25. Baron, later Count, Friedrich Beust (1809–86) became Austrian foreign minister in 1866 and subsequently prime minister and chancellor. He negotiated the Compromise of 1867 with the Hungarians. As prime minister of Saxony until 1866, and subsequently during his Austrian service, he was known as an opponent of Bismarck's policies.

26. Czech-inhabited Moravia in the ninth century became the nucleus of a short-lived
    empire which included present-day Czechoslovakia as well as parts of Poland and
    Hungary. It was at this time that the Czechs adopted Christianity.

    Stefan Dušan (ruled 1331–55) brought medieval Serbia to the height of its
    power and in 1346 proclaimed himself emperor. His state disintegrated after his
    death, however, and, like the rest of the Balkans, Serbia soon came under the rule
    of the Ottoman Turks.

27. Adam Mickiewicz (1798–1855) was the great Polish romantic nationalist poet of
    the nineteenth century. Bakunin met him in the 1840s in Paris, where Mickiewicz
    for several years held a chair in Slavic literature at the Collège de France and
    propounded a mystical, messianic view of Polish and Slavic destiny.

28. Czech Bohemia separated from Moravia in the tenth century and became part of
    the Holy Roman Empire. At the end of the twelfth century Bohemia became an
    independent kingdom within the empire, and in the fourteenth century Prague for
    a time became the capital of the empire itself.

29. The Hussites were followers of Jan Hus, the Czech religious reformer who was
    burned at the stake by order of the Council of Constance in 1415. His views in
    many ways foreshadowed the Reformation of the sixteenth century. The Hussite
    wars which followed his death were a religious as well as Czech nationalist revolt
    against the Catholic and German Holy Roman Empire; they devastated much of
    central and eastern Europe for some twenty years. The Hussites, and Protestant-
    ism in general, were brutally and definitively suppressed in the Czech lands by the
    Habsburgs during the Thirty Years War in the seventeenth century.

30. Bakunin groups together these disparate episodes of Russian history because each
    could be read as an assertion of local autonomy, initiative, or rebellion against the
    central government. Novgorod and Pskov in the middle ages were independent
    Russian city-states with close commercial ties to the West through the Baltic. They
    were annexed by Muscovy at the end of the fifteenth and beginning of the sixteenth
    centuries.

    During the Time of Troubles at the beginning of the seventeenth century, a
    period of social upheaval, political collapse, and foreign intervention, a Polish army
    invaded Russia and captured Moscow. With the boyar-dominated central govern-
    ment paralyzed, a popularly supported militia force arose spontaneously in the
    Volga River region to the east of Moscow, drove out the Poles, and in 1613
    established the new Romanov dynasty.

    In the mid-seventeenth century a Cossack-led rebellion of the Orthodox
    peasantry of Ukraine, which was under the control of Poland, against the Polish
    (and Catholic) landowners of the region led to Russia's annexation of left-bank
    (i.e., east of the Dnieper River) Ukraine as well as the city of Kiev.

    Stepan (Stenka) Razin and Emelian Pugachev led the two most extensive
    peasant rebellions in Russian history, in the 1670s and 1770s, respectively.
    Bakunin takes up these peasant rebellions again in Appendix A of the present
    work.

31. General, later Count, Michael Muravev (1796–1866) was appointed Governor-
    General of Vilna in March 1863 and charged with the suppression of the Polish
    insurrection and the pacification of Russia's Polish territories. In addition to
    executions and deportations, Muravev instituted a policy of ruthless Russification
    of the area during his two-year tenure. For his efforts he came to be called
    Muravev the Hangman, an epithet Bakunin uses subsequently.

32. August Bebel (1840–1913), of authentic working-class origin, was one of the
    founders and foremost leaders of the German Social-Democratic Party.

33. The fifth Congress of the International, held at The Hague in September 1872,

saw the final schism between the followers of Marx and Bakunin. Bakunin is referring to the resolution voted by the majority of the congress to insert in the International's statutes recognition that the proletariat must establish itself as "a distinct political party," and that "the conquest of political power" must become the great task of the proletariat. The decisions of the congress were subsequently repudiated by most of the national federations of the International.

34. After two rebellions against Turkish rule beginning in 1804, Serbia became an autonomous principality within the Ottoman Empire. Its status was recognized in the Treaty of Adrianople of 1829 between Russia and Turkey, and it was placed under the protection of Russia. The Treaty of Paris of 1856 guaranteed the integrity of Serbia under the protection of all the major powers. It became a sovereign kingdom in 1878.

    Montenegro was the one part of the medieval Serbian Empire that remained independent after the Turkish conquests of the fourteenth and fifteenth centuries, thanks to its mountainous location. In the nineteenth century it formed an independent kingdom, and in 1918, like the Kingdom of Serbia, it became part of the new nation of Yugoslavia.

35. Count Camillo di Cavour (1810–61) was prime minister of the Kingdom of Sardinia. A brilliant statesman, he was the mastermind of Italian unification. He achieved his objective just two months before his death, when Victor Emmanuel was proclaimed king of a united Italy.

36. "The crown of St. Wenceslas" was the term for the lands of the ancient Kingdom of Bohemia, consisting of Bohemia, Moravia, and Silesia, which came under Habsburg rule. Similarly, the Kingdom of Hungary was called "the crown of St. Stephen."

37. Jan Žižka (1358?–1424) was the military leader of the Taborite sect. Drawn largely from the Czech peasantry, the Taborites were one of the most radical elements of the Hussite religious and national revolt of the fifteenth century. A brilliant military innovator, Žižka devised unconventional techniques for his untrained forces. Elsewhere, Bakunin glorified him as a revolutionary hero in terms similar to his praise of Razin and Pugachev.

38. Bakunin, it will be remembered, participated in the Slav Congress held in Prague in June of 1848, as well as in the popular insurrection which broke out during the congress and was suppressed by Windischgrätz.

39. František Palacký (1798–1876) was a Czech historian and political leader whose monumental history of the Czechs played a major role in stimulating Czech national pride. He was a leading spokesman of Austro-Slavism, the belief that a politically reformed and federally structured – but not dismembered – Austrian state would be the best protection for the Slavs against Russia, on the one side, and Germany on the other. Palacký's son-in-law, František Ladislav Rieger (1818–1903), a journalist, and František August Brauner (1810–80), a lawyer and economist, were also leading Czech political figures. All three were sometime members of the Austrian parliament and stood for the conservative Czech nationalist program of autonomy for the lands of the Bohemian crown.

40. In 1867 a Slav Congress was held in Moscow in conjunction with a Slavic ethnographic exhibition. The congress was a privately organized endeavor supported by pan-Slav circles in Russia, notably the Slavic Benevolent Committee of Moscow, which had been formed to lend philanthropic assistance to the south Slavs. Over eighty non-Russian Slavs attended, most of them from the Austrian Empire, with the Czechs forming the most important delegation. The delegates were received by Alexander II in St. Petersburg. There were no Polish delegates, but Rieger in fact expressed forceful support for the Poles while in Moscow.

The journey to Russia was a demonstrative expression of the disillusionment with the Habsburg monarchy which the Czechs, as well as other Austrian Slavs, had experienced as a result of the Compromise of 1867. "Dualism" divided the administration of the empire between the Germans and the Magyars, at the expense of the Slavs in both parts of the monarchy. Of the Slavic minorities in the empire, only the Galician Poles benefited from the new arrangements; in return for their support of the government in the Austrian parliament they were granted a greater degree of local autonomy.

41. In 1871 Emperor Franz Joseph considered granting national recognition to the Czechs by, in effect, placing Bohemia on the same footing as Hungary. The proposal was abandoned under pressure from both Germans and Magyars, however, severely undermining the conservative Czech nationalist position.

42. Alexander II, the son of Nicholas I, came to the throne in 1855 and was assassinated in 1881. In 1861 he emancipated the serfs (the "peasant reform" to which Bakunin refers below) and inaugurated a series of far-reaching changes designed to modernize Russia's institutions, military forces, and economy. As Bakunin indicates later on, William I of Germany (1861–88) was Alexander's uncle, the brother of Alexander's mother.

43. Bakunin is referring to the group of Russian army officers who, upon the death of Alexander I, staged an unsuccessful rebellion in December 1825 and thus came to be known as the Decembrists. Their ostensible aim was to prevent Nicholas I from coming to the throne, but more broadly they wished to liberalize Russia's institutions. The conspirators formed two independent secret societies, the Northern Society, in St. Petersburg, and the Southern Society, based in Kiev. Pavel Pestel (1793–1826), Sergei Muravev-Apostol (1796–1826), and Mikhail Bestuzhev-Riumin (1803–26), were leaders of the Southern Society, which was the more radical of the two; they were among the five Decembrists hanged by Nicholas I. The Society of United Slavs, also composed of army officers stationed in Ukraine, originated as a separate underground group but merged with the Southern Society shortly before the rebellion. Its program included unification of all the Slavic peoples in a federal republic.

44. In an oft-quoted remark, Frederick the Great said of Maria Theresa in regard to the first partition of Poland, "she wept and still she took."

45. Alexander Aleksandrovich, the son of Alexander II, who succeeded to the throne as Alexander III in 1881 and ruled to 1894.

46. The major fortress of Belfort in Alsace was returned to France upon completion of its 5 billion franc indemnity payment to Germany.

    Thiers, who had been in power since early 1871 and had been elected president of the new Third Republic in August of that year, was voted out of office on May 24, 1873. The monarchist majority of the National Assembly chose Marshal Marie Edmé Patrice Maurice de MacMahon (1808–93) to succeed Thiers as president.

47. Field-Marshal Ivan Paskevich (1782–1856) was one of Nicholas I's most trusted military subordinates. A hero of the Turkish War of 1828–29, Paskevich subsequently suppressed the Polish insurrection in 1831 (for which he was created Prince of Warsaw and, as viceroy of the Kingdom of Poland, became its virtual ruler) and the Hungarian rebellion against Austria in 1849.

48. Bakunin is referring to Russia's isolation in the Crimean War of 1854–56. Russia was defeated on her own soil by a coalition of England, France, and the Kingdom of Sardinia. As Bakunin ironically phrases it, Austria showed its "gratitude" for Nicholas's help in quelling the Hungarian rebellion of 1849 by adopting an anti-Russian position. Prussia had been "offended" by Nicholas's opposition to Prussian unification of Germany. In 1850 he had supported Austria in forcing Prussia

to renounce, in the Convention of Olmütz, creation of a Prussian-led German Union. During the Crimean War, Prussia maintained an ambiguous neutrality. Nicholas died in 1855, as Russia was going down to defeat.

49. Bohdan Khmelnytsky (1595?–1657), Hetman of Ukraine, led the Cossack uprising against Poland which resulted in Russia's annexation of left-bank Ukraine and Kiev in 1654.

50. The cities of Vilna and Grodno in Lithuania, and Minsk in White Russia, as well as the provinces of Podolia and Volhynia in western Ukraine, were all territories Russia acquired in the partitions of Poland.

51. The Congress of Vienna in 1815 established the Polish city of Cracow as a free city, the one part of Poland not in the possession of the three partitioning powers. In 1846 it was annexed by Austria. The significance of the year 1841 is not readily apparent; perhaps Bakunin meant 1831, when the insurrection against Russian rule ended the autonomy of the Kingdom of Poland.

52. A line from Pushkin's "To the Slanderers of Russia," a patriotic poem written in 1831 in response to French critics (including General Lafayette) of Russia's suppression of the Polish insurrection.

53. The Old Believers, or schismatics, were the sizable part of the Russian population that broke away from the official Orthodox Church in the mid-seventeenth century in a dispute over reform of church rituals. Withdrawing to the frontier regions of the empire and dwelling in their own self-contained communities, they rejected the legitimacy of the established church, and hence of its defender, the tsar. Some Russian revolutionaries, including Bakunin at one point, viewed the Old Believers' alienation from the existing order as a potential revolutionary force, but they soon discovered that the Old Believers were interested only in religion, not politics.

54. Franciszek Duchiński (1817–93), a Polish émigré writer and scholar, expounded the so-called Turanian theory, according to which the Great Russians were a non-Slavic, "Turanian" or Asiatic people distinct from the "Aryan" and European Slavs.

55. Count Dmitry Miliutin (1816–1912) served as Alexander II's minister of war from 1861 to 1881. In that position he effected a sweeping modernization of the Russian military, including improvements in officer training and the introduction of universal conscription and a reserve system.

56. Magdeburg Law was a system of municipal self-government that gave considerable autonomy to the towns. Originating as the charter of the city of Magdeburg in the thirteenth century, it became a model for hundreds of medieval towns not only in the rest of Germany but in large parts of Eastern Europe.

57. The three parties were the National Liberals, the left-liberal Progressives, and the Social Democrats.

58. Bakunin is referring to Napoleon III's failure to supply anything more than diplomatic protests against Russia's suppression of the Polish insurrection.

59. Prince Alexander Gorchakov (1798–1883) served as chancellor (i.e., foreign minister) of the Russian Empire from 1856 to 1882.

60. Georg Herwegh (1817–75), a German political poet, was a representative of "Young Germany," a movement which sought to apply democratic principles to Germany. His poem "Die Deutsche Flotte" was published in 1841. Bakunin became closely acquainted with Herwegh in Dresden in 1842.

61. Riga and Revel (the Russian name for Tallinn) are Baltic ports in Latvia and Estonia, respectively. Kronstadt, a naval base on an island just off St. Petersburg, was the home of Russia's Baltic Fleet.

62. Maimachin (or Maimachen), present-day Altan Bulak in Mongolia, was a major center of Russian–Chinese trade.

228

63. By the Treaty of Peking in 1860, China ceded to Russia the Amur River and Ussuri River regions, vast territories which included a sizable stretch of Pacific coastline.

64. The Duke of Brunswick was the commander of the Prussian army that invaded revolutionary France and was defeated at the battle of Valmy in September of 1792.

65. Heinrich Heine (1797–1856) was one of the greatest of German lyric poets. In 1831 he moved to Paris and became the leading figure of the literary movement Young Germany, which sought to propagate democratic and progressive French ideas in Germany.

66. The September Massacres (September 2–7, 1792) were mob lynchings of suspected counter-revolutionaries held in French jails. They were a prelude to the execution of the king in January 1793 (the queen was executed later in the year) and to the period of the Terror under Maximilien Robespierre and his colleagues in the Committee of Public Safety in 1793–94.

67. Baron Heinrich Friedrich Karl vom und zum Stein (1757–1831) served as prime minister of Prussia in 1807–08. The far-reaching program of social, military, and administrative reforms instituted during his brief tenure, including the abolition of serfdom, revived and modernized Prussia. At Napoleon's insistence he was removed from office and went into exile in Russia.

68. Fichte's *Addresses to the German Nation* of 1807–08 exalted German nationalism and urged the regeneration of Germany through a system of liberal national education.

69. Bakunin is referring to Theodor Schmalz (1760–1831), a professor of law and one of the leading proponents of post-Napoleonic reaction in Prussia. His pamphlet was one of the works burned at the Wartburg Festival which Bakunin describes below.

70. As the last Holy Roman Emperor, Francis II (1792–1806), and as the first emperor of Austria, Francis I (1804–35).

71. Bakunin's source for this quotation, as well as for much of the information on German history in this section of *Statism and Anarchy*, seems to have been the work by Wilhelm Müller to which he refers below (see n. 82). Bakunin was not fastidious about what he placed in quotation marks, and he freely mixed paraphrase with direct quotation. For the German text of this and other quotations used by Bakunin, see Lehning, ed., *Archives Bakounine*, III, pp. 427ff. I have followed Bakunin rather than the original in making the translations.

72. Gerhard Johann David von Scharnhorst (1775–1813), a Prussian general, reorganized the Prussian military, introducing universal conscription and devising the highly effective reserve system to which Bakunin refers above.

73. The German Confederation, which was set up by the Congress of Vienna in 1815, was a loose federation of all the German states, including Prussia and Austria but excluding their non-German territories. The Confederation had a Diet which met in Frankfurt under the presidency of Austria. The German Confederation lasted until the Austro-Prussian War of 1866, when it was superseded by the North German Confederation, which excluded Austria.

74. Schwarzenberg's plan was actually put forth in 1849 and rejected by the Frankfurt parliament.

75. Count Aleksei Andreevich Arakcheev (1769–1834) was a general and one of Alexander's most trusted subordinates. Widely regarded as a martinet, he was placed in charge of the brutal system of military colonies Alexander devised after the Napoleonic Wars and was frequently blamed for the increasingly reactionary character of the last years of Alexander's reign.

76. Bishop Rulemann Friedrich Eylert (1770–1852) was an advisor to Frederick William III on church affairs and a supporter of political reaction in the post-Napoleonic period.

77. Prince Wilhelm Ludwig Georg von Sayn-Wittgenstein-Hohenstein (1770–1851), a supporter of Metternich's policies, served as head of the Prussian police (not as prime minister) from 1812 to 1819.

78. Baroness Barbara Juliana von Krüdener (1764–1824), the widow of a Russian diplomat, was a novelist and religious mystic. Alexander met her in Germany in the summer of 1815, and for a brief time she seems to have exerted a considerable influence over him. She claimed credit for the idea of the Holy Alliance, but the strain of mysticism and religious piety in Alexander's personality had begun to manifest itself several years earlier.

79. The festival at Wartburg Castle, near Eisenach in Saxe-Weimar, was held in October 1817 to celebrate the three-hundredth anniversary of Luther's *Theses* and the fourth anniversary of the battle of Leipzig. It had a considerable impact on Germany as the first public protest against the order established in 1815.

   Ernst Moritz Arndt (1769–1860) was a poet and professor of history. His patriotic songs, of which the most famous was "Where Is the German's Fatherland?," had earned him considerable popularity during the Napoleonic period. He was dismissed from the University of Bonn in the growing wave of reaction in 1820.

   Friedrich Ludwig Jahn (1778–1852), called the *Turnvater*, or "father of gymnastics," was the founder of the *Turnverein*, a gymnastic association aimed at the physical and moral regeneration of German youth. It became a popular vehicle for the expression of German nationalism.

80. On March 23, 1819, Karl Sand, a young, mentally unbalanced theology student, stabbed to death the German dramatist August von Kotzebue, an agent in the service of Alexander I. On July 1, Karl Löning attempted to murder an official named Karl von Ibell. Sand was executed in 1820, and Löning committed suicide in prison. Metternich made use of these incidents to secure adoption by the Diet of the German Confederation a few months later of the Carlsbad Decrees, which dissolved student societies and gymnastic associations, placed the universities under strict supervision, and introduced rigid censorship.

81. Ludwig Börne (1786–1837), a writer of democratic views who, with Heine, initiated the Young Germany movement, is sometimes regarded as the father of German political journalism. Bakunin used these words in slightly different form in an unpublished manuscript of 1872 directed against Marx. See Lehning, ed., *Archives Bakounine*, II, pp. 216–17. As usual, in both cases he was paraphrasing rather than quoting precisely.

82. Wilhelm Müller (1820–92) was a liberal historian. His *Political History of Recent Times: 1816–1875, with Special Reference to Germany* was first published in 1867.

83. Bakunin is in fact referring to the *July* Revolution of 1830 (July 27–29, known as the Three Glorious Days), which saw the dethronement of the Bourbon Charles X and his replacement by Louis-Philippe of the House of Orleans. (The *June* Days of Paris, which Bakunin refers to below, occurred in 1848.) The Italian revolutions of 1830–31 were undertaken in the hope of aid from the new government of Louis-Philippe, but none was forthcoming.

84. That is, between the supporters of Isabella II and the adherents of her uncle, Don Carlos, the pretender to the throne. Maria Cristina of Naples was the mother of Isabella (born 1830) and became regent when her daughter assumed the throne in 1833. See n. 20.

85. The Reform Act of 1832 extended the franchise to the middle classes and redis-

tributed seats in parliament to make it a more representative body.

86. Prince Alfred zu Windischgrätz (1787–1862), the governor of Bohemia, shelled Prague in June 1848 to suppress the insurrection that followed the Slav Congress. In October of the same year (not 1849), he besieged Vienna in the course of putting down an insurrection there.

87. Johann Georg August Wirth (1798–1848) was a Bavarian democrat and journalist. In his speech at the Hambach Festival (which was attended by Polish refugees, among others), he called for the deposition of princes, the liberation of Poland, Hungary, and Italy as well as Germany, and the creation of a federal republic of Europe. He was subsequently tried and imprisoned for this speech.

88. A pre-parliament, consisting for the most part of liberals from the south and west of Germany, convened at Frankfurt at the end of March 1848 to plan elections for a national parliament. The Frankfurt parliament, or National Assembly, that was subsequently elected consisted of over 500 deputies, belonging mainly to the liberal upper middle class and including some fifty professors. The Frankfurt parliament convened in May 1848 and set about trying to unify Germany into a federal state on the basis of liberal principles. Increasingly coming into conflict with its liberalism, however, was the parliament's insistence that all territory inhabited by Germans be included in the new national empire, including provinces populated largely by Czechs, Poles, and Danes. At the end of March 1849 the assembly elected Frederick William IV of Prussia as emperor, but he refused to accept a crown offered by an elected assembly. This essentially marked the end of the assembly's activities, and it began to disintegrate. In June its remaining members moved to Stuttgart, where they were dispersed by Prussian troops.

89. Börne in the years 1830–33 sent to Germany a long series of satirical *Letters from Paris*, in which he extolled French conditions and contrasted the militant French democrats to the submissive Germans. Heine in 1832 published his reports from Paris under the title *French Conditions*, in which he also described French liberty in glowing terms and satirized the benighted condition of his countrymen.

90. Baron Karl vom Stein zum Altenstein (1770–1840) served as Prussian minister of culture from 1817 to 1838. Baron Wilhelm von Humboldt (1767–1835) was a leading proponent of liberalism in the years before 1815. As Prussian minister of education in 1809–10 he reformed the school system and was one of the founders of the University of Berlin.

91. Victor Cousin (1792–1867) was a philosopher, educator, and political liberal. He had studied in Germany and began to popularize Hegel's philosophy in the late 1820s, especially in his influential lectures.

92. Ludwig Büchner (1824–99) was a German philosopher noted for his materialist interpretation of mind and the universe. His book *Force and Matter*, published in 1855, was widely regarded as the foremost expression of materialism.

93. The League of the South was a regional defense association formed at the time of Napoleon III's defeat. It combined national defense with radical and federalist views and was opposed by moderate republicans like Gambetta.

94. Bakunin is referring to the political leadership of the Spanish republic of 1873–74. Both Emilio Castelar y Ripoll (1832–99) and Francisco Pi y Margall (1824–1901) of the Federal Republican Party served briefly as president during this period. The cantonalist revolts, local separatist movements which Bakunin supported, were suppressed by the forces of the republic under Castelar.

95. A Customs Union (*Zollverein*) dominated by Prussia was established in 1834. It came to include most of the states of Germany but excluded Austria, thereby helping to prepare the way for German unification under Prussian leadership.

96. Frederick William IV (1840–61) was the brother-in-law of Nicholas I of Russia

(his sister was Nicholas's wife). In 1858, because of the king's mental instability, his brother became regent and at Frederick William's death in 1861 succeeded him as William I.

97. Alphonse Marie Louis de Lamartine (1790–1869), a French poet and political figure, was the author of *The History of the Girondists* (1847). Louis Blanc (1811–82), a leading French socialist, wrote a twelve-volume *History of the French Revolution*, which began to appear in 1847. Jules Michelet (1798–1874), one of the greatest French historians of the nineteenth century, wrote an impassioned and influential seven-volume *History of the French Revolution*, which also began to appear in 1847.

98. Arnold Ruge (1802–80), a philosopher and democrat, was a leading figure in the development of the Left Hegelians. Bakunin became friends with Ruge while living in Dresden in 1842, and it was in Ruge's journal *Deutsche Jahrbücher für Wissenschaft und Kunst* that Bakunin published his 1842 article "The Reaction in Germany."

99. Lorenz von Stein (1815–90) was a German economist and sociologist who taught at the University of Kiel and later at Vienna. His *Socialism and Communism in Contemporary France*, first published in 1842, introduced early French socialist ideas to the German democrats. In his "confession" Bakunin claimed that the book had had an enormous impact on him and impelled him to the further study of the French democrats and socialists.

100. Wilhelm Christian Weitling (1808–71), a tailor from Magdeburg, active first in Paris and then in Switzerland, was the first German proponent of communism. In Paris, he had been a member of a secret society called the League of the Just. He was imprisoned in Zurich in 1843 for spreading communist propaganda and for blasphemy (he had published a work which depicted Jesus as the precursor of communism) and was then handed over to the Prussians. After his release he eventually made his way to America, where he participated in the labor movement and died in New York.

101. Johann-Kaspar Bluntschli (1808–81) was a conservative law professor and political figure in Zurich. In 1843, he published a report on the Weitling affair which implicated Bakunin, who had been living in Zurich and had met Weitling. The Russian government, now alerted to Bakunin's activities, investigated further and in February 1844 ordered him home. His refusal precipitated his trial *in absentia* and a sentence of banishment to Siberia.

102. The Young Hegelian circle to which Bakunin refers was the Doctors' Club, located in Berlin, not Cologne. Marx studied at the University of Berlin from 1836 to 1841 and received his doctoral degree from the University of Jena in 1841. The leading figure in the Doctors' Club was Bruno Bauer (1809–82), a lecturer in theology at the University of Berlin. He was removed from his post in 1842 for writings in which he denied the historical existence of Jesus and the historical reality of the gospels. His brother Edgar (1820–86) was a journalist and historian whose anti-authoritarian writings earned him four years in prison. Max Stirner (1806–56), the pseudonym of Johann Kaspar Schmidt, was a philosopher and secondary-school teacher whose book *The Ego and Its Own* (1845) is the most extreme expression of anarchist individualism. Marx and Engels subjected the Bauers and Stirner, among others, to severe criticism in *The Holy Family* and *The German Ideology* of 1845–46.

Marx spent the latter part of 1842 and the first part of 1843 in Cologne. The journal Bakunin is referring to was the *Rheinische Zeitung für Politik, Handel und Gewerbe*, which was financed by a group of liberal industrialists in the Rhineland and published articles on political and economic subjects directed against the policies of the Berlin government. Marx contributed to it and in October 1842 became its editor-in-chief. When the journal was suppressed in the spring of 1843 (partly in response to a complaint by Nicholas I), Marx moved to Paris.

The "nihilists" Bakunin mentions were the group called the Freemen, consisting of former members of the Doctors' Club and other literary and philosophical radicals who met in the cafés of Berlin and engaged in various antics intended to shock respectable society. For a time they collaborated with Marx on the *Rheinische Zeitung*, but he soon broke with them.

103. This is a reference to the League of the Just, with which Wilhelm Weitling had been affiliated. See n. 100.

104. Moses Hess (1812–75), a pioneer German socialist, was instrumental in founding the *Rheinische Zeitung* and was a contributor to it. He was a major link between Left Hegelianism and socialism, introducing the radical Young Hegelians to socialist doctrines and influencing both Marx and Engels. Marx later repudiated Hess's idealistic version of socialism.

105. Count Claude-Henri de Saint-Simon (1760–1825), a French nobleman who fought in the American Revolution, was an early socialist. He was one of the first proponents of social planning to maximize industrial production, advocating public ownership of industry and capital, with control over labor and the resources of society to be vested in scientists, industrialists, and engineers.

Pierre-Joseph Proudhon (1809–65) was an important figure in the development of socialism and especially of anarchism. Of working-class origin and largely self-educated, he achieved fame with the publication in 1840 of a work entitled *What Is Property?* – a question to which he gave the resounding answer, "property is theft." Hostile to both the state and modern capitalism, he developed a system called "mutualism," in which society would be organized into free federations of voluntary economic associations. Proudhon and Bakunin became close friends during Bakunin's stays in Paris in the 1840s, and Proudhon strongly influenced Bakunin in the direction of anarchism, although the latter did not accept all of Proudhon's ideas. In 1846, Proudhon published a two-volume work entitled *System of Economic Contradictions, or the Philosophy of Poverty*, which was critical of socialism. In 1847, Marx responded with a bitter attack which he called *The Poverty of Philosophy*.

106. Blanc advocated the building of a new socialist order through the creation of state-supported "social workshops" which would gradually replace private enterprises. He served as a member of the provisional government set up in February 1848 after the expulsion of Louis-Philippe and was instrumental in establishing the ill-fated National Workshops.

107. Marx was expelled from Paris in February of 1845 (not 1846) and was joined in Brussels by Engels a few months later. The "secret society" to which Bakunin refers came somewhat later. The Central Committee of the League of the Just had moved from Paris to London. In 1847 the organization was renamed the Communist League, and it was at this point that Marx and Engels joined it and wrote the *Communist Manifesto* as its program.

108. The Old Catholic movement arose among German clergy and laymen who separated themselves from the Roman Catholic Church in protest against the decisions of the Vatican Council of 1870, particularly the declaration of papal infallibility.

109. Count Eduard von Reichenbach (1812–69), a Silesian noble, was a well-known democrat of Breslau and a friend of Bakunin. Julius Stein was the author of a history of the city of Breslau. Johannes Ronge (1813–87) was the leader of what was actually called German Catholicism. Excommunicated for his letter to Bishop Arnoldi of Trier, he and his colleagues founded a number of "German Catholic"

congregations which rejected papal authority and other elements of Catholic orthodoxy and propagated a form of primitive communism. (Johannes Tetzel was the friar whose sale of indulgences in 1517 outraged Luther and touched off the Reformation.)

110. The Friends of Light, founded in 1841, was a German Protestant movement which criticized Lutheran dogmatism and sought a return to simple Christian virtues and the spirit of the Reformation. Both the Friends of Light and the German Catholic movement contributed to the rise of political radicalism in Germany prior to 1848.

111. When the National Assembly voted on June 22, 1848, to close the National Workshops, which had provided public-works jobs for many of the unemployed, a worker insurrection ensued and was brutally suppressed by the forces of the republic. The number of casualties ran into the thousands, and thousands of other insurgents were subsequently deported. To Bakunin, as well as to many other radicals, the Paris June Days (23–26) of 1848 provided incontrovertible proof that the bourgeoisie and the proletariat, which had cooperated in the overthrow of Louis-Philippe in February, were in fact irreconcilable enemies, and that parliamentary democracy could serve only the interests of the bourgeoisie, not the workers.

In April of 1834, labor unrest in the silk industry of Lyons had led to a full-scale insurrection, which in turn touched off an uprising in Paris. Both were suppressed with considerable loss of life.

112. The text has "Baron Islagish," evidently a printer's error. Count Josip Jelačić (1801–59), a Croatian nobleman, was appointed Ban, or governor, of Croatia in 1848 and was one of the military commanders who suppressed the uprising in Vienna and the revolution in Hungary.

113. Joseph Maria von Radowitz (1797–1853), Prussian general and statesman, was a friend and confidential adviser of Frederick William IV. At the end of 1850 he served briefly as Prussian foreign minister (not prime minister, as Bakunin states below).

114. Archduke John (1782–1859), an uncle of the Austrian emperor but known for his progressive views, was appointed *Reichsverweser*, or imperial viceregent, by the Frankfurt assembly.

115. Louis-Eugène Cavaignac (1802–57) was minister of war in the provisional government and was given dictatorial powers to suppress the June Days uprising.

116. Count Friedrich Wilhelm von Brandenburg (1792–1850), a son of King Frederick William II, served as prime minister (minister-president) of Prussia from November 1848 until his death two years later.

117. The first line of a patriotic Prussian song written by Bernard Triersch in 1830.

118. Count Otto Theodor von Manteuffel (1805–82) succeeded Brandenburg as Prussian prime minister upon the latter's death in November 1850 and signed the Olmütz Convention. He served as prime minister until 1858.

119. Prince Karl Anton von Hohenzollern-Sigmaringen (1811–85) served as Prussian prime minister from 1858 to 1862.

120. The Count of Chambord (1820–83), the grandson of Charles X, was the Bourbon pretender to the French throne.

121. Both Carl Schurz (1829–1906) and Gottfried Kinkel (1815–82), a poet and professor of art history at Bonn, participated in the uprising in the Grand Duchy of Baden in the spring of 1849, the last act of the 1848 revolution in Germany. Schurz, after escaping from prison, in turn freed his friend and teacher Kinkel, who had been sentenced to prison for life. Schurz made his way to America, where he had a distinguished career as a military man, diplomat, and politician. Contrary

234

to Bakunin's chronology, Schurz was appointed minister to Spain in 1861 and served as senator from Missouri from 1869 to 1875. He was later Secretary of the Interior under Rutherford B. Hayes.

122. The *Neue Preussische Zeitung*, founded in 1848, voiced the extreme anti-democratic views of the Prussian aristocracy. It was popularly known as the *Kreuzzeitung*.

123. Rudolf Virchow (1821–1902), a pathologist, was one of the founders of the Progressive Party.

   Franz Hermann Schulze-Delitzsch (1808–83), an economist, was also a leading figure in the Progressive Party. He was best known as the founder of a system of workingmen's cooperative associations, which Bakunin discusses below. Both Virchow and Schulze-Delitzsch were deputies to the Prussian Diet.

124. The League of Peace and Freedom was a middle-class democratic organization which grew out of a pacifist congress held in Geneva in 1867. Bakunin served on its central committee and tried to persuade it to adopt his social and economic principles. When the attempt failed, he and his adherents withdrew from the League and formed the Alliance of Social Democracy.

125. Bakunin never wrote a sequel to this work.

126. Bakunin is referring to the Association of German Workers' Societies (*Verband deutscher Arbeitervereine*), which was founded in 1863 under middle-class auspices to counter Lassalle and took a non-political stance. Under the influence of Liebknecht and Bebel it drew closer to the Marxist position and at its fifth Congress in Nuremberg in 1868 adopted the statutes of the International as its program. In 1869, the majority of the Association entered the Social-Democratic Party.

127. See the *Manifesto of the Communist Party*, Part II.

128. Lassalle's critique of Schulze-Delitzsch was entitled *Mr. Bastiat-Schulze von Delitzsch, the Economic Julian, or: Capital and Labor*, published in 1864. Marx's work in question is his *Contribution to the Critique of Political Economy*, only the first volume of which was published in 1859.

129. Marx's comment appeared in a footnote to the preface of the first German edition of volume I of *Capital*, 1867.

130. Bakunin is paraphrasing the passage at the end of Part II of the *Communist Manifesto* which lists ten measures to be adopted by "the proletariat organized as the ruling class." The "state engineers," however, are his own addition.

131. A reference to the fact that most of the national federations belonging to the International subsequently repudiated the decisions taken at the Hague Congress of 1872.

132. The Intransigents were the radical wing of the Federal Republican Party. They opposed the monarchy of Amadeo I and favored mass insurrection over parliamentary methods.

133. The Nuremberg Congress was actually the fifth Congress of German Workers' Societies. The Social-Democratic Party was founded in 1869 at Eisenach. See n. 14.

134. Technically, Bakunin is referring to the International Brotherhood, which he had founded in Italy in 1866. He created the International Alliance of Social Democracy only after withdrawing from the League of Peace and Freedom. Below, in reference to events in 1869, he speaks of the Alliance of Social Revolutionaries rather than the Alliance of Social Democracy. In one of his writings he claimed that the Alliance had changed its name when the Germans adopted the term Social-Democratic for their new party. In fact, the Alliance of Social Revolutionaries was a new organization which Bakunin founded in Zurich in September of 1872, essentially as a successor to the Brotherhood and the Alliance of Social Democracy. He referred to it earlier in regard to Bakuninist activity in Spain. (See

n. 21.) He started using the name Alliance of Social Revolutionaries only in 1872, but here he appears to be using it retroactively to refer to the Alliance of Social Democracy.

135. This was a collection of articles by Bakunin and others, published in Zurich. It was issued as volume II of the Publications of the Social-Revolutionary Party, of which *Statism and Anarchy* formed volume I.

136. Amand Gögg (1820–97) was a German democrat who had taken part in the revolution in the Grand Duchy of Baden in 1849. He served as vice-president of the League of Peace and Freedom and also as a member of the central committee of the People's Party.

   Charles Lemonnier (1806–91) was a professor of philosophy and an exponent of Saint-Simonianism. He was an influential member of the League of Peace and Freedom.

137. A reference to the so-called *Kulturkampf*, a series of anti-Catholic laws which Bismarck began to introduce in 1871 and which included restrictions on Catholic worship and education and the expulsion of the Jesuits.

138. This may be a reference to the short-lived Ruble Society of 1867–68. The group's intention was to send itinerant schoolteachers to the villages; their teaching, discussions, and public readings would be based on books to be published legally by the society. They were to be financed in part by dues paid to the society by sympathizers in the intelligentsia, on the basis of 1 ruble per head. This was one of the many currents of thought and activity that would generate the "to the people" movement of 1874. Bakunin could have learned about this group from one of its members, German Aleksandrovich Lopatin (1845–1918), the man who in 1870 exposed the mythical nature of Sergei Nechaev's revolutionary claims.

139. Mirtov and Kedrov were both pseudonyms of Peter Lavrovich Lavrov (1823–1900), one of the foremost theorists of Russian Populism. Under the name P. Mirtov he published his highly influential *Historical Letters*, which first appeared in 1868–69. In this work, Lavrov urged the young intelligentsia to repay the moral debt it owed to the people for its material comfort and intellectual development. The work played a major role in inspiring the "to the people" movement of 1874.

140. Peter Iakovlevich Chaadaev (1794–1856) was one of the leading Russian intellectuals of the 1830s. In 1836 he published the first of his *Philosophical Letters*. It depicted Russia as a moral and intellectual desert, devoid of history and of culture, a condition Chaadaev attributed to Orthodoxy's eleventh-century rupture with Catholicism, and hence with the dynamic forces of Western civilization. For this essay, Emperor Nicholas had Chaadaev officially declared insane. In 1837 Chaadaev wrote an essay ironically entitled *Apology of a Madman*, to which Bakunin alludes here. In it, Chaadaev tempered his earlier pessimistic diagnosis and suggested that Russia's lack of historical traditions might be an advantage – as it was in the case of Peter the Great, who was able to write his Westernizing reforms freely on the "blank page"of Russia.

141. *Forward!* (*Vpered!*) was a journal and later a newspaper published by Lavrov, who left Russia in 1870, and a group of Russian collaborators. It was published from 1873 to 1876, first in Zurich and then in London. The third version of the group's editorial program was circulated in March of 1873 and then published in the first issue of the journal in August of that year. In sharp contrast to Bakunin, *Forward!* saw little possibility of an immediate popular uprising and advocated a gradual, educational program of intellectual preparation of the Populist revolutionaries themselves and socialist propaganda of the peasants. Without naming them, Bakunin criticizes the Lavrovists and their "preparatory" program below.

   The program of the *Forward!* group referred to the hopes of some in Russia for a legal, or constitutional, revolution, which would transfer power from the emperor to some parliamentary body, such as the Governing Senate, but it expressed hostility to such proposals and affirmed its own trust in an eventual popular insurrection. The Governing Senate had been established by Peter the Great in the early eighteenth century. An appointed body with no legislative power, in the nineteenth century it had certain administrative functions in the central government of the Russian Empire and also served as the supreme court of the judicial system.

142. The False Dmitry was a pretender to the Russian throne during the Time of Troubles at the beginning of the seventeenth century. Claiming to be Ivan the Terrible's youngest son, Dmitry (who had in fact died in mysterious circumstances in 1591), he was proclaimed tsar in 1605 but was overthrown and murdered in the following year.

In the early years of the reign of Tsar Alexis (1645–76), economic distress and official corruption generated unrest in a number of Russian towns. There was a serious revolt in Moscow in 1648, followed by rebellions in other cities, including Novgorod in 1650.

143. Sergei Gennadevich Nechaev (1847–82) was the militant but pathological young revolutionary with whom Bakunin had an ill-fated collaboration in 1869–70. Extradited from Switzerland to Russia as a common criminal in 1872, Nechaev was tried for the murder of one of the members of his revolutionary circle in Moscow. He was convicted and sentenced to solitary confinement in a fortress, where he died. Dostoevsky used the Nechaev affair as the basis for his novel *The Possessed*.

144. Etienne Cabet (1788–1856) was an early French socialist. In 1840 he published a widely read utopian novel entitled *Voyage in Icaria*, which described an ideal society organized on communist principles. In 1848, the first band of "Icarians," joined later by Cabet himself and other adherents, set out from France for America to establish a colony based on Cabet's ideas. After an unsuccessful attempt to settle in Texas, they moved to Nauvoo, Illinois. Their colony, called Icaria, was beset by internal dissension and soon split, but remnants of it survived until 1895.

145. A reference to the peasants' dissatisfaction with the terms of the serf emancipation of 1861 and their widespread belief that a new and more generous emancipation would be proclaimed.

146. Bakunin created the Slavic Section of the International in July 1872. It had fifteen or twenty members, mostly Russians along with a few east European Slavs. In August of 1872, Bakunin drew up the program for the Slavic Section. It neatly summarizes the main ideas Bakunin would develop in *Statism and Anarchy* in the following year.

Bakunin originally drafted the program in both Russian and French versions. Only the French version of the original draft has survived, and it differs slightly from the Russian text appended to *Statism and Anarchy* in 1873, which is translated here. See Lehning, ed., *Archives Bakounine*, III, pp. xviii–xix, and, for the 1872 French text, pp. 185–86.

147. The Jura Federation, composed mainly of artisans in the watchmaking trades in the Jura Mountains region of Switzerland, was a major stronghold of Bakunin's adherents in the International.

Index

Beust, Baron Friedrich, 34, 173, 224
Bismarck, Prince Otto Eduard
  Leopold von, 8, 36, 48, 59, 92, 126,
  173, 191, 236; character of, 168–
  72; and Frederick the Great, 9–10,
  169; and Lassalle, 180–81, 184;
  and Marxists, 138, 184, 194, 196;
  and Napoleon III, 102, 114, 170–
  71, 195; and Poles, 40, 65, 84–86,
  88; and reaction in Europe, 3–5, 12,
  194–97; and Russian Empire, 37,
  61, 89, 95, 101–02
Blanc, Louis, 140, 232, 233; and
  Marx, 142–43
Bluntschli, Johann-Kaspar, 141, 232
Börne, Ludwig, 141, 230; *Letters from
  Paris*, 129, 231; quoted, 124
Brandenburg, Count Friedrich
  Wilhelm von, 160, 170, 234
Brauner, František, 58, 59, 226
Büchner, Ludwig, 131, 231

Cabet, Etienne, 213, 237
Castelar y Ripoll, Emilio, 138, 182,
  231; quoted, 184
Catherine II (the Great), empress of
  Russia, and partitions of Poland, 12,
  65
Cavaignac, Louis-Eugène, 157–60,
  234
Cavour, Count Camillo di, 55, 226
Chaadaev, Peter, 205, 236
Chambord, Count of, 168, 234
Charles Albert, king of Italy, 55
Consorteria, 31, 224
cooperatives, 174–75, 201–03
Cousin, Victor, 130, 231
Czechs, xviii, 38, 56–60, 225, 226–27

Decembrist uprising, 64, 121, 227
Duchiński, Frantiszek, 76, 228
Dušan, Stefan, emperor of Serbia, 38,
  53, 56, 225

Engels, Friedrich, 7, 146, 184, 232,
  233; character of, 143; and German
  Social-Democratic Party, 50; *see
  also* Marx, Karl: works
Espartero, Baldomero, 29, 224
Eylert, Bishop Rulemann Friedrich,
  230; quoted, 117

Favre, Jules, 4, 5, 221
Feuerbach, Ludwig Andreas, 131
Fichte, Johann Gottlieb, 105, 130,
  131; *Addresses to the German Nation*,
  108–09, 229
Forward!, 208, 236–37
France: decline of state in, 14–26, 68–
  69, 190, 194–95; Government of
  National Defense, 4, 18, 221; July
  Revolution, 125–26, 129, 230; and
  social revolution, 18–26, 157, 159;
  see also June Days of Paris; Paris
  Commune
Francis I, emperor of Austria, 229;
  quoted, 110
Franco-Prussian War, xxvi, xxix, 3, 12,
  16, 18–19, 43, 74, 95, 189–91, 221,
  223
Frankfurt National Assembly, xviii,
  129, 149–54, 160, 162, 229, 231;
  composition of, 149, 231
Frederick II (the Great), king of
  Prussia, 107, 111, 113, 169;
  character of, 9–10; and partitions of
  Poland, 12, 65, 227
Frederick William III, king of Prussia,
  107–08, 109, 127, 130, 230;
  character of, 117; and German
  liberalism, 111–18
Frederick William IV, king of Prussia,
  152–53, 160, 162–63, 165, 231,
  232, 234; character of, 139–40,
  151; quoted, 163
Freemasonry, 106, 221

Gambetta, Léon, 4, 15, 18, 22, 23–25,
  48, 137, 182, 183, 221, 231
Garibaldi, Giuseppe, 8, 30, 55, 138,
  195, 222
General German Workers'
  Association, 173–76, 185, 222
German Confederation, 112, 115–16,
  124, 127, 128, 154, 163, 165, 170,
  172, 229, 230
German Customs Union, 130, 139,
  231
German National-Liberal Party, 85,
  167, 228
German People's Party, 172–73, 181,
  186, 188, 190, 223, 236
German Progressive Party, 85, 167,
  174, 228, 235

Index

Liebknecht, Karl, 17, 50, 185, 188, 189, 191, 223, 235
Löning, Karl, 123, 230
Lopatin, German, 236
Louis-Philippe, king of France, xvii, 125, 230, 233, 234; *see also* France: July Revolution

MacMahon, Marshal Marie Edmé Patrice Maurice de, 68, 227
Manteuffel, Count Otto Theodor von, 165, 166, 170, 234
Maria Theresa, empress of Austria, and partitions of Poland, 65, 227
Marx, Karl, xv, 7, 109, 146, 187, 223, 232–33; and Bakunin, xvii, xxiv, xxvii, xxxi–xxxii; and Blanc, 142–43; character of, 141–43, 177, 182; and German Social-Democratic Party, 50, 185, 188–89, 196; and Hegel, 131–32, 138, 142–43, 232, 233; and International, xxviii–xxix, 175, 182, 185, 188, 194, 225–26; and Lassalle, 147, 175, 176–77, 180, 184, 222–23; and Proudhon, 142, 233; and the state, 17, 24, 137–38, 184; and "state communism," xxxi, 33, 180–81, 235. Works: *Capital*, xxiv, 176, 235; *Civil War in France*, 221; *Communist Manifesto*, 146, 176, 184, 233, 235; *Contribution to the Critique of Political Economy*, 235; *The German Ideology*, 232; *The Holy Family*, 232; *Inaugural Address*, 176; *The Poverty of Philosophy*, 233
Marxists, xxx–xxxi, xxxvi; and Bismarck, 138, 194; and International, 51, 188–89; and pan-Germanism, 138, 148, 189, 194; and the state, 13, 147–48, 177–79
Mazzini, Giuseppe, 8, 30, 54–55, 70, 138, 222; and International, 5–6, 222
Metternich, Prince Klemens Wenzel von, 10, 33, 66, 110–11, 117, 118, 120, 126, 130, 230
Michelet, Jules, 140, 232
Mickiewicz, Adam, 38, 225
Miliutin, Count Dmitry, 77, 228
mir, see peasant commune, Russian

Müller, Wilhelm, 229, 230; quoted, 125
Muravev, Count Michael, 40, 72, 83, 84, 225
Muravev-Apostol, Sergei, 64, 121, 227

Napoleon I, emperor of France, 9, 27, 29, 74, 120, 122, 159, 170, 189; and Germans, 27–29, 107–09, 110, 111, 113, 229
Napoleon III (Louis Napoleon), emperor of France, 8, 14, 16, 34, 55, 82, 87, 159, 183, 189–90, 221, 223, 228; and Bismarck, 102, 114, 170–71, 195
Narváez, Ramón María, 29, 224
Nechaev, Sergei, xxiii–xxv, 212, 236, 237; "Catechism of a Revolutionary," xxiv
New Catholicism (German Catholicism), 143–44, 233–34
Nicholas I, emperor of Russia, xix–xxi, 10, 75, 127, 130, 139, 162–63, 165, 222, 231–32, 233; character of, 168; and Hungarian uprising, 11, 34, 222, 227; and Olmütz Convention, 163, 166, 227–28; and pan-Slavism, 64, 69–70, 72
North German Confederation, 172, 229

Ogarev, Nicholas, xii, xxii
Old Believers, 75; and Bakunin, 228
Old Catholicism, 143, 233
Olmütz Convention, 163, 165, 166, 170, 227–28, 234

Palacký, František, 58, 59, 86, 226
pan-Germanism, 16, 29, 37, 66, 74, 96, 103, 122–23, 144, 161, 190–94, 196–97, 218; and naval power, 92–93, 94, 191, 192; and Slavs, 36, 43–45, 151
pan-Slavism, 11, 67, 76–77, 102, 218; and Austrian Slavs, 37–38, 42–45, 64, 72–73; and Russian government, 37, 64, 69–70, 72–73, 88–89, 223, 226
Paris, Treaty of (1856), 95, 97, 223, 226

Cambridge Texts in the History of Political Thought

Titles published in the series thus far

Aristotle *The Politics* (edited by Stephen Everson)

Bakunin *Statism and Anarchy* (edited and translated by Marshall Shatz)

Bentham *A Fragment on Government* (introduction by Ross Harrison)

Bossuet *Politics Drawn from the Very Words of Holy Scripture* (edited and translated by Patrick Riley)

Cicero *De Officiis* (edited by M. T. Griffin and E. M. Atkins)

Constant *Political Writings* (edited and translated by Biancamaria Fontana)

Filmer *Patriarcha and Other Writings* (edited by Johann P. Sommerville)

Hobbes *Leviathan* (edited by Richard Tuck)

Hooker *Of the Laws of Ecclesiastical Polity* (edited by A. S. McGrade)

John of Salisbury *Policraticus* (edited and translated by Cary Nederman)

Leibniz *Political Writings* (edited and translated by Patrick Riley)

Locke *Two Treatises of Government* (edited by Peter Laslett)

Machiavelli *The Prince* (edited by Quentin Skinner and Russell Price)

J. S. Mill *On Liberty* with *The Subjection of Women* and *Chapters on Socialism* (edited by Stefan Collini)

Montesquieu *The Spirit of the Laws* (edited and translated by Anne M. Cohler, Basia Carolyn Miller and Harold Samuel Stone)

More *Utopia* (edited and translated by George M. Logan and Robert M. Adams)

Paine *Political Writings* (edited by Bruce Kuklick)